THE Critique
OF Domination

THE Critique OF Domination

The Origins and Development of Critical Theory

TRENT SCHROYER

George Braziller

NEW YORK

ACKNOWLEDGMENTS

Parts of this book have appeared as follows:

"Toward a Critical Theory for Advanced Industrial Society," in *Recent Sociology #2* (Macmillan: London, 1970) Hans Peter Dreitzel (ed.); also reprinted in *Radical America*, April, 1970, also reprinted in *Revival of American Socialism*, George Fisher et al. (ed.), Oxford University Press, 1971. This paper was originally presented to a special session of the Socialist Scholars Conference, September 7, 1969.

"Marx and Habermas," in *Continuum*, Spring-Summer, 1970.

"The Tradition of Critical Theory," in *Critical Anthropology #1*, Summer 1970. This paper was presented on April 15, 1970 to the General Seminar of the Graduate Faculty of the New School.

"The Paradox of Alienation in the Western Image of Man: A Hegelian Perspective," in *Abraxis #2*, Winter, 1970.

"A Reconceptualization of Critical Theory," in *Radical Sociology*, D. Colfax and J. Roach, (eds.) (New York: Basic Books, 1971).

"Toward a Critical Theory of Society," Paper read to the Sociology and Philosophy Section of the American Sociological Association in Washington, D.C., Fall, 1970.

Review article, "On the Frankfurt School of Marxism," in *Telos #6*, Spring 1971.

Paper presented to the Columbia Faculty Seminar on Social and Political Thought in Habermas's "Reflections on Knowledge and Cognitive Interests," January 1972, and published as "The Dialectical Foundation of Critical Theory" in *Telos #12*.

"The Politics of Epistemology," in *International Journal of Sociology*, Winter 1972.

"Neo-Marxism and the Marxist Tradition. The Continuity of the Marxist Critique of Capitalism," paper presented to the Political Sociology Division of the Southern Sociological Conference in New Orleans, April 1972.

"The Need for Critical Theory"/"Marx's Crisis Theory" in *Telos #13* and *#14*, read in part to the "Criticism of Sociology" section of the National Meeting of the American Sociological Society in New Orleans on August 30, 1972.

The author and publisher wish to thank the following for permission to reprint certain materials included in this book from the publications listed below:

Beacon Press—for the passages from: *Knowledge and Human Interests* by Jürgen Habermas, (1970), pp. 68, 196, 284; *Eros and Civilization* by Herbert Harcuse, (1955), pp. 52, 96–97; *One Dimensional Man* by Herbert Marcuse, (1964), pp. xv, 35, 168–169, 10, 74.

Chapman and Hall—for the passages from *Economics and Ideology* by Ronald L. Meek (1967), pp. 136, 142.

Doubleday and Company, (Anchor Books)—for passages from *Hegel, A Reinterpretation* by Walter Kaufmann, (1966), pp. 49–50.

Contents

THE Critique
OF Domination

INTRODUCTION

The Need for Critical Theory

The Critique of Domination

The critique of domination, or the reflective critique of socially unnecessary constraints of human freedom, is as old as the Western concept of reason. In classical Greek philosophy the notion of reason (*nous*) was developed in relation to the "seeing" of the invisible in the visible, or of the essential in the appearing. For example, in Plato's famous cave allegory the painful re-turning to the sun (i.e., beauty, truth) involved a recognition of the mystifications and domination of conventions (*nomos*) over man's potentialities. Only a turning around of the soul could restore the knowledge of the difference between the appearances created by the false light of the fire (maintained by the guardians of convention) and the true source of essential reality. In Plato's myth the unconcealment of truth, of actuality, required a reflective negation of the appearances of conventional life. Plato's concept of negative reason is best illustrated in his presentation of the person and the dialogic method of Socrates. Plato mythically depicts Socrates' "inner voice" (the symbol for reason) as always saying no, and while this does not exhaust the concept of reason it is clearly its major function. Or, the Socratic method of dialogue is presented as discovering the essential by ruling out what it is not (e.g., justice, love, etc.). With the Socratic method Plato shows the basic concept of reason as a critique of conventional mystification which releases a changed praxis (action) in the individual's life.

This concept of negative reason and its associated concept of the dialectical relatedness of theory and action established the framework for the modern forms of the critique of domination. For example, in Hegel it became the critique of one-sided social-cultural forms that distort human spontaneity and, in Marx, the critique of political-economic forms that separate and block the essential productive processes of society. In these critiques of domination, the concept of rational critique remains inseparable from the moral community and, therefore, from human action.

Today the critique of domination has suffered the fate of being identified with the "communist" world's alleged blueprint for world revolution. This association has blocked and obscured the real potential of critical reflection which, following its modern reconceptualization in critical philosophy (i.e., Kant, Fichte, Hegel, etc.), can be called *critical theory*. While Marx inherited this classic tradition of criticism and comprehended its radical reformulation in German idealism more clearly than the "Marxists" have, he neither developed its final form nor adequately realized its utopian "moment" as a theory of emancipation. Contemporary critical theorists, such as Marcuse, Habermas, Sartre, and Henri Lefèbvre continue to try to work out the foundations for a critical theory that would retain its ties to classical philosophy but would have the role of effecting a more critically oriented type of social science theory and research. This book constitutes another such attempt. In a sense, all the efforts to found a genuinely critical social science involve both the sphere of philosophical reflection and the ongoing attempt to either update or transcend Marx's concrete realization of a political-economic critical theory of society. Indeed, as a theory, Marx's critique has become a material force within the planning mechanisms of the contemporary world. In a way, today's social theorists are all "Marxists" in their one-sided stress upon the *objective necessity* for economic development as the first priority for all societies and as the variable on which social development hinges. This emphasis, once a genuinely radical concept for emancipation of an international proletariat, may now be the means for their permanent suppression and domination.

A contemporary critical theory must, therefore, begin with a critique of Marx's work. Whereas Marx's highly successful realization of an epochal crisis theory (i.e., *Capital*) may have justified his claim that philosophy must be abandoned in order to realize its ideals, we are now faced with the objective necessity of *returning* to a reflective critique of that very theory. We have only to recognize that almost all of the theorists reformulating critical theory have attempted to restore to it a social-cultural component, converging thereby on the greatest current deficiency of Marx's work. In confronting the present situation we will also realize that the objective dynamics of capitalist development do not, in themselves, produce "the class struggle." We have to see, finally, that in today's scientized civilization the character of domination is broader than economic exploitation and alienation.

Reforming critical theory means a radical returning to its roots in order to restore the intent of critical reflection in the context of the present. The critical imagination has itself been locked into a sterile faith, guarding the fire of Marx's theory. In a way the guardians of this fire, like those in Plato's allegory of the cave, have produced shadows that conceal and distort reality. A return to the origins of critique should not become an antiquarian exercise in the exegesis of the sacred texts of the critical tradition— knowledge of Hegel, Marx, Lukacs, Gramsci, etc., will not restore the *telos* (i.e., the purpose) of critical theory. To begin again from the present is to recognize that the dynamic of centralized state societies now requires an increasing utilization of scientific information, management theory and the integration of scientific and technological development. To regain any access to contemporary forces of change is to comprehend science and technology as forces of production and to recognize that critique must be reformulated within this context. The Marxist conception of critical theory and its political potential is now surpassed by the evolution of late capitalism. Those who continue to deduce their current analysis and activity from Marx do so more as an act of faith than as critical, rational action.

In the following endeavor to begin a rethinking of the meaning of critical theory, there is no intent to discredit Marx. His *Capital* remains a monumental example of critical theory, despite its inadequateness for a broader formulation of critique. In order to restore the vitality of Marx's contribution we must reevaluate his work, not embalm it as a public icon that conceals the domination actualized in his name. With no disrespect for Marx's revolutionary spirit, contemporary "Marxists" may be the last to recognize the dialectics of emancipation in our time and among the first to try to block them in the name of revolutionary necessity. Just as past moments of liberated human existence were routinized into rigid forms that contradicted the spiritual insights of their fusion, so today's mechanistic Marxism seems to stand in direct opposition to the intent of critical theory. For this reason critical theory must absorb Marx or wither away as a living contradiction of his intent.

The Present Situation of Domination: The American Empire

Despite the growing similarity of capitalist and socialist imperial systems, the American-dominated world capitalist system remains the basic framework for global development. Evolution of capitalism has continued and become a world-wide system that increasingly sets up new social forms such as the world bank or the multinational corporation. This system sets the ground rules for social-economic development not only in the "free" world but to some extent also in the socialist world.

The contradictions of capital accumulation and uneven social-cultural development have not been transcended in the American civilization but are actually deeper and more universal than ever. The depth of this crisis can be seen in the greater and greater resources and efforts at rationalization that are needed for continued economic growth, international stability, and internal mass loyalty. But perhaps the clearest indicator of this crisis was the United States' continued attempt to determine the fate of South Vietnam. While not economically necessary for America, the involvement demonstrated the massive interlock of international and domestic domination, as well as the growing incapacity of the American state to reorient its policy. At the same time the split within the nation on the issue of war, and the continuation of the war under a facade of lying and deception was a clear indication of the depth of state capitalist domination over the society.

During the sixties the landing of men on the moon and the spontaneous founding of the "Woodstock nation" stand as antithetical symbolic events that represent the zenith of American technical progress and the affirmation of a communal sentiment that is in direct opposition to the enforced domination of state-corporate capitalism. These polar events mark the basic contradiction of a civilization that is increasingly committed to technological progress at the cost of reproducing social dislocations, isolation and opposition. The main drift of the American empire is an ever deepening commitment to the generation of new administrative systems and social control technologies for the "stabilization" of international and domestic "social problems." The commitment is at once undiscussed and obligatory as the basis for political decision. This new ideology of "scientific politics" appears to be in fact the end of ideology; it is universally applied and apparently beyond refutation, as in the case of Vietnam.

Despite the failure of American "know-how" and technology in Vietnam we continue to believe that social problems and conflicts can be "managed." Precise quantification and systematic decision-making are held as the essential basis for *purposive rational* action despite repeated political and military failures. To the liberal notion that cultural ideals should not determine political decision (the fabled separation of fact and value) has now been added the technocratic claim that the production of adequate information is actually the substance of *all* rational decision. Traditional liberal political practice is being replaced by the *technocratic strategy* in which politics and science are related integrally as the means for a more efficient and effective decision-making process.[1] In this way we have indeed left behind the ideology of cultural values and are now guided only by the "neutral" standards of purposive rational action, or what could be called *instrumental reason*.

Introduction

No doubt continued faith in the American destiny derives from our confidence that as the leading industrial nation we are justified in taking the role of global policeman of the "free" world. However, despite this confidence and the power of American technical resources, the reality of America's role in history would appear to be more complex and less flattering. Beginning earlier in the century, perhaps over Dresden or Hiroshima, and then every day over Vietnam, we have lost our innocence. The early American cultural ideal of the Adamic man is no longer viable, although we resist confronting this reality. Our defenses against a growing American destructiveness have resulted in an open willingness to murder those who express their guilt and despair, as in the cases of Kent State, Attica, and Southern University. "Law and order," the new political ideal, has become the instrumental end of our legal and judicial systems and the ideals of justice and freedom seem irrelevant as we repress those who act upon their conscience.

Is irony or tragicomedy at work in American history? Today one can envision an Asian intellectual musing about "those inscrutable Americans who are always trying to save face." We seem to experience Vietnam and the last decade as if the American way of life is now more than ever the hope of history. Intensification of this belief correlates with renewed efforts to create the appropriate instrumental means for control. Hence a decade of civil disobedience has resulted in a massive reinforcement of our police system; early disasters in Vietnam propelled a "systems" reorganization led by Robert McNamara. More recently this American instrumental reaction to failure resulted in governmental attempts to muzzle the news media and to deny the reality of American barbarism by making dissent appear treasonous.

As a people we seem to be involved in a pathological syndrome which reacts with new technical levers to moral and social unrest ("law and order"); with violence to any opposition ("national security"); and with a repressive authoritarianism to any attempt to open up communication about the ends, ideals, or goals of our civilization ("treason"). We conceal this reality from ourselves by generating scientistic rationalizations that simply define the normative issues as beside the point and reorganize for a more effect-tive instrumental *control* of the situation. We avoid a public re-examination of the standards for political judgment and force individuals who see the necessity for this to become criminals (e.g. Daniel Ellsberg). The American political, economic, and military institutions, and now the scientific community, have been integrated into this societal avoidance pattern.[2]

Such a collective defense mechanism is no doubt the result of a complex overdetermination of social, economic, and political factors, but the naive scientism of our technocratic guidance systems appears to be the emergent cultural element that promotes and conceals this delusory behavior. In short, we are wedded to an instrumental concept of reason whose one-sidedness blocks our capacity to recognize the sociocultural significance of our acts and lowers our ability to act intelligently in novel situations. Consequently, as a people we are becoming less able to reformulate our identity and less capable of recognizing the need for reexamination of our values, actions, and institutions.[3]

Discussion and reexamination of these issues have taken place; as, for example, the debates about the consequences of technological society, the social necessity of economic growth, and the ecological costs of industrial production. However, in each of these debates the problem has been confronted only partially. The root of the problem seems to be posed most totally by the twentieth century philosophical discussion about the crisis of Western reason (e.g., Husserl, Habermas, et al.) and, in a derivative way, by the intellectual minorities who point to an internal crisis in sociology, political science, economics, and so forth.[4] In these philosophical and methodological debates there is a growing concern about the adequacy of our social theory.*

Only the extension of these discussions will enable us to confront the consequences of our scientized civilization. With this in

---

* "Social theory" is used here in a way which refers to the philosophical presuppositions and general theoretical models which inform social science. In this sense, social theory is exemplified by the social science paradigms of behaviorism, structural-functionalism, Marxism, phenomenology, systems theory, etc. All of these theories inform scientific practice in various fields of social science. The following analysis attempts to move at the level of a comparative analysis of social theory.

mind, state-guided economic growth, or external guidance of the Third World's "modernization" become tragic instances of the unintended domination of man* by a belief in the power of instrumental reason and management. Domination, or coerced control of human behavior, is the result of denying *cultural* sovereignty and liberty to people to interpret their own needs. In short, insofar as social theory is guided by an instrumental notion of reason, we are unable to understand the meaning of cultural reality and thereby indirectly destroy or impoverish it. Technocratic strategy, and its allied social theory, seem to be active forces for the destruction of culture and the domination of man,[5] as, for example, in the applications of modernization models developed from a theory of pattern variables, or achievement motivation that cannot conceptualize, or measure, their by-products of domination.[6]

The influential comparative sociology of Max Weber is more sensitive to this reality. Weber was aware that the basic trend of the industrial world, which he expressed as the general process of "rationalization," involved a disenchantment and secularization of our world views while actualizing bureaucratic structures whose potential for domination increased with the size and scope of their function. Yet despite this painful consciousness of the inseparability of rationalization and the potential for domination, Weber, and other less sophisticated social theorists, have stressed that there is no alternative and that our collective survival depends upon the possibilities presented by the extension of all kinds of purposive rational action systems.[7] This thesis is too simplistic and one-sided.[8] If we accept it, we are led into a stoic acceptance of the social necessity of separating political decision from ethics, science from values, and social theory from the systematic analysis of utopian possibilities. We are all asked "to see how much we can stand," and admit the "rational" necessity of the extension of centralized management strategies to more and more areas of

---

* In order to satisfy the conflict between methodology and non-chauvinistic language the term "man" is used to refer to historical men and women. In contexts where the reference extends to universal generic-man the term "mankind" or 'the human species" is used.

human life. This assumption has been so reinforced by positivist philosophy, by our intoxication with the technical powers of science and technology, and by the development of business management techniques that it has become an unquestionable standard of social policy. To successfully challenge this position requires a major re-examination of the foundations of social theory, the social consequences of a state-guided industrial order, and an investigation of alternative modes of inquiry and social-cultural organization. This task has only begun, but it is undertaken most appropriately at this point by social theorists.

The Ideological Function of Social Theory

Never before has society allocated so much of its resources to the "production of knowledge," nor been so dependent upon "mental works." Today, in the advanced industrial nations, the social sciences have taken on a new and more crucial role. The ongoing, interlocked development of social science and an information-dependent society produces a qualitatively new configuration of the economic and the sociocultural processes. But these new relations do not give us a "post-industrial cybernetic service society"[9] which has the capacity to regulate itself; an image held by some of the most influential social theorists who claim that, in the last decade, advanced industrial society has taken a quantum jump into a new era. Celebration of our "leap into freedom" has produced new concepts for the emergent era, e.g., "post industrial,"[10] "post-civilized society,"[11] "the technocratic age,"[12] etc. All of these concepts stress the necessity for the institutionalization and extension of science and technology and their importance for economic growth and social development. These theories emphasize that "progress" is now dependent upon meeting the "technical imperatives" of an industrial system.[13] They result in a direct or indirect advocacy that we meet "the challenge of the technological potentialities" inherent in industrial systems. The possiblity of a decentralized model of social development, of the maximization of public discussion about local and regional needs, of paths out of the consumer society, of alternative low level technologies—these options do not seem to be part of the "challenge" of the new era. If, however, we approach the question of rational "planning" in a way which involves cultural sovereignty and the right of groups and peoples to interpret their own needs, centralized "cybernetic service" institutions, or even the consumer goods that require these structures, might not be considered necessary. What is the nature of the "necessity" for increasing rationalization of society in order to stimulate economic growth? What are the material *and* social costs of alternative models of development? What are the technical means and options available to groups who want to control their own production and/or drop out of the consumer society? Until we have a social science that treats these questions as seriously as organization for greater economic growth is treated, we will not have an *objective* (there is no *neutral*) social science.

The "post-industrial society" image of contemporary society is treated here as false and ideological to the extent to which it permits historical domination to appear as a natural process. Insofar as contemporary science uncritically promotes this image, it becomes not only, in Marxist terms, a factor of production, but an ideological relation of production. In a new guise, this technocratic celebration of instrumental progress perpetuates the grim determinism of an earlier industrial ideology. Whereas the first industrial societies understood their development in terms of the "economic necessities" of the market, today we conceive our chances for "development" as linked to the internal "needs" of the industrial system.[14] In the earlier market-ideology, history was reduced to the necessity of *natural law*; in the current image of "post-industrial" society, the internal dynamic of social change has been elevated to the status of *cybernetic process*. Both societal self-images imply that chances for human liberation are related to the capacity of man *to adapt to* an externally imposed "natural" necessity. (It is natural to destroy our environment in order to reduce the cost of production!)

Just as the earlier capitalist image of social development has been exposed by Marx as an ideological justification of private ownership of the means of production, so the contemporary images of advanced industrial society (i.e., the U.S.A. and the Soviet Union) can be shown to be a justification of the perpetuation of private power and privilege. Both of these images are instances of societal bad faith in that they continue the man-is-a-pawn-of-natural-necessity theme. It is this type of consciousness that permits the setting of undiscussed national goals that take for granted the "necessity" for a massive war machine ("national security"), unparalleled waste and destruction of resources and labor (the "free enterprise" system), while remaining unable to meet the health and educational needs of the population. The possibility that man might be active in establishing the goals, as well as the technical means, for social development is merely a utopian ideal in a context which depicts him as passively adjusting to imposed necessities. William Leiss has put this point succinctly:

Through a curious process of inversion, the means (technological innovations) come to govern the ends (values and norms); men become the "objects" rather than the "subjects" of their own activity. It is not that men are experiencing an essentially novel phase of social development, for most men have passed through the historical record as the objects of forces which they neither comprehended nor controlled; the paradox is that this persistent phenomenon should be *revalued* and now be regarded as bursting with "the promise of new freedom." The element of passivity in these conceptions of technological development is the unintended admission of the truth that most men remain the objects of their practice, i.e., that their productive activity somehow results in new circumstances to which perforce they must adapt themselves.[15]

The utopian hope for the activation of populations becomes a rational alternative, however, when we recognize that societies dependent on manipulative consumerism can only resolve their emergent "problems" by the growth of state controls. For example, the problems created by a corporate capitalist system of production, e.g., a permanent "under-class," ecological destruction, urban decay, must be constantly remedied in an ad hoc manner by the creation of welfare programs and state bureaucracies. The adequacy of state intervention becomes questionable, when one recognizes that it is constrained in meeting social needs by its uncritical commitment to produce the conditions for expansion and growth in the private economic sector. An unquestioned acceptance of the societal priorities established by huge corporate and state complexes blocks a *societally rational* response to "social problems."[16]

The Marxist framework is relevant, in a reformulated manner, for conceptualizing the increasing contradiction between the dynamic of corporate capitalist production and the needs of the people within the system. The deeper the contradiction, the more the technocratic strategy is urged upon society as the only "rational" response to the crisis. One concern of contemporary critical social research is to reveal that the adoption of business strategies (cost effectiveness, the planning-programming-budgeting system, etc.) by state planning mechanisms is *not* "rational" in terms of meeting the needs of the public. It is, in fact, "rational" only as a business strategy that maximizes the cost-benefits of state resources and services—*after the needs of the private economic sector have been met.* It is a peculiarly capitalist and highly partisan form of "rationality": socialism for the rich and capitalism for everyone else (as in the case of the recent wage freeze). Contemporary state intervention secures the private corporate system by supporting more than half the research and development costs, supporting the training of educated labor, and maintaining an effective demand by massive (and socially wasteful) state expenditures. Despite the ideological veil of technocratic rhetoric, contemporary organized capitalism is best described as rational management for the perpetuation of capitalist economic growth. Only secondarily, is it a social accounting of the existing state budgets for increasing public needs. And despite growing opposition, such as that of ecology and consumer groups, local and regionally deprived minorities, our social science continues to work out technocratic solutions for corporate and state management.

While ostensibly maturing in its research techniques and becoming increasingly freed from value judgments, it is obvious that the drift of contemporary social science is toward the service of existing administrative systems. Too often the knowledge produced becomes useful only as a means to control "social problems" and to re-establish a social equilibrium that takes for granted the existing institutional constellation. Methodologically we have begun to recognize that insofar as social science knowledge is generated in a way which presupposes existing societal arrangements as so many "initial conditions," the knowledge produced will be "true" only as a set of propositions that contribute to the *control* of these conditions. This methodological argument is more carefully formulated elsewhere;[17] for now, it is sufficient to state the thesis that lies behind this perspective: contemporary establishment social science is essentially a science of managerial rationality. We need a social science that is capable of recognizing the ways in which existing structures exploit, alienate, and repress human possibilities. We need a critical science whose primary focus is the critique of domination. Such a science would not be limited by scientistic blinders; it would attempt not only to assess the human costs of social planning but would also be committed to the investigation of alternative modes of social organization in which individual freedom and development would be standards of rationality.

The Alternative: Critical Theory

We begin to rethink the meaning of social theory from a position that views the main trend of industrial civilization as an increasing utilization of state support for a permanent revolution of scientific and technological innovation to serve the specific purpose of mediating conflict and controlling social change. We have called this trend the *technocratic strategy* and its notion of rationality that of *instrumental reason.*

If we were to take seriously the technocratic strategy, we would be led to believe that an age-old ideal of reason had been realized. That is, insofar as the production of knowledge is now fundamental to societal change, we seem to have unified theory and practice in a way dreamed of by philosophers throughout western thought.

Introduction

By unifying knowledge and production, societal guidance and social reproduction, we have broken into a realm of freedom heretofore inaccessible to man.

In ancient Greek philosophy, it was held that theory relates to life as an exemplar whose illumination releases an ecstatic mimesis and a consequent reorientation of activity. *Theoria* was dialectically related, on the one hand, to the dialogue between the active man within society and, on the other, to the theoretical transcendence of human thinking. In this sense, theory was emergent from, yet transcended, human relations and led back to the spontaneity of life itself. This relationship was the origin of the ideal of the unity of theory and practice.

Twentieth-century philosophical reflection has presupposed this ideal in its criticism of the pseudo-unity of the technocratic strategy. Except for the continued reformulations of positivist philosophy, something like a major convergence of contemporary philosophy seems to have emerged. Phenomenology (Husserl),[18] existentialism (Heidegger),[19] neo-Marxism (Habermas),[20] and hermeneutic philosophy (H. G. Gadamer),[21] have all generated a critique of what we have called "instrumental reason." Each has based its reflective critique on an attempt to recover the ancient truth that thinking and action (praxis) are in some sense an intended unity; hence all are speculative reconstructions of the relationship of knowledge and life, thinking and action. Whether the source of the contemporary crisis is conceptualized as "objectivism" (Husserl), "technicity" (Heidegger), or "instrumental rationalization" (Habermas), the essential point is that the modern industrial world has severed theory from the practice of life.[22] All these viewpoints converge in their critique of the modern identification of knowledge and/or reason with the products of strict science. This philosophical consensus points to a growing cultural regression where social values and norms are replaced by technical rules which mystify the social world (e.g. I.Q. scores which reify the process of education). Interaction of persons is determined more by technical rules and less by the spontaneity of human subjectivity. The technical universe surrounds the person as an ever ready definition-of-the-situation—it is a permanent spectacle to which we can "tune in" at any time. What appears to these philosophers as a cultural crisis is more seriously a crisis of human subjectivity itself. The very meaning of a "person" is undergoing a transformation which may be an unintended consequence of the technocratic strategy and its one-sided concept of reason.

A critical social theory begins from the position that a codified scientific method is not an adequate foundation for the validity of truth claims.[23] Only in a reconstruction of the self-formation of developmental processes is there objectivity about the relation between these processes and our cultural understanding of them. Only by an explicit awareness of the dialectical reciprocity of history and culture can we attain an adequate grasp of the immediacy of the present. We approach "social facts" from a cultural perspective which is not neutralized by research techniques since these may themselves conceal our prejudgments of the "data." Our social inquiry begins from and returns to the immediate and we must become aware of the influence of our cultural situation. This cannot be achieved by the development of a "sociology of knowledge" but by the extension of the Hegelian-Marxist method of phenomenological reconstruction. As a first approximation of this method it is necessary to over-simplify it by describing Hegel's critical philosophy as expressed in the *Phenomenology of Spirit*.

Reflection upon the genesis of knowledge is for Hegel the beginning of critical awareness. Beginning from the immediacy of a given consciousness, and by reconstructing the self-formation of this consciousness, we observe how at every stage standards of the preceding one disintegrate and new ones arise. Critical reflection therefore goes beyond the abstract distinction made by Kant between theoretical and practical reason (now enshrined in the fact-value distinction). Hegel's phenomenological method goes beyond the critique of knowledge and involves a critique of reified consciousness that binds life to habitual social forms.[24] The method of critical philosophy was therefore radicalized by Hegel to the critique of the successive stages in the self-formation of the subject. Each critical reconstruction is a self-understanding that breaks down the constraints of past forms of consciousness. An adequate comprehension of the present requires both a critique *and* retention of the past stages within a theory of the totality. With Hegel the reflective critique of the limits of knowledge (the method of German idealism) became a critique of false consciousness. It is but a step, taken only by Marx, to conceive of this phenomenological critique of consciousness as an immanent method for the critique of ideology.

For Hegel, critical philosophy is a reconciliation of the objective conflicts inherent in the institutions of society (objective spirit) and the forms of consciousness (absolute spirit) basic to the historical activity of man. Ultimately, the role of philosophy is the critical comprehension of the historical genesis of these conflicts, and the resulting mediation will be the basis for a reunification which effectively "respiritualizes" that which has become comprehensible. (Of course, Hegel assumed that the philosophical mediation would eventually be concretely universalized by the actions of the man aware of this truth.) Critique reconstructs the constitutive genesis of the *existing* in order to recognize the *actual*, or the universal possibilities that are objectively present in the existing.

Analogously for Marx, a reconstruction of the genesis of capitalism illuminates the historical origins of the development of universal commodity exchange.[25] Having shown how it has become immanently possible to conceive of human labor as equivalent to the value of its product (the question which classical political economy did not ask and conceived of as a *natural* relation), Marx goes on to demonstrate that the *actual* dynamics of capitalism make equal exchange between wage labor and capital impossible. The critique at the same time defines an immanent potential that the bourgeois ideology conceals—the objective possibilities that are inherent in the socialization of the means of production. Critique thus anticipates the emancipation of man from both the constraints of nature and of repressive social power. The intent of the critique is to promote conscious emancipatory activity.

Construction of a critical theory follows the principle of an immanent critique. By first expressing what a social totality holds itself to be, and then confronting it with what it is in fact becoming, a critical theory is able to restore the actuality to a false appearance. Thus, the ideology of "equivalence exchange" identified by Marx as the self-image of capitalist society is contradicted by the formulation of the "developmental laws of capitalism." The phenomenal appearance of capitalism is negated by its own structural tendencies, which Marx shows intensify human exploitation and alienation.

Critical theory therefore attempts to restore missing parts of the historical self-formation process to man and, in this way, to release a self-positing comprehension which enables him to see through socially unnecessary authority and control systems. By uniting lost experiential dimensions of both individual and collective pasts, critical theory anticipates a release of emancipatory reflection and a transformed social praxis. In this self-reflective recognition of "pseudo-necessity," the conditions needed to perpetuate unnecessary social roles and institutions are removed and man can actualize new possibilities for human development. Yet the methodological ideal of critique remains an undeveloped and residual dimension of Marx's work; except for the early need to distinguish between the philosophical mode of critique undertaken by Hegel and the left-Hegelians, and a materialistically-conceived form of critique. With this, Marx unfortunately blocked the later Marxists' understanding of the method of critical theory. He so totally polarized materialistic and idealistic forms of critique that he sometimes seems to have made culture an automatic by-product of material progress.[26]

These vacillations in Marx himself have theoretically permitted the regression of Marxism behind Marx. Lack of methodological clarity has made possible a mechanical form of critique that approximates a left technocratic ideology which is equally willing to predict five-year plans for a "bureaucratic socialism" or revolutionary strategies for power-taking.[27] In both types of "predictions," the intent of critique has, ironically, been replaced with its opposite. Enlightenment and emancipation from unnecessary domination have been subordinated to the dialectics of accumulation—now celebrated as non-alienating due to the "socialist" mode of economic development. In a strange reversal, this type of left technocratism continues the illusion of the industrial epoch, and man is still perceived as a pawn or a cadre of history.

Marx's form of critical theory is thus in some ways less dialectical than Hegel's "idealistic" one. Hegel's philosophy united theory and history in a radically new way. Thought and will, theory and action are comprehended as reciprocally related within the developmental dialectics of "reason in history." Philosophy itself is the critique of "abstraction" (reified thought and social relations) in the context of social discord, or crisis. Hegel's radical combination of philosophical and social analysis is usually overlooked, especially by Marxists who polarize materialism and idealism. In its attempt to comprehend the origin and consequences of the disruption of dialectically related self-consciousness and cultural systems Hegel's critique contained a theory of cultural alienation which precedes and today supplements Marx's theory of the alienation of work; it is a more fundamental theory of alienation which is more sensitive to socio-cultural processes. Marx's work is rooted in Hegel's thought and, while achieving a lasting critique of Hegel (namely the claim to absolute knowledge), he seems to fail to achieve the total sublation (*Aufhebung*) that he claims. A more adequate critical theory of society must reconstruct Hegel and Marx together in order to attain a more flexible and truly dialectical theory.

It can be shown that Marx's critical theory has underestimated the socio-cultural and overstressed the economic and political.[28] In Marx, and the socialist tradition in general, it is assumed that the critique of domination must yield a political action program that will restore a proletarian "public." However, unlike the theories of Hegel or Habermas, this theory of emancipation is unable to give an adequate account of *the objective need* to recognize domination. Marx has not really shown why emancipatory struggle is necessary and has reduced the problem to economic determinism; that is, forced cooperation of workers in the midst of a mechanizing production process is held by Marx to result in the growth of socialist consciousness. Later Marxists have therefore always been faced with an unanswerable question: namely, "how is consciousness of domination possible?" But Marx provides no theory of why recognition of domination is necessary, although Hegel has expressed it in his notion of the "causality of fate" and Jürgen Habermas has systematically developed in it his communication theory of society. Because of this deficiency, Marx is unable to really unite his profound critique of capitalist development and his theory of revolution. In attempting to overcome the abstract critical theory of the left-Hegelians and to transcend the positivist traditions of political economy, Marx reduced the cultural moment of his dialectical social theory to the vanishing point. The problems created by this "missing link" in Marx's critical theory have made possible the emergence of mechanical forms of Marxism that justify centralized party mechanisms as the only mechanisms that can promote the recognition of domination (the theory of the vanguard). To answer the same problem (but equally reductive), Herbert Marcuse grasps for the biological source of rebellion. Both the theory of the vanguard and the "revolt of the instincts" are measures of the desperation of critical analysis which cannot conceptualize the internal tendencies in social-cultural processes that ensure recognition of domination. Given this systematic failure, Jürgen Habermas's communication theory of society is theoretically progressive in its conception of the recognition of domination as an objective possibility of symbolic communication. However, Habermas's critical theory has lost its relation to Marx's materialistic critique.

The primary intent of this book is to relate the political-economic and the cultural forms of critical theory. In order to do this, the discontinuity of Marx's materialist critical theory and the evolution of the cultural critiques of the Frankfurt school of Marxism (i.e., Max Horkheimer, Theodor Adorno, Herbert Marcuse, Jürgen Habermas) must be transcended in a broader conception of critical theory. By discarding Marx's labor theory of value as the normative foundation of critique, Frankfurt restored the cultural component of a dialectical social theory and yet never regained its link to Marx's work nor was able to develop a new theory of emancipation. In this sense the developing work of Jürgen Habermas is the most significant advance in the creation of a critical theory since Marx. But it will be argued here that a broader framework for critical theory is necessary, one that neither Marx nor Habermas has entirely realized.

Whereas the cultural dimension can be restored to critical theory—and twentieth-century anti-Leninist Marxism has done this in a variety of ways—the conception of the link between critique and emancipation has not been adequate. This is especially true of Habermas's work which, at present, views the ideal of non-repressive communication sedimented into the normative structure of the scientific community, as most pertinent, in the long run, for liberation. A self-consciousness of communication that is free from domination (that which is presupposed by rational discourse) is held to be the model to be used for the critique of power distortions of everyday communication. This model, and the historically specific critiques based upon it, can potentially, Habermas believes, feed back and promote a reorganization of other social institutions. Although this is a powerful formulation for a critical inquiry, the formalism of Habermas's utopian ideal should not be taken as the limit of reason.

In another formulation Habermas's new critical theory remains too narrow because it has, until now, avoided a systematic development of its own formalistic utopian moment. Critical theory cannot ignore the utopian anticipation of the objectively possible. To its tradition of negative critique there must be restored the systematic anticipation of socially emergent alternatives. While critiques of the contradictions of capitalist development and systematic investigation of cultural constraints remain the substantive problems of negative critiques, there must be an equal attempt to reassess new social-cultural claims for emancipation. Without relating the social-economic transformations to emancipatory struggles, critical theory remains a contemplative activity.

Only within such a broad conception of critical theory can such a utopian moment be developed. This statement will be called "revisionist," "reformist," "utopian," and "idealistic" from an orthodox Marxist perspective—criticisms that may be founded since the theoretical controls that adhere to this perspective are considered here to distort the emancipatory intent of critical theory. There can be no separation of critical theory and emancipatory struggles on the level of both social and personal existence. To restore spontaneous, free existence, whether on the societal or personal level, is to regain a sense of totality and the capacity to begin anew. Ultimately the critical consciousness is manifest in its acts, and in its readiness to reflect upon them. Critique, action, and reflection inscribe an ever renewable circle that cannot be stopped arbitrarily or adequately expressed in a formalistic theory.

Indeed, if critical theory is ever to become a force for change, it must do so by transforming our consciousness about the developmental tendencies of both societal and personal processes. It is not enough to claim, as traditional Marxists do, that critique relates to the recognition of objective possibilities for the creation of "socialism." Whereas the notion of the socialist alternative of industrial development was at one time a revolutionary conception, it is today a vague concept that can no longer express the concrete ideal of a liberated society. We need to reflect on the meaning of emancipation in the context of the 1970s and reconceptualize the conditions of liberation from a higher level of industrial domination. And we must anticipate the social forms that will enable us to realize freedom. Historically the term "socialism" has always meant the centralized control of production in order to create economic and social equality. However, in practice this theory, as a material force, has meant the authoritarian destruction of the more revolutionary spontaneity of people who, in the midst of a revolutionary situation, regain the power to interpret their own needs and begin to restore the social basis for human community and individual development.[29]

If emancipation from domination means freedom to use the infinite possibilities of an advanced civilization, it cannot be anticipated as the acquisition of power. Liberty to participate in the control of production, freedom to become involved in meaningful work, liberty to use leisure time in a non-coerced or manipulated manner, freedom to encounter others and nature in relationships that are not functionally determined—these are among the necessary options for the development of autonomous social individuals. These goals are not directly implied by the centralist revolutionary theory of Marxism-Leninism, and are, in practice, explicitly disallowed. This repressive theory of revolution must be discarded and replaced by a new model of emancipation. No abstract utopianism is suggested. But we cannot restrict analysis and emancipatory struggles by the standards set by the reality principle of "socialist" society. In critique, and anticipation of the possible, we must give, as the graffiti of the May 1968 Paris revolt proclaim, "Power to the Imagination!"

The Plan for this Book

Critical theory is not a subject that suggests an easy method of presentation. The basic assumptions of critical philosophy and of everyday life do not necessarily correspond in a scientized civilization. Presentation of the background of critical theory is therefore a necessity even if this may be common knowledge to some.

The first part of the present volume, on the category of alienation, is an attempt to demonstrate that the interest in critique is universal and that some form of critical theory—even in mystified theological versions—has always been present in western thought. Hegel's synthesis of critical philosophy is presented as an attempt to show the untenability of all past forms of critical theory (i.e., the critical analysis of the unhappy consciousness) and to establish the basic problematic for a critical theory of society. The continuity of Marx's work is discussed around his formulation of a theory of the alienation of work in Chapter Two.

The second part is perhaps the most difficult and the most important section of the book. The ideal of critique is reconstructed, beginning with Kant's discovery of the method of transcendental reflection, in contrast with today's positivistic concept of knowledge. The argument traces the development from Kant through Hegel to Marx and attempts to build a nonscientific philosophy of science and a non-objectivistic image of knowledge; these concepts are crucial. Discussion of the relation of Max Weber and social theory to critique; elaboration on the meaning of a dialectical theory; and, finally, a presentation of Habermas's metatheory for critical theory complete the section.

The third part tries to reconstruct and reunite the crisis theories of Marx and contemporary cultural Marxists. An attempt to begin, as a first approximation, the critique of contemporary American society is presented as a model for a broader form of critical theory than has hitherto been attempted.

The influences on my thinking may be useful for the reader. I am deeply indebted to *parts* of the work of Jürgen Habermas which, in my opinion, opens up a new era for the critical philosophy of the social sciences and for critical theory too.

The criticism and encouragement of many people have enabled me to complete this book; I will mention only a few. I would like to express my gratitude to Murray Bookchin, Stanley Diamond, Cliff DuRand, Martin Jay, Martin Sklar, Jeremy Shapiro, Shierry Weber, and Albrecht Wellmer for demonstrating in their relations to me the meaning of critical theory. If I did not see or hear their messages, it is my failure.

Jo Ann Averill, Emily Boardman, Frank Miata, and Karl Schibel have helped me with the present work. I am grateful for Leita Kaldi's endless patience in preparing the manuscript for publication. Finally, I would like to thank Edwin Seaver for his sustained encouragement and Victoria Newhouse for her editorial skill.

I: *THE CATEGORY OF ALIENATION AND THE IDEA OF CRITIQUE*

*C*hapter One is essentially a brief history of ideas presented in an attempt to prove that the category of alienation has always been a primary concept in western thought and has been used in different ways to describe or diagnose the human condition. For example, assessment of states of melancholia, insanity or, generally, alienatio mentis were culture-determined assessments of the maladies confronting humanity. But in all these cultural perspectives there existed a fundamental ambiguity which duplicated the basic dualisms inherent in the early onto-theological conceptions of man. The systems of spiritual guidance that used ideas of alienation were mystified equivalents of what later became critical theory, but they were unable to develop because of their inadequate conceptions of the objective context on the one hand, and of subjectivity on the other. Their inner circularity (what Hegel called "bad infinity") can be expressed as "the paradox of alienation" which subsisted in all pre-Hegelian concepts of alienation.

These early forms of alienation are discussed for two reasons: first, to show that the interest in assessing alienation as domination by the "other" is a constant throughout the history of western thought and can be taken as a universal interest in the use of knowledge for emancipation; second, the Hegelian critique of these pre-critical concepts of alienation (as expressed in his general critique of the "alienated soul") demonstrates the scope of his dialectical concept of alienation that is logically presupposed by all later critical theory. Hegel's critique of the alienated soul shows that it results in the endless vacillations of the contemplative, who is confronted with a paradox which he never really faces: contemplation has become both a means of "transcendence" and a possible disease of the soul. We will see that this "ecstasy-melancholy" duality can be interpreted, following Hegel, as a demonstration of how pre-modern thought was unable to develop a principle of subjectivity that enabled man to negate his alienation. Hegel's dialectical idea of alienation places the moment of domination within the experience consciousness (both individual and collective) has with itself, and alienation becomes a recurrent phase in the process whereby human life externalizes itself, comes to experience things-in-themselves and overcomes this polarity by the conscious "alienation of the alienation." For Hegel the "moment" of the alienated soul is, logically and experientially, an incompatible relationship between psyche, polis, and cosmos. It is impossible for the alienated soul to be "at home" in the present world since its way of representing self and others is, as yet, unable to attain a "reconciliation." Hegel thus reaffirms a dialectical rationalism which had been lost in the medieval and modern separation of the vita activa and vita contemplativa. It is from this point of view that we must begin to interpret contemporary theories of alienation; all refer to this basic alienation of the natural unity of knowing and doing.

In the second chapter, the contrast of Hegelian and Marxian concepts of alienation also permits a comparison of their dialectical theories of society. Most important in the writings of the early Hegel, unknown to Marx, is a general dialectical theory of the relationship of the system of natural needs, the community of mutual recognition, and the reflective self-consciousness of man. Hegel's early concept of alienation was applied to the disruptions in these dialectically related processes, e.g., his assessment of the positivity of religion; Marx's later theory of the dialectical relatedness of natural needs, the processes of human production, and the self-consciousness of man repeats Hegel's theory from a different perspective. The common basis of both theories is the radicalization of critical philosophy into a "phenomenological" (in the Hegelian sense) critique of society. These two theories can be contrasted as theories of cultural (Hegel) and work (Marx) alienation and are not logically as different as later perspectives assume. However, the real difference appears in the way in which *the critique of alienation is conceived in relation to emancipatory action: while Hegel retains the necessity for the diffusion of critique through the processes of high culture, Marx sees critique as a means to further mass struggle against domination. In short, whereas Hegel and Marx share a common type of critical social theory, they differ on the relationship of critique to these processes. It is ironic that just where Marx is more precise about the intent of critique—the relationship of domination and enlightenment—his theory is also more ambiguous than Hegel's.*

1

Pre-Modern Origins and Hegel's Theory of Cultural Alienation

*Das Wahre war schon längst gefunden
Das alte Wahre, fass es an!*
("*Vermächtnis*"—Goethe)

The Divided Image of Man in Western Thought

*T*he "Great Chain of Being", a concept which permeates Western thought, forms the cosmological framework for a discussion of the category of alienation. Plato's *Timaeus* can be interpreted as outlining the elements of this doctrine although other conceptions are added in its subsequent development.[1] In the *Timaeus* we are introduced to the idea of God, or the Demiurge, who has created the world by emanating outside himself thus forming the world as a hierarchy of angels, demons, heroes, average men, vulgar men, animals, vegetables, minerals, and prime matter. In creating the world God in effect *alienated* the world from himself; he created the world as *otherness*.

Medieval teleology is linked to this cosmological scheme. Rocks are meant to be rocks and hence fall toward the earth. Animals are meant to be animals and hence lust after each other for the purpose of procreation. Angels are meant to be angels and thus have their given realm in the heavens. But man presents a problem. According to Christian theology man is created in the image of God. Yet this very theology, having absorbed the classical cosmology, saw man as ontologically alienated from God by being part of that "otherness" created by Him in the beginning. The gap between the ontological otherness of the world and the special status of man is bridged by the concept that man *ought* to escape this otherness and return to the Godhead. Thus St. Augustine's *Confessions* opens with:

You have made us for thee, O God, and we
cannot rest until we rest in thee.

In Western thought man is thus the paradox of nature whose purpose, or telos, is to reunite with God, but whose nature is firmly rooted in the "otherness" of the corporal world. "At home" in the earthly world is to be estranged from his essential divinity, while striving for reunion with God is to experience his own "otherness" as a prison. Man is that wretched creature whose tragic duality condemns him to endless struggle and homelessness. To be man therefore is to be both a sick animal—since total immersion in the sensate world is impossible—and a futile passion —since striving for divinity is ontologically impossible. The vacillations within the Western image of man can be seen as a circling about these poles, duplicating and re-turning to this fundamental metaphysical ambiguity which haunts its beginnings.

It is impossible to reconstruct here the history of this ongoing contradiction in the philosophical anthropology of the West.[2] Instead we will focus on the idea of alienation as it has appeared and reappeared. This strategy has several advantages:

1. The idea of alienation has been traced both etymologically and philosophically; we can briefly summarize this work in view of establishing the hypotheses of this chapter.

2. Alienation is a useful category for a comparison of contemporary and pre-modern consciousness about man.

Etymological Origins of the Idea of Alienation[3]

Nathan Rotenstreich finds that the Latin word *alienatio* has two meanings: first a denotative legal meaning and then several metaphoric or "psychological" meanings. Our interest lies not with the legal root, in which "alienation" refers to the transfer or conveyance of property to another, but with the metaphorical meanings which deal with the unity of consciousness. The first metaphorical meaning is the Latin *alienatio mentis,* or the German *Bewusstlosigkeit,* which indicates a loss of sanity, the ability to concentrate, etc. What is lost is some form of independence; a unity is disrupted. The second metaphoric meaning of the Latin term *alienatio* assimilates the classic Greek ideas for change and disturbance as mediated by ecstasy. This meaning leads to "the ecstatic literature on contemplation":

... *alienatio mentis in St. Augustine is the act of elevation from the senses and not the act of forlornness of the mind.* Being an act of elevation it reaches the divine realm, and ceases to be a negative act of estrangement, thus becoming a positive act leading to the achievement of union with God. Yet this achievement is still ... outside the mind, the latter to be taken in its discursive meaning, maintaining the separation between the knower and the known.[4] (italics mine)

Alienation in this context is thus an ecstatic elevation: a positive achievement of man, not his denial of himself.

In all of his research Rotenstreich seeks to contrast the modern idea of alienation with its earlier etymological forms. Specifically, he wants to contrast the Christian idea of ecstasy as an *alienatio mentis* with the modern use of alienation by Hegel, Marx, etc. He finds that the earlier ecstatic positive evaluation contrasts with modern perspectives that see alienation as "an improper transcendence" (Hegel), a "fictitious one" (Feuerbach), or else a "terrifying one" (Marx).

While Rotenstreich has greatly illuminated some of the origins of the category of alienation, his thesis of discontinuity is unacceptable and misleading. It will be shown, first, that there is a common structure to the idea of alienation which allows us to talk of it as a unit-idea of Western thought; and second, that Rotenstreich's contrast obscures an ambiguity inherent in the Christian tradition's image of man. The argument will be advanced by developing these counter theses.

The Unit-Idea of Alienation in Western Thought

In the Christian literature on ecstatic contemplation, ecstasy was considered a necessary "alienation" so that man *could gain a unity* that is impossible as long as he is *confined to the knower-known dualism* of everyday consciousness. Early as well as later usages of the term *alienation* have a normative focus—that is, a unity or wholeness *should* be achieved, and some form of "transcendence" is felt necessary for this reunification. The constant presence of these two characteristics is here taken to constitute the irreducible core of a unit-idea of alienation, one which is fundamental to all Ancient, Medieval, Renaissance and modern formulations. Rotenstreich's contrast thus obscures the common framework upon which the various ideas of alienation can be compared.

In the numerous variations of the idea of alienation two characteristics subsist: there is a concept of an essential unity (e.g. fulfillment of the image of man, immersion in the "One," reconciliation with externalized "others," etc.) and a designation of the processes which disrupt unity (e.g. humors, furies, passions, vices, sin, capitalist society, etc.). Upon the basis of these common characteristics it is possible to generalize that alienation is a deprivation of the "one" by the "other"; a non-being or unformedness of the one due to the appropriation of the other. Various formulations of the idea are simply different ways of conceptualizing the "one" and the process of appropriation.

The Ecstasy-Melancholy Duality:
Paradox of the Alienation Category

Rotenstreich's isolation of the ecstatic origin of alienation is unwarranted since both metaphorical meanings must be taken together if we are to be consistent with Medieval usage of *alienatio mentis*. Christian and Renaissance thought, especially, reveal an attitude toward the life of contemplation which contains the dual meaning of *alienatio mentis*. Internal to these thought systems is the philosophical framework of the ancient "Great Chain of Being" which, above all in its Neo-Platonic reformulation, sees the possibility of both the soul's elevation *and its descent*. Thus, within the Christian literature on contemplation, *alienatio mentis* was indeed seen as the *furor divinus* which accompanied the striving to ascend to the Godhead. But this same *furor divinus* might have been viewed by others as an insanity or estrangement from self and world, and thus as a movement "downward." The irresolvability of this epistemological problem constantly promoted profound ambivalence. The other side of the contemplative's striving to climb the spiritual ladder to God is the possibility of encountering a different type of *alienatio mentis*, generally called *melancholia*, which resulted in loss of sanity and concentration. Rotenstreich's two metaphoric meanings are different sides of the same matter. What might be an elevation could become a descent; what might seem to be the highest human experience could also be the most serious disease.

For example, in the Christian traditions, infused with the Pauline contrast of spirit and flesh, movement away from the baser forms of human life toward God was a process of becoming "unalienated" (from God). In the highest stage of this movement "upward," that of ecstasy, the mystic claims he becomes one with God. But this could be an alienation from the human world, from the point of view of the Greek's concern with the "mean" or that of the "philosophies of resignation" (e.g. Stoicism). The ambiguity as to the basic nature of man (capable of ascending toward God in an ecstatic alienation, or in so being possessed by passions that one is alienated from the "limit") is thus reflected in the paradox of alienation.

But the paradox is deepened by the epistemological problems. If man has a determinate form, then he is alienated if he allows passions to make him "miss the mark": but on the other hand, the highest men, such as Socrates, often experienced ecstasy. Even in the Greek image of man there is an epistemological-ethical problem of how to distinguish between the highest experiences and the baser passions.

From the point of view of the classic Greek tradition an "ecstatic elevation" may not be "positive," but an indication of a "frenzy" which takes man beyond the limit of humanness, and alienates him from his fellow man and hence from the human world. Even in Plato's system there is an ambivalence toward ecstatic alienation. In the *The Phaedrus* Plato develops his fourfold theory of the "divine furies": prophetic madness, religious madness, poetic madness, love madness. Love "madness" is the most extensive and complex of Plato's depictions of "madnesses." It is clearly what has been called ecstasy by later mystics, and yet Plato also implies that there are very "negative" consequences of this madness.[5] But in general Plato continues the Greek belief that "ecstasy" is necessary to ascend to the realm of wisdom.[6] Erwin Rohde summarizes the core experience of the "positive" Greek view of ecstasy:

> The extraordinary phenomena transcending all normal experience were explained by saying that the soul of the person thus "possessed" was no longer "at home" but "abroad," having left its body behind. This was the literal and primitive meaning understood by the Greek when he spoke of the "ekstasis" of the soul in such orgiastic conditions of excitement. This ekstasis is a brief madness, just as madness is a prolonged ekstasis. But the ekstasis, the temporary *alienatio mentis* of the Dionysiac cult was not thought of as a vain purposeless wandering in a region of pure delusion but as a *hieromania*, a sacred madness in which the soul leaving the body, winged its way to union with the god.[7]

The "negative" side of the Greek perspective is illustrated, however, by Aristotle's theory of genius which, when applied to Socrates, implies the melan-cholic, or the presence of too much black bile.[8] Hence the heirs to the classic Greek tradition inherit an ambivalent characterization of ecstasy: from Plato it can be an ecstatic elevation; from Aristotle it can be a disease of the soul.[9] Here is the same problem that we encountered in the above dissussion of *alienatio mentis*.

The Greek ambivalence becomes but another factor in the later paradox. In the medieval image man could be misled by his passions not toward God but away from him, and thus again the problem became one of how to distinguish movements "upward" from movements "downward." Paradoxically in both of these frameworks what may be a sign of the highest perfection (the unalienated state) could also be the most dangerous mode of alienation.

In the work of the thirteenth century writer Arnoldus du Villanova, for example, a heroic lover who yearns for the beautiful female or for the immersion in God can be stricken by a loss of concentration and consciousness.[10] What might be an ecstatic elevation could also become a melancholic passion which leads not to God but to a low form of human dis-ease. This is the paradox of contemplative ecstasy: an *alienatio mentis* which represents God's grace and an elevation beyond the human realm could be mistaken for an *alienatio mentis* that is actually a cast-down-ness to an animal-like incapacity to transcend the emotions of the moment.

A more important example is Marsilio Ficino (1433–1499), an Italian philosopher, physician, and scholar, who was one of the leaders of Renaissance Platonism. Ficino uses the category *alienatio mentis* for a comprehensive analysis of passions, furors, humors, etc., and he is thought by some commentators to have resolved some of the dualistic contradictions of the western tradition. More specifically he has been given credit for "reconciling" Neoplatonism with the medieval tradition:[11]

as far as we know, Ficino was the first writer to identify what Aristotle had called the melancholy of intellectually outstanding men with Plato's divine frenzy.[12]

But even the resurgence of the classic tradition in a foremost Renaissance scholar of Plato was insufficient to resolve the contradictions of the *alienatio mentis* debate. In his commentary on Plato's *Ion*[13] Ficino provides a complete theory of alienation which accounts for three types of *alienatio*, and gives them each a place in a comprehensive hierarchical framework. He places the human soul in the central position of the cosmos as the bond which links the highest and lowest beings through its infinite aspiration and thoughts. The soul is capable of a four-fold ascent or descent, and the movements along this scale were classified by Ficino as illness and divine inspiration.[14] The four stages of descent are the intellect, reason, opinion, and nature. *Insania* for Ficino is a downward alienation from the first two to the two lower ones. But the *divine furor* can enable the soul to rise again by unifying and pacifying the stage "below" while ascending to a "higher" level. At the lowest level poetry calms and harmonizes the soul. But there is too much diversity in the world and the soul must therefore ascend to the stage of mystery where a "higher" unity can be achieved. Here the soul must be unified by reason—but this too must be transcended, and hence the *furor amatorius* helps the unified soul to merge with the supreme Unity itself.

The system works both ways: at the lowest level the *furor poeticus* (an ascent) can be a *furor melancholicus*[15] (a descent). The poet-philosopher can be alienated "upward" or "downward" depending upon his mode of activity. At the highest stage the furor of love can also manifest itself in two ways: the one drawing us up to beauty, the other casting us downward. Only divine love can unify the soul.

When applied to the figure of Socrates the complications of this scheme appear.[16] What Aristotle had called Socrates' melancholy is according to Ficino an *alienatio . . . ab humoris morbis* and not an *alienatio . . . a Deo*. But this is true only in an exterior sense, for inwardly Socrates did not succumb to this melancholic agitation, but was involved in the *amor copia* of the higher realm! Thus the poet-lover Socrates is an embodiment of both of these realms at once! He reflects on the lower levels the physical symptoms of the melancholic, but at the same time he is inwardly unified in a realm of tranquility. One wonders if this magnificent synthesis is philosophically tenable.[17]

Historically, as might be expected, the tenuous resolution of the paradox of alienation produced by Ficino was not to last, and future discussion opened again the contradiction which he had so laboriously attempted to bridge.[18] What Nathan Rotenstreich wanted to accept as the pre-modern form of alienation-ecstatic elevation (a positive alienation)—and contrast with modern ideas (negative alienation), must now be seen as too simplistic. Ecstasy can be "positive," but it might also be "negative." We do not know how to distinguish infallibly true ecstasy from false, nor are we sure that contemplation always helps us "ascend."[19] What seems to be a clear division of pre-modern alienation has become a paradox.

In what Rotenstreich calls "the ecstatic literature on contemplation" there are combined fundamentally philosophical ideas (the Platonic opposition of the realm of ideas and the realm of existence and its implicit epistemological problem of how man is to ascend from the one to the other) and fundamentally theological conceptions (the Pauline antithesis between the Flesh and the Spirit). In following the word linkages back to the Christian ecstatics Rotenstreich has failed to see that the meanings given to the term *alienatio mentis* often depended upon metaphysical systems that had become entwined in Christian theology, making the theological discussion of ecstasy into a syncretistic complex.

To repeat: throughout the history of the category of alienation there persists a basic logical form. Some essential unity has been disrupted, sometimes by the domination of another. The various therapeutic systems that emerged were based upon different conceptions of what is the essential reality, the ideal state of human existence. But continued failure to identify accurately what was a positive or negative alienation made spiritual guidance rather unstable. For example, in testing Joan of Arc, the church was concerned with whether she was possessed by an evil demonic force or was indeed, as she claimed, in ecstatic communication with the divine. As usual, the incapacity to solve this problem resulted in the "test" of fire which would "prove" the case. How can we know even when the ecstatic "knows" that he is unalienated, or if he is, isn't he still "alienated" from us?

Given the components of the Western tradition, the "mean" or limit of tranquility translates itself into a dictate that man "ought not to be alienated"; but given the ideal of a Logos and/or Eros that carries man "upward" toward the "essential reality" or toward God, the command is reversed and man is confronted with "thou should be alienated." The observer can not know if other men are alienated "up" or "down"; surely this medieval and

Renaissance debate underlies the later synthesis of the "tragic vision" of man.

Given the course of pre-modern theories of alienation, the Human Condition is one of encountering "otherness," or domination, at every point; man is challenged by the recalcitrance of his own materiality as well as beaconed by the promise of his spirit's capacity to ascend to joy. But life experience forces him to recognize that immersion in the "one" may pass over into the control by the "other." He hovers, therefore, between the Scylla of the human world's deadening "security" and the Charybdis of the beckoning of his yearning spirit. He must choose. But the soul yearns for the *telos* that will point the way, for a definition of what is most essential and what is the necessary path. Frustrated attempts are suffered as melancholy, and man is thus cast back into the endless dialectic from which he has more and more difficulty emerging. This point has been put more comprehensively by William James who sees the universal consequences of the need for *telos*. "The real core of the religious poem" is the deliverance of man from a sense of *anhodenia* or "loss of appetite for all life's values," which in its extreme form "leads to desperation absolute and complete, the whole universe coagulating about the sufferer into a material and overwhelming horror, surrounding him without opening or end."[20]

Hegel's philosophy, especially as developed in the *Phenomenology of Spirit*, addresses itself precisely to the endless vacillations of the alienated soul. He implies only melancholy can result from philosophical contradictions that "determine" the experience of man trying to judge what is essential, and how to recognize domination.

Long before Hegel's dialectical reformation of the idea, however, there appears in Christendom a rejection of the Christian formulation. Giordano Bruno, in the fourth dialogue of *The Heroic Frenzies*, criticizes the spiritual yearning inherent in the contemplative experience of melancholy:

. . . . you transgress when, seduced by the beauties of the intellect, you leave the other part of me in danger of death. Whence have you engendered this perverse and melancholy humor of breaking certain natural laws of the true life, a life you hold in your power, for an uncertain life that is nothing if not a shadow beyond the limits of the imaginable? Does it seem natural to you that creatures should refuse the animal or the human life in order to live the divine life when they are not gods but only men or animals?[21]

But Bruno was suppressed, and the alienation paradox continued to have an impact on European ideas, transforming itself in different thought systems, but generally retaining its initial pathos up to the modern era.

The Hegelian Conception of Philosophy and the Problem of Alienation

The central motif of Hegel's thought is the reconciliation of man with his world, the mediation of all alienations, and the restoration of man to himself in his "otherness" (history, society, culture). The need for speculative reunification of the totality is most acute at those unique junctures in human history when the discords and dislocations that are ever present in history reach a critical point:

when the power of unification disappears from the life of men and opposites have lost their living relation and reciprocity and gain independence, then the need for philosophy originates.[22]

The need for philosophy emerges when the oppositions have become "independent" and can no longer be expressed meaningfully in terms of existing cultural systems.

The need for speculative synthesis, or reconstruction, issues from the crisis of the social whole—a radically new conception of the ground of philosophy, which historicizes the classical notion that philosophy begins in the experience of wonder. For Hegel philosophy begins in crisis, in the discord that presses upon the individual in a fragmenting social whole:

Philosophy springs on the one hand from the living originality of the spirit who in it has restored through himself the rent harmony and given form to it through his own deed; on the other hand, from the particular form of the bifurcation from which the system issues. Bifurcation (or discord) is the source of the need for philosophy.[23]

A genuine philosophical comprehension is more, however, than a new world view; it is a transformation of human experience itself in that expression and understanding of the conflict and discord become possible. Such comprehension is not directed toward reinstituting a past golden age nor does it imply a blueprint for the transformation of the present into some future Ideal. It is a speculative reconstruction of *the totality* that objectifies the requirements of the present. The complexities of the totality, the tyranny of ossified institutions and the hopes for the future all make the grasp of reality in the present the most ambitious task that human reason can achieve:

To comprehend what is, this is the task of philosophy, because what is, is reason. Whatever happens, every individual is a child of his time; so philosophy too is its own time apprehended in thoughts. It is just as absurd to fancy that a philosophy can transcend its contemporary world as it is to fancy that one individual can overleap his own age, jump over Rhodes. If his theory really goes beyond the world as it is, and builds an ideal one as it ought to be, that world exists indeed, but only in his opinions, an unsubstantial element where anything you please may, in fancy, be built.[24]

Philosophy as a critical theory must be developed therefore, against both Kant's distinction between theoretical and practical reason, and the romantic yearning for the "ought." Both of these philosophies stress a dualism of "is" and "ought" which Hegel rejects as surmountable in the Identity of Reason and Being:

"What is universally valid is also universally effective; what ought to be, as a matter of fact, is too; what merely should be, and is not has no truth."[25]

What ought to be *is*, in so far as it is contained as a concrete potentiality in the given state of affairs. What merely should be is contained in the present only as an abstract possibility and is not an objective possibility. Hegel does not mean that we are always in the midst of "the best of all possible worlds," that what *exists* is *actual* and rational. This is an erroneous interpretation of the famous line: "what is rational is actual and what is actual is rational." The existing is, in itself, not rational, only the unique power of human comprehension can penetrate historical alienations and express what is objectively possible:

Actuality is always the unity of universal and particular, the universal dismembered in the particulars which seem to be self-subsistent, although they really are upheld and contained only in the whole. Where this unity is not present, a thing is not actual even though it may have acquired existence. A bad state is one which merely exists; a sick body exists too, but it has no genuine reality. A hand which is cut off still looks like a hand, and it exists, but without being actual. Genuine actuality is necessity; what is actual is inherently necessary.[26]

This distinction between existence and actuality destroys the image of Hegel as counseling us to affirm the existent as rational. It also sets forth the basic intent of critical theory.

For Hegel philosophy must mediate the "here" and "now" in such a way that the abstractions of the past do not become more real than the moment. At the same time, the philosopher must see the moment without being swept into a pathos of an Ideal future. To be aware of the "eternal moment" requires a continual reconciliation of the residues of the past and the prejudices for the future. This conception is most powerfully stated in the preface to *The Philosophy of Right*:

What lies between reason as self-conscious mind and reason as an actual world before our eyes, what separates the former from the latter and prevents it from finding satisfaction in the latter, is *the fetter of some abstraction or other which has not been liberated* (and so transformed) into the concept. To recognize reason as the rose in the cross of the present and thereby to enjoy the present, that is the rational insight which reconciles us to the actual, the reconciliation which philosophy affords to those in whom there has once arisen an inner voice bidding them to comprehend, not only to dwell in what is substantive while still retaining subjective freedom, but also to possess subjective freedom while standing not in anything particular and accidental but in what exists absolutely.[27] (italics mine)

The liberation from "abstraction" is essentially, in Marxian terms which are apt here, the de-reification that is a necessary condition for de-alienation. For example, the word or deed, in representing an individuated self in a changing public world, may be taken by others as an adequate representation of the person—or the person himself might view this externalization as totally representing him. Such an imputation of "fixedness" to a potentially infinite capacity is what Hegel calls "abstract thinking," later described as a reification in Marxian terminology. Hegel himself pointed out the presence of such ongoing reifications in a very lively article entitled "Who Thinks Abstractly," written for a Berlin newspaper. He recounts the reaction of various classes to the event of a murderer being led to execution, and evaluates the identification of the common populace:

This is abstract thinking: to see nothing in the murderer except the abstract fact that he is a murderer, and to annul all other human essence in him with this simple quality.[28]

Recognizing the ubiquitousness of "abstract thinking" it is likely that many—if not most—externalizations result in a failure to understand the "other" and thus distort self-reflection.

For Hegel philosophy is "what is most antagonistic to abstraction, and it leads back to the concrete." The critical method is the only reliable guide for man in the constant flux of the human world:

Science alone is theodicy: it keeps one both from looking at events with animal amazement, or ascribing them, more cleverly, to accidents of the moment or of the talents of one individual—as if the destinies of empires depended on an occupied hill—and from lamenting the triumph of injustice and the defeat of right. . . .[29] (italics mine)

Only a Science of Reason (i.e., critical theory) can transcend the alienated thinking of one-sided ("abstract") views of history that lead man away from recognizing what is real in the "appearing."

The Concept of Cultural Alienation

The externalization of subjectivity into a public world typifies Hegel's idea of alienation; once manifested, human words and deeds have lives of their own. Man loses himself insofar as he divests himself in "things," or in the "in-them-self-others" of human creativity. But these alienations can themselves be "alienated" by the human agent's ability to recognize himself in his otherness, though remaining with himself. For example, one can comprehend the religious motive and recognize its inherent truth without becoming involved in either the false consciousness of religion or the will to destroy it. But historical alienations are not always comprehended and instead become ongoing "reifications" of the existing world. The "cunning of reason" in history is that the rarity of man's knowledge of the actual truth of human activity constitutes one of the necessary conditions for man's continuing efforts to transform the world in accordance with his practical reason. It is the division between the desire to bring order into the world and our theoretical understanding of order which motivates us to continue to form, or cultivate our worlds.

But emancipation requires the unity of impulse and reflection and Hegel insists that the reason and the will of man are not separable faculties:

> Spirit is in principle thought, and man is distinguished from beast in virtue of thought. But it must not be imagined that man is half thought and half will, and that he keeps thought in one pocket and will in another, for this would be an empty idea. The distinction between thought and will is only that between the theoretical attitude and the practical. These, however, are surely not two faculties; the will is rather a special mode of thought, thought translating itself into existence, thought as the urge to give itself existence.[30]

Will is the internal imperative of thought to give itself external existence, to negate a given state and aim toward making it conform with the interior determination. Will is therefore the intention of reason and as such it results in actions that would transform material and social realities and so realize the rational. Theory and practice, thought and will are two drives (*Treibe*) of the human animal that together constitute the *telos* of man—to impose upon reality a form which makes it conform with reason. The end of human life is the transformation of the irrational into the rational, of the void into order.

The function of thought is to subject the impulse of will to its critique; only through their unification is practical reason comprehended and given its universality:

> . . . it is in the **will** that the intrinsic finitude of intelligence has its beginning; and it is only by raising itself to become thought again, and endowing its aims with immanent universality, that the will cancels the difference of form and content and makes itself the objective, infinite will. Thus they [i.e. Kant and Fichte] understand little of the nature of thinking and willing who suppose that while, in willing as such, man is infinite, in thinking he, or even reason itself, is restricted. In so far as thinking and willing are still distinguished the opposite is rather the truth, and the will is thinking reason resolving itself to finitude.[31]

In short, free self-conscious life is possible only by thought absorbing will and willing itself. Insofar as thought remains directed by desire it results in false consciousness, or the alienated soul.

To be aware, however, of the need to create the rational is at the same time to be aware of an "in-itself-ness" that is, from the point of reason, separated from the Idea. Thus "will" always posits a difference that separates the ego from the non-ego and must be overcome:

> The variegated canvas of the world is before me; I stand over against it; by my theoretical attitude to it I overcome its opposition to me and make its content my own. I am at home in the world when I know it, still more so when I have understood it. So much for the theoretical attitude. The practical attitude, on the other hand, begins in thinking, in the ego itself, and it appears first as though opposed to thinking because, I mean, *it sets up a sort of diremption.* Insofar as I am practical or active, i.e. insofar as I do something, I determine myself, and to determine myself simply means to posit a difference. . . . If I now let these determinations and differences go, i.e. if I posit them in the so-called external world, they none the less still remain mine. They are what I have done, what I have made; they bear the trace of my mind.[32]

The nature of human experience is a divesting of self into "others" and the return to self. This is true for all levels of the *Geist* in Hegel's philosophy and as such it is a general formative principle of spiritual life. In the most general sense then we can call this recurrent moment of externalization cultural (*Bildung*) alienation, the fundamental definition of which could be taken from the section of the *Phenomenology* entitled "Spirit in Self-Estrangement: the Discipline of Shaping a World":

> The spirit of this world is spiritual essence permeated by a self-consciousness which knows itself to be directly present as a self-existent particular, and knows that essence as an objective actuality over against itself. But the existence of this world, as also the actuality of self-consciousness, depends on the process that self-consciousness diverts itself of its personality, by so doing creates its world, and treats it as something alien and external, of which it must now take possession . . .[33]

Alienation of the individual self-consciousness is the means by which he produces, or creates, himself—but these externalizations must be re-appropriated before he can *realize* himself. Again the movement is circular: self-awareness—externalization—reappropriation—self-awareness. The circular process is possible as a function of the fact that in the humanly produced world the reappropriation is essentially the capacity to comprehend one's own words and deeds.

Philosophizing within the tradition of transcendental philosophy, Hegel shows that the emergence of self-consciousness is not a process which can develop out of the isolated ego but presupposes the "process of recognition." In so constituting the "ego" Hegel has taken what was for Fichte a logical ground and demonstrates that in order to have a "me" we must have a "we"; in this sense what was logical also becomes "cultural." *Mutual-recognition* is both the transcendental condition of intersubjectivity and the empirical process whereby the speakers of ordinary language are able to communicate with each other. Disruptions of the process of mutual-recognition, such as the emergence of relations of domination (e.g., master and slave) break the open communication process and are thus alienations.

Hegel's notion of alienation can be interpreted as focusing upon the dialectical relatedness of self-consciousness and mutual-recognition systems. If available systems of "mutual-recognition," such as the mores or laws of a society, make it impossible for man to recognize the other, or himself, as a potentially free self-conscious agent, these systems are "cultural alienations." In the same way, if the processes of self-reflection are systematically limited there results a set of alienated action patterns which express this self-estrangement. The mutual reciprocity of self-consciousness and mutual-recognition systems is the basis for what we call Hegel's critical theory of cultural alienation. Concentration upon this theoretical linkage is a selective reconstruction from Hegel's more comprehensive project of a transcendental ontology. Such interpretation is necessary if the implications of Hegel's thought are to be realized by social theory. A few examples from his early writings will demonstrate the constant presence of this theory of cultural alienation.

The "Positivity" of Religion and the Causality of Fate

In the *Early Theological Writings* religion is always approached as complex *social* phenomena and never as mere schemes of believed-in ideas. The concern is with how this social phenomena binds the social totality together in a moral unity, or whether its domination by Church, or State, transforms the vital moral fibre of the community of believers into a dogmatic thing-like structure.

An important evaluative standard which is more prominent in the later theological essays is the Kantian notion of a rational religion. That is, a religion based entirely upon the conscience of an autonomous moral agent. The significance of this ideal is central to the idea of "positivity," a critical concept for the evaluation of the authenticity of historical religions:

The conception of the 'positivity' of a religion has originated and become important only in recent times. A positive religion is contrasted with natural religion, and this presupposes that there is only one natural religion, since human nature is one and single, while there may be many positive religions. It is clear from this very contrast that a positive religion is a contranatural or a supernatural one, containing concepts and information transcending understanding and reason and requiring feelings and actions which would not come naturally to men; the feelings are forcible and mechanically stimulated, the actions are done in order to form obedience without any spontaneous interest.[34]

I: *The Category of Alienation and the Idea of Critique*

Once a religious system becomes embedded in a Church, the moral law becomes "a given"; something that stands over and against the men who "have this systematic web woven around them from youth up." In so constraining every thought, emotion and action, the historical religion deadens "life" by pre-defining its every response. This general assessment of the consequences of the transformation of a living faith into a dead system of statutes, dogma, and codified moral rules is seen by Hegel as a domination of the human conscience by a "life-denying" authority. For example, Hegel's assessment of the contradiction of the Christian church, which commands not only actions (as in Judaism) but also feelings, is that it promotes:

(a) self-deception, i.e. the belief that one has the prescribed feelings,
. . . (one common form of this is) the ordinary self goes on acting . . .
alongside the spiritual self . . . the man is not a unity at all . . .
(b) the result of this self-deception is a false tranquility which sets a
high value on these feelings manufactured in a spiritual hothouse and
thinks much of itself on the strength of these; for this reason it is weak
where it should be powerful, and if a man recognizes this for himself,
he sinks into helplessness, anxiety (Angst) and self-distrust, a physical
state which often develops into madness.[35]

As early as 1795 Hegel was aware of the manner in which the coercive imposition of religious systems produces a disrupted, or alienated self-consciousness.

The gradual transition in Hegel's early writing on this very problem of positivity of religion is what is most relevant for our concern with his theory of cultural alienation. In the essay "The Spirit of Christianity and its Fate" (1878–79) Hegel changes his approach to the positivity of religion with a reinterpretation of the "moral teaching of Jesus." The emergence of Jesus in the midst of the Judaic world was a product of, and an opposition to, the Jewish faith. He did not "fight merely against one part of the Jewish faith; he set himself against the whole." He did this by healing on the Sabbath, which broke all Jewish law. Hegel thus begins by defining religious practice as the "endeavor to unify the discords necessitated by our development," making the ideal existent and confirming it in a deed. In this act Jesus denied the "duty" of the Sabbath but realized the urge for unification in religious practice as well as the meeting of human need. Thus the unification of human needs and of the religious urge becomes "love" which Jesus actualizes in his life by healing. Finally, by making virtue triumph despite the laws, he placed the sphere of morality not in the external world but within the community of man and his individual needs.

For Hegel the religious urge is not a pure subjectivity; we cannot root religion in the "law of reason" as Kant has tried to do. This simply replaces the external positivity with an internal one; rather than being a slave to an alien God, man is a slave to himself. Man remains a duality in either case: as God-man or reason-will.

Hegel calls this duality the *fate* of the Christian community in that the love for God, settling over the whole, chokes off the unity of life:

Since the love of the group had overreached itself . . . and was now filled with an ideal content but was deficient in life, the bare ideal of love was something 'positive' for it; it recognized it as set over against itself and itself as dependent on it.[36]

Hegel concludes the essay by anticipating his analysis of the Unhappy Consciousness in the *Phenomenology*.

it is fate that church and state, worship and life, piety and virtue, spiritual and worldly action, can never dissolve into one.[37]

Eighteen hundred years of "sorrow and suffering" has thus been the fate of the Christian Church.

Hegel tries again and again in these early essays to formulate a philosophical resolution of the suppositions that divided the moral community. The hint of a solution emerges from the mystery of the Eucharist:

Yet the love made objective, this subjective element become a *thing*, reverts once more to its nature, becomes subjective again in eating.[38]

Hegel compares this mysterious circle of religious experience with the circle of thought become "thing" (as written down) and its vanishing in the *understanding*. This circle is the source of Hegel's later phenomenological method, but here he treats it as a secret of the inner law of spirit itself. In these early essays it is most developed with a reflection about the dogma of the trinity in which the connection of the Father, the Son, and the Holy Spirit is seen as the circle of mankind in faith, alienation and *self-produced unity*. (This same trinitarian speculation can be discovered in a crucial section of the *Phenomenology* in which the Lord has the servant serve and through terror and servitude the bondsman produces his own world which is an objective unification of self.) In these essays Hegel suggests that the Christian Community could have found its unity in the Community-of-faith which had developed into an objective history producing a basis for life. That is, the division between spirit, and the history of the Christian community as an objective community of need and religious urge could have been unified by *understanding* this alienation:

... what is a contradiction in the realm of the dead is not one in the realm of life.[39]

The Christian, therefore, could have seen that love of God could become love of man. In the same manner, recognition of need, as a unity of natural relationships, as well as the urge for unification, could have formed the basis of a unified Life that *recognizes itself as spirit*; this is, in fact, Hegel's early dialectical theory of society. The natural dependence of man forms a physical basis for life, while the "loving circle" which "tied one member to another" formed the possibility of an understanding of the unity of man and God.

Within the living whole there are posited at the same time death, opposition and understanding, because there is posited a manifold that is alive itself and that, as alive, can posit itself as a whole.[40]

The cultural basis for unification is in the opposition between the *subjective consciousness* of spirit and the *objective configuration of love* which unites the real human community. (Distortions of either the symbolic interaction system or self-consciousness will therefore disrupt religious authenticity.) Hegel argues that to understand this self-identity we need a speculative science that can understand *spiritual causality*,[41] which we can now regard as the unique causality of dialectically-related sociocultural systems and self-reflection. But "spiritual causality" is described in the early essays as the dialectical movement of the fate of Christianity; faith, positivity, and construction of a real basis of Life are seen as the moments of the cycle. The possible resolution of the alienation of the Christian era depends for the young Hegel upon the development of reflection and its necessary base in increased communality. Neither increased self-consciousness nor real community were able to develop, however, since they reciprocally presuppose each other. But the history is now "comprehended"; development of the infinite subject from the finite required the alienation of the Christian people—which was a suppression of finite life until it became infinite life. Hegel therefore finds the Christian religion of fundamental importance for the emergence of Western civilization. The Judaic religion resulted in a rigid positivity which did not promote the necessary spiritualization, and the Greek harmony remained a unity of immediacy and could not become spiritual. The alienation of man in the Christian epoch has been the means by which nature has become spiritualized and the unity of life established. Hence domination of the servant by the Lord has, for Hegel, been the means by which man produced his world in which he then recognized himself. This is the real basis for the section on lordship and bondage that has so absorbed Marxists.

Hegel's early speculations on the unity of spirit and life have provided the foundation for numerous later attempts to generate a philosophical anthropology,[42] and have influenced Dilthey's last attempts to generate an adequate methodology for the human sciences.[43]

The Phenomenology of Spirit

In the preface to the *Phenomenology*, there is a vivid descriptive statement about the nature of the "true" which philosophy investigates:

I: *The Category of Alienation and the Idea of Critique*

The true is thus the bacchanalian whirl in which no member is not drunken; and because each, as soon as it detaches itself, dissolves immediately—the whirl is just as much transparent and simple repose.[44]

In the pages of the *Phenomenology* the stages of the spirit's *Bildung* are encountered as detached unstable parts of the whirl, the coming to be and passing away that is history. As parts they are transparent in their incompleteness and one-sidedness. However, the whole can be experienced when the parts are conceived as a dynamic movement from the lowest human experience up to the moment of philosophic-science. That is, the end of the *Phenomenology* is presupposed by the beginning.

What makes the *Phenomenology* important for the theory of alienation is that Hegel is committed to show how each appearance of the Spirit changes over into another because of the internal principle of that "stage." The dynamic of history is transitory because of its one-sidedness and its capacity to be transformed by the contradictions that are inherent in it. Thus Hegel must demonstrate how the stages in themselves constitute the changes that come about; what is latent becomes manifest because of the concreteness of the set of forces that emerge internally. The presentation and internal critiques of the cultural gestalt's self-consciousness, such as lordship and bondage, Stoicism, skepticism, and the Unhappy Consciousness, as well as the modes of practical realization of self-consciousness, such as "the man on the make," "the man of heart," "the man of virtue," the cult of "players of the game," are especially brilliant and penetrating analyses of the dialectical relatedness of cultural patterns and self-consciousness. The analyses always depict both the social situatedness and the dynamic consequences of the internal contradiction. The point of these reconstructions is always the "necessity" of the cultural configurations, resulting in their *inner instability* for individuals formed by these alienated cultural forms.

Hegel's Theory of the Unhappy Consciousness

Hegel is one of the moderns who is aware of the history of the paradox of alienation. He reexamines it in his philosophical analysis of the *ungluckliches Bewusstsein* (unhappy consciousness).[45] Significantly, he deals with the paradox as a phase of the human spirit's quest for knowledge and, contrary to the ecstatic assumption, he holds that transcendence of the subject-object polarity is possible within the human realm. But more precisely Hegel's concern is really twofold, in keeping with the twofold theme of the *Phenomenology*: first, the experience of consciousness as it moves from natural consciousness to scientific knowledge; and secondly, the history of the spirit's development (*Bildung*).

In the original introduction Hegel indicates this twofold concern:

. . . this exposition . . . may be taken as the pathway of the natural consciousness which is pressing forward to true knowledge. Or it can be regarded as the path of the soul, which is traversing the series of its own forms of embodiment, like stages appointed for it by its own nature. . . .[46]

The consciousness of each individual must pass through the stages that, historically, the *Weltgeist* has transversed. However, the Hegelian ontogenetic theory is not an automatic development; its fundamental principle is that consciousness must develop as a result of its experience with itself. "Progress" is not inevitable, for men may possess more information than the ancient sages and yet still be caught in the same types of experiential contradictions that dominated another age. Throughout the *Phenomenology* when Hegel constructs gestalts of the *Bildung* of the spirit he often takes several periods that are widely separated in history and builds a composite example of that "stage." For example, in the section entitled "Spirit in Self-estrangement," Hegel treats the period of early Christianity, the Renaissance, and the Enlightenment as having manifested similar spiritual characteristics. This example forces a reassessment of the popular belief that Hegel held a linear theory of development of the *Weltgeist*; his position in the *Phenomenology*, as in the *Logic*, is that the experience of consciousness has no rigid temporal sequence. Absolute knowledge remains as the end, however, and though the order is not fixed, there are "necessary moments" which must be passed through if this goal is to be attained.

Hegel leads up to the discussion of the alienated soul by showing the development of thought which logically precedes it. The movement of thought goes from the pure notion of freedom, as expressed in Stoicism, to the expression of an unrecognized duality (skepticism), and is finally brought to the point where the duality is explicitly recognized in the Unhappy Consciousness.

Consciousness of life, of its existence and action is merely pain and sorrow over the existence and activity; for therein consciousness finds only consciousness of its opposite as its essence—and of its own nothingness. Elevating itself beyond this, it passes to the unchangeable. But this elevation is itself the same consciousness. It is, therefore, immediately conscious of the opposite, viz. of itself as single, individual, particular. The unchangeable, which comes to consciousness, is in that very fact at the same time affected by particularity, and is only present with this latter.[47]

No matter how the alienated soul tries to elevate itself toward God (the unchangeable), its "infinite yearning" (the *furor divine*) must fall back unreconciled with God and self. The Unhappy Consciousness ends with a sense of nothingness before the eternal "other" and in the self-nullification of knowing itself as a union of self and other. Although the medieval contemplative is the prototype for this experience of inner division, it is a recurrent phase of all human experience.[48] Hence all consciousness is doomed to be "unhappy" simply because it is the nature of man as spirit to be constantly yearning to transcend his given state. The irony of human existence is that in this struggle victory really means to lose again, because one only confronts new oppositions.

But for Hegel the melancholia of human consciousness stands not as a proof of the innate recalcitrance of human nature, but as evidence of its limitless potential. For Hegel man is that creature who constantly brings to the world the *unrest* of entertaining opposed possibilities that differ from the "given." He repeatedly *denies* the external determination of his life and struggles to "realize" (in the double sense of "come to know" and "produce") that which is concretely potential for him in the world. The very process of life is the continuity of the struggle for realization, the reflexiveness of consciousness upon this process, and the consequent resurgence of spirit to alienate itself.

Hegel's concept of the Unhappy Consciousness can be interpreted historically as a philosophical analysis of the dominant spiritual malady of the medieval period. But the reference can be broadened. In the preface to the *Phenomenology* Hegel constructs a parallel between the tragic impotence of the Unhappy Consciousness and the spiritual poverty of the secularized member of bourgeois society. The Unhappy Consciousness is the inevitable result of the contradictions of Christian dualistic thought. The bourgeois person is the spiritually impoverished individual of an atomistic civil society. Both are types of spiritual deprivation and loss of freedom that represent to Hegel "stages" in the ascendance of the Christian principle of the infinitely free person. In the first case the loss is in freedom of thought; in the second there is a concrete loss of freedom. What concerns us here is Hegel's analysis of the contradictions in the dualistic mode of thought which are implicit in the experience of melancholy.

Hegel's major point is that the Unhappy Consciousness is characteristic of a mode of thinking within which it is impossible to attain genuine freedom of reason. Though an advance over previous ideas of freedom which restricted it to those who were privileged by birth or status, the Christian idea of freedom is abstract. It does not see, as the Greeks emphasized, that man is part of nature and is determined as much as he determines. The Christian idea of freedom culminated in an experience of nothingness before the eternal-other, revealing the limitations of conceiving freedom as a property of the isolated individual. For Hegel the Greek and Christian experiences of freedom had to be synthesized.

Hegel returned to the Greek conception of the social as the necessary realm of freedom. In the Greek world freedom was an accepted characteristic of the political realm: a conception which is the *opposite* of the notion of inner freedom in which man may escape from eternal otherness and "feel" free.[49]

Hegel's Resolution of the Paradox of Alienation

The idea of alienation in both pre-modern and Hegelian formulations is a theoretical attempt to transcend a rapidly changing world and affirm the values that are held necessary for the maintenance of a human world. We have seen that the idea of alienation appears in theoretical systems in what could be called the critical function of these general idea schemes. That is, the conception of an essential reality is applied to existing conditions in an attempt to mediate between the given and the "real." This has been the case throughout pre-modern and modern usages. The Hegelian idea assumes the Greek ideal of a social ethos, but now stated in a new philosophical framework (the critical philosophy of subject) and modified by the universalization of the idea of freedom. Like the classic Greek ideal, Hegel's theory is applied as a critical model to the current social totality. Thus two ages separated by over 2,000 years utilized what is essentially the same *Eidos* for a critical assessment of historical transformations.[50] In both, the Greek "mean of beauty" remained the definition of the manner in which the individual should be related to the totality, or the particular to the universal.

Hegel saw in the Greek experience a culture where man was the center, in process and in end. The wealth of man was not in his dependence on a transcendent deity, but in the degree of independence and self-sufficiency which he himself attained. The world-denying aspects of early Christianity were unknown to them, and thus Hegel points out that it was "their country in its living and real aspect; this actual Athens . . . was a necessity of life without which existence was impossible." Hegel contrasts the Greek social ethos with the individualistic ideal of the Enlightenment which is based on a mechanistic materialism. Whereas the Enlightenment ideal was constructed in an attempt to overcome feudal alienation, its logical culmination was the terror of the French Revolution. In a similar manner Hegel also opposed the views of Kant and Fichte who saw the nature of social life from the standpoint of the free ego and the requirements of an individualistic morality.

But most importantly, Hegel opposed the deification of Greek and Medieval "Ideals" and the attempt to return to these past social forms. For example, Herden, von Humboldt, and Hölderlin had viewed Greek values in light of a new Germany; they stressed the likeness of the two peoples and upheld the possibility of a new Periclean age. Not so with Hegel who saw the significance of the sharp antithesis of the Greek ideal to the present age, and not in its likeness. Although it is true that Hegel, as well as the romantic movement, saw an idealized Hellas, he did not use this ideal as an excuse for an estrangement from bourgeois society, nor conceive the role of philosophy to be "edifying." (Hegel directs this charge against the romantics of his day who saw the divine as a way of transcending contemporary spiritual poverty, e.g. F. Schlegel, Schliermacher, et al.) Hegel thus stands aside from both neo-classicism and romanticism, and argues for the unity of social life, but not as a restoration of the past, nor as a pose for a romantic estrangement from the totality.

Hegel is led to this independent posture partly by an awareness of the experience of the "alienated-soul," which is an "overdetermined" alienation of the pre-modern world. There man had lost both unity of self and world; he is "homeless" in this world and unable to enter the transcendent world of his own volition. Alienation thus expressed a two-fold loss: loss of unity of self *and* loss of a social world, a cosmos,[51] which is the necessary condition for the reunification of self. For Hegel man must have a "home" in both an objective and subjective sense. Loss of one may turn into loss of "the other."

It is this dialectical relation which underlies Hegel's own assessment of alienation in the bourgeois world. His diagnosis of the alienation of the unhappy consciousness and of bourgeois society are analogous. In both, alienation must be overcome by a "leap" into a new world in which reason can reunify man and cosmos.[52] In bourgeois society as well as in the case of the alienated soul it is necessary to retain the total experience of man and his world in consciousness and generate a new consciousness forged from the critical grasp of the past applied to the contemporary experience. In this sense it is instructive to see how Hegel approached the problem of the normative presuppositions of a human cosmos.

On the one hand there is the Christian idea of the free individual, and on the other the ancient Greek idea of the *polis*, in which man experiences himself as a part of a moral totality. Although Hegel changed his position on how the resolution of this opposition was to be achieved and eventually came to view the Christian principle of subjectivity as a higher manifestation of the "spirit," he never lost his sense of the aesthetic perfection of the Greek experience. Whereas an understanding of freedom was advanced by the development of Christianity, the zenith of man's experience of harmony of self and world remains the ancient Greek *polis*, especially the Periclean Age in Athens:

> When man began to be at home with himself, he turned to the Greeks to find enjoyment in it. Let us leave the Latin and Roman to the church and to jurisprudence. Higher, freer philosophic science, as also the beauty of pure untrammelled art, the taste for, and the love of the same, we know to have taken root in Greek life and to have created therefrom their spirit. If we were to have an aspiration, it would be for such a land and such conditions.[53]
>
> It is in this . . . spirit of homeliness, in this spirit of ideally being-at-home-with-themselves in their physical, corporate, legal, moral and political existence; it is in making what they are to be also a sort of Mnemosyne with them, that the kernel of thinking liberty rests; and hence it was requisite that Philosophy should arise amongst them. Philosophy is being at home with self, just like the homeliness of the Greek; it is man's being at home in his mind, at home with himself.[54]

This is the ideal that Hegel holds up to the present age and finds that man no longer lives in a moral totality. The principle of subjectivity which was actualized in the Reformation and the French Revolution has now come to dominate the objective world in the form of an individualistic civil society. If we consult Hegel's first system of philosophy, the so-called "Jenenser" System, we find an analysis of the fragmentation of life in the midst of bourgeois institutions which anticipates Marx's later work in an amazing manner. Thus, as early as 1801–1806, that period when Hegel worked out his first complete system of philosophy, the present age was found lacking when compared to the unity of the Greek *polis*:

> [*the individual*] *is subject to the complete confusion and hazard of the whole.* A mass of the population is condemned to the stupefying, unhealthy, and insecure labor of factories, manufactories, mines, and so on. . . . The conflict between vast wealth and vast poverty steps forth, a poverty unable to improve its condition. Wealth becomes . . . a predominant power. Its accumulation takes place partly by chance, partly through the general mode of distribution. . . . The utmost abstractness of labor reaches into the most individual types of work and continues to widen its sphere. *This inequality of wealth and poverty, this need and necessity turn into the utmost dismemberment of will, inner rebellion and hatred.*[55] (italics mine)

In bourgeois society, man is reduced to a non-human existence because he is subjected to an inhuman totality. Hegel's concern with the poverty of the spirit in his age as well as his analysis of the "alienated soul" reveals the political nature, and the Greek origin, of his humanism. There has been a terrible loss of human experience in the new totality:

> By that which suffices the spirit (of the present age) one can measure the extent of its loss.[56]

Thus, in the preface to the *Phenomenology* (added after the book was finished) he contrasts the impoverishment of the spirit in the Medieval era with the "Present Position of the Spirit."

> The significance of all that is, lay in the thread of light by which it was attached to heaven; instead of dwelling in the present as it is here and now, the eye glanced away over the present to the divine, away, so to say, to a present that lies beyond. The mind's gaze had to be directed under the compulsion to what is earthly, and kept fixed there; and it has needed a long time to introduce that clearness, which only celestial realities had, into the crossness and confusion shrouding the sense of things earthly, and to make attention to the immediate present as such, which was called experience, of interest and value. Now we have apparently the need for the opposite of this; man's mind and interest are so deeply rooted in the earthly that we require a like power to have them raised above that level. His spirit shows such poverty of nature

that it seems too long for the more pitiful feeling of the divine in the abstract, and to get refreshment from that, like a wanderer in the desert craving for the merest mouthful of water.[57]

The portrait of the "Unhappy Consciousness" is a spiritualized analogy to the present state of malaise which stupefies human activity. There is a sense of urgency which pervades Hegel's work —a need for true philosophy *now*.

Hegelian philosophy is perhaps the most ambitious attempt in the history of Western thought to transcend the objectivistic necessity that haunts dualistic and materialistic thought. But, as Marx showed, in its final form of a philosophy of identity, Hegel continues the (idealistic) tradition of classic rationalism in a reaffirmation of the power of reason to attain freedom.

2
Marx's Critique of the Alienation of Work

> *"It may be said that each person changes himself to the extent that he changes and modifies the entire complex of relationships which center in him. From this aspect, the real philosopher is the political person, the active man who modified his environment, the sum total of his relations."*
> —*A. Gramsci*

*N*o attempt is made in the following pages to assess the "influences" on Marx's "development." Our concern is to effect an interpretive reconstruction of the early critical theory of Marx, which is both different yet continuous with the more fully developed critique of the post-1850 period. Marx's development will be viewed therefore from a perspective roughly coincidental with that of Avineri.[1] There is no need to try to repeat this exemplary interpretation, whose purpose differs from ours. We will endeavor to show that Marx's work was from the beginning a historical critique of constraints on consciousness, and in this sense always approximated the form of a *critique of ideology*. Marx's critical theory was therefore the beginning of critical science.

Marx's Phenomenology of Work

Marx asserts that Hegel was correct in recognizing that man actively constitutes himself in history, but that he was wrong in conceiving of this constituent dialectic as fundamentally "spiritual." Although Hegel had recognized the self-creation of man through the process of work, he had comprehended the latter as abstract mental labor. Following Feuerbach's method of transformational criticism, Marx claimed it was not consciousness that was fundamental to the creation of man's collective species-powers, but those species-powers that have generated consciousness in the historical dialectic of need and work. The moving "negative" dialectic of work is the means by which man satisfies the needs which confront him as an active natural force. In acting back on these needs, historical man extends the range of control over nature and creates a collective material base (a "humanized nature") which reflexively transforms human needs and, thus, the range of possible human consciousness.

Marx is neither a materialist ("matter" is fundamental to consciousness) nor an idealist (consciousness is fundamental to matter). He adheres to a position in which nature is basic to mind, but man's activities mediate the natural processes and create a unity that is in neither the subject nor the object. The subject-object schema of materialism and idealism is transcended in a radicalization which conceives the humanization of nature and the naturalization of man as proceeding via the synthetic "fire" of human labor which constitutes an objective world that man can comprehend reflexively, thereby recognizing new human possibilities.

In the first thesis on Feuerbach, Marx's early polarization of materialism and Hegelian idealism is later modified in a half-step backward toward the transcendentally-conceived Hegelian phenomenology. After claiming the defect of all materialism to be that sensuousness is conceived only as an object of perception, Marx asserts vulgar materialists do not conceive it as:

> . . . *sensuous human activity*, practice (praxis) . . . Hence, in opposition to materialism the *active* side was developed by idealism—but only abstractly since idealism naturally does not know actual, sensuous activity as such. Feuerbach wants sensuous objects actually different from thought objects: but he does not comprehend human activity itself as *objective* . . . Consequently he does not comprehend the significance of "revolutionary," of practical-critical activity.[2]

In short, Feuerbach's materialism (and we today could add Engels's and Lenin's, too) retained the same dualism between material-object and thought-object that subjective idealism held. The term "active" mediates between subject and object and points to the constitutive synthesis (work) which unifies the subject and object into an "objective" process. Work as "material synthesis" has changed the form of the materials into a new historical objectivation of man.[3]

Marx's "critical-materialism," or his phenomenology of work, is best illustrated by looking forward to *Capital* where he defines values and use-value as forms given to matter by the activity of man under the social relations of commodity production. Man deposits his productive activity in the "crystals of value." The social forms that man creates through his historic activity is what has to be comprehended and thus, in *Capital*, Marx proceeds to reconstruct the genetic-historical process through which man created the value form, the commodity form, the money form, and so forth. In this way, Marx's phenomenological reconstruction of the critical praxis which historically creates social forms anticipates Georg Simmel's notion of "sociation" as the associational synthesis which constitutes ever new social patterns.[4] (This transcendentally-conceived notion of constitutive synthesis was rediscovered by George Lukacs, who studied under Georg Simmel.)[5]

But the definitive source of Marx's conception of work is Chapter VII of *Capital*, entitled "The Work Process." It is an attempt to create a dialectic of objective (*gegenständlich*) activity, and represents a synthesis of materialism and Hegel's logic of self-activity. For Marx, work is both a world building and a self-realizing activity. The work dialectic is that purposive activity which, step by step, tries to achieve the changes desired, and is characterized by an open reciprocity of end and means as the work proceeds. Just as work is the "outwardizing" of human potential as objectivations of human subjectivity in the public world, so too is the rational insight and reflexive understanding that accompanies the reciprocity of work the "inwardizing" side. As man produces, he comes to know his own powers and limitations. Work is a "making" which also reflexively "forms" man and society. Alienated work de-forms man by making the product contradict the intention of purposive activity, or by negating the dialectic of work and thereby denying the reflexivity of work.

Perhaps the definition of work in *Capital* best expresses this dialectic:

We presuppose labor in a form that stamps it as exclusively human. A spider conducts operations that resemble those of a weaver, and a bee puts to shame many an architect in the construction of her cells. But what distinguishes the worst architect from the best of bees is this, that the architect raises his structure in imagination before he erects it in reality. At the end of every labor-process we get a result that already existed in the imagination of the laborer in its commencement. *He not only effects a change of form in the material on which he works, but he also realizes a purpose of his own that gives the law to his modus operandi, and to which he must subordinate his will.* And this subordination is no mere momentary act. Besides the exertion of the bodily organs, the process demands that, during the whole operation, the workman's will be steadily in consonance with his purpose.[6]

Here again we have the Hegelian notion of the unity of theoretical and practical reason, but now it is in the context of a transcendentally-conceived notion of work praxis. This definition stands at the opening of the chapter on "The Labor Process and the Process of Producing Surplus-Value." The above quote is followed by a short statement which points out that:

the less man is attracted by the nature of the work and mode in which it is carried on, and the less, therefore, he enjoys it as something which gives play to his bodily and mental powers, the more close his attention is forced to be.[7]

Marx then proceeds to describe the capitalist production process—*which obviously does not meet the criterion* set forth on the first page of the chapter. Work becomes alienated labor (*entfremdete arbeit*), when it is a repetitive, stultifying toil whose major demand upon the worker is the constant need to remain attentive. Such toil negates the capacity of man to use his self-productive capacity. The capitalist laborer must deny his active powers by the need to remain an effective part of the machine process, to imitate the new totem ritual of endless repetition of precisely defined operations.

Marx concludes that work under capitalism is its own negation;

it is the exhaustion and debasement of man, not his self-realization. Under the conditions of capitalist production which separate man from his means of production (and, therefore, from nature) and from his own active powers (and, therefore, from his power for social transcendence), Marx asserts that man is alienated from his species-being. No more absolute kind of alienation is conceivable. The accumulated techniques and culture are no longer utilizable by man for his self-development; in an odd reversal of this movement the very power of these developments cut man off from his own potential. This is because alienated labor turns "species-life into a means of individual life," making survival of the individual the point of the universal character and potential of man. Civilization's collective consequence and, therefore, its "meaning," is that it enables the *individual* to alienate his labor! Under conditions of alienated production there is an inversion of history, the communal character of man becomes only a means to the survival of the individual and the potential of man becomes identified with individual capacity to sell labor power. In order to demonstrate that alienated labor is not the historical nature of work, Marx reconstructs phenomenologically the changing relations between civil society and the state.

The Critique of the Class Basis of the State and Civil Society in the Capitalist Epoch

In 1843 when Marx arrived in Paris, he had lost his country and he truly believed that German despotism and backwardness were shaping a major tragedy. From the period when Marx became editor of the *Rheinische Zeitung* he was directly involved in interpreting the social dislocations that accompanied the transition from feudal social forms to the first imperfect foundations of a market society. His analyses of the Rhineland "wood fetish" (October 1842) and the Moselle wine farmers (January 1843) were, for him, prime instances of the social costs of this transition.[8] Where once the dead wood in the forest had been an object for communal use, the new market forces had transformed it into an economic value that land *owners* now used the law to protect. The intensity of this emergent conflict is represented in the fact that five-sixths of all prosecutions in Prussia dealt with wood theft and the rate was higher in the Rhineland![9] The Moselle wine farmers were also being ruined as the tariff barriers were broken down by the extension of customs unions (the *Zollverein*). Marx's articles argued that the objective circumstances of the Moselle Valley demonstrated the need for a political debate in order to mediate the irreversible losses for the ruined farmers; he suggested a political debate in the press to consider redress.

As a result of this critique of the state, the newspaper was suppressed and with it Marx's radical democratic position was denied further representation. This state suppression drove Marx back to a renewed investigation of the relations between the state and civil society. These studies involved the completion of the critique of Hegel and the systematic study of the French Revolution.[10]

During this period the central point of Marx's critique of the German state was expressed in the famous essay, "On the Jewish Question." Here Marx drew a distinction between political emancipation and human emancipation and held that the first goal (i.e., the achievement of the bourgeois rights of man) was, for nineteenth-century Europeans, not equivalent to the restoration of a human world and relationships. Insofar as capitalist civil society guarantees the "rights of man," social processes become a framework in which man is forced to conceive of himself and others as egoistic monads controlled by a "natural necessity" (i.e., man conceived as driven by egoistic need and private interests). For Marx, the irony of political emancipation from feudal controls is that it reduces "citizenship" to a means of preserving civil society. Thus, the dissolution of the old society and the emergence of the constitutional state—which guaranteed the rights of equality, liberty, security, and property—also inverts the relations between the citizen and the private person. Now the rights of man are identified within the personal needs and inclinations of the "natural" man and these are the basis for the operation of the "political."

But these civil rights are not the rights of the citizen and, according to Marx, man is thereby degraded and separated from his community and his authentic species-being.

Material emancipation from the constraints of feudalism therefore fulfilled only the ideals of civil society, not the idealism of the ethical state. Following Rousseau, Marx claims that true human emancipation is the restoration of the human world and the freedom for man to discover himself in his relations with others. The new constitutions of the capitalist states secured the rights of man at the cost of his political freedom. They secured the rights of contract but not man's freedom to discover his realization in a society with other men. In short, human rights secured only the right to sell and to enter into contracts and, in doing so, turned human relations into a means for securing and protecting market relations. Political emancipation permitted only the emancipation of the economic processes and further denied and intensified human alienation.

Marx's argument was not, however, that the modern state was a reflection of property interests, but only that its claim to represent the general good could be shown to be a cloak for class interests.[11] Modern society separates the private man from the citizen in a radical way and creates an abstract polarization of the private and public. This separation of the private sphere of material production resulted from the breakdown of feudal social relations and to this extent placed the new entrepreneurs in a position of public power over the means of production. For a brief time there existed a sphere of "the public" which mediated between the private sphere of material reproduction and the sphere of public power. Existing as a literary public (coffee houses, literary salons, etc.) and the assembly of citizens who step out of their private roles of entrepreneurs and take the role of defining the common interests of the society, the bourgeois public can be defined as those private men who meet and attempt to discuss the general rules for the protection and aid of the private economic sphere.[12] This is the period in which liberal political philosophy defined the public sphere as the social space in which political debate and reason replaced the arbitrary decisions of absolute monarchs. This philosophy assumed that the public interest was identical to the national interest despite the restrictive conditions placed upon citizenship (e.g., male, property, education), and thus an equivalence was made between men as property owners and men as citizens. Whereas the economy was self-regulated ("the invisible hand"), the bourgeois public sphere was supposedly regulated by rational debate and decision.

In these reflections are the final fusing of Marx's philosophic perspective and historical consciousness of the crisis of his time. During this period he is constantly drifting away from the left Hegelian critique of religion, which, nevertheless, he claims remains the premise of all critique. But he now sees the unmasking of all "unholy alienations" to be the point of critique. The intent of critique is to expose the power relations that are concealed by the veil of ideas or social forms which block a more adequate recognition of human possibilities. For example, the repressive state authority which permitted land owners to use legal structures for their economic advantage blocked the recognition of the need for political mediation of market disruptions of traditional society. The intent of critique is here intended to point out the illegitimacy of state authority insofar as it permits a one-sided resolution of the emergent conflict between land owners and the poor who need wood. Critique is directed toward the exposure of alienating power relations that are concealed behind an ideology claiming that justice is possible.

For Marx, critique is no longer an end in itself, as the left Hegelians assume; it is a means to the struggle against social domination. Critical theory is therefore a theoretical moment of the struggle against domination, e.g., the backwardness of the German state and ideology. The critique of German backwardness was, to Marx, the critique of a present history that was actually the past history of France and England.

Marx's critique was not abstract left Hegelian "criticism"; it referred instead to the actual struggles of groups that experienced the domination of the new age. Critique, or a critical theory, is intended to show a world why it struggles and can do this only by breaking through the false consciousness of the age and actualizing the needs that are not represented in the public. Critique can become a material force only by gripping the masses and showing them that class domination and exclusion of their needs contradicts the objective social possibilities. Only in recognition of the socially unnecessary deprivations imposed on them by *historical* domination, not absolute or natural necessity, can they regain an experience of the totality of their existence. Critical theory serves as a radicalizing force by the restoration of the *meaning* of the otherwise mystified image of a self-regulating economic necessity. In this sense it is a retotalizing force which restores the possibility for autonomous subjectivity.[13] These reflections on the meaning of critique are best illustrated in Marx's application of it to the basic categories of bourgeois society.

The Appearance and Actuality of Bourgeois Production

In Marx's early phase (circa 1844), he develops the foundations of his critical synthesis in overlapping works (e.g., "The Economic-Philosophic Manuscripts," *The Holy Family, The Poverty of Philosophy, The German Ideology*). These can be viewed as so many reflections on the basic categories of the capitalist system, which were also the period's cultural postulates. For example, the categories of work, or production, or the meaning of "common life" or of "society" were constantly being investigated in these analyses. The outcome is the documentation of how consciousness embodied in social relations becomes a self-fulfilling prophecy which inverts the actual historical relations and reinforces the domination of a dynamic class division of labor. These analyses also confirm the centrality of the Hegelian method of transcendental critique, within a phenomenological framework, that begins from the immediacy of everyday life.

We can unify much of Marx's critical reflections on the crucial category of production (or work) if we see them as so many attempts to answer the transcendentally posed question: How is alienated labor possible? That is, what are the historical conditions which make it possible to conceive of work as an "economic equivalent"? In his early criticisms, Marx shows that the concept of work, or production, in classical political economy presupposes the following:[14]

1. Work is the pain imposed by natural necessity that men must endure in order to satisfy their individual needs;
2. Under the market relations of capitalist society, work is the equivalent that can be exchanged for products that can satisfy needs;
3. The exchange of economic equivalents becomes the definition of human relatedness—you want my product and I want yours—and that relation of egoistic desire is our essential reality.

All production under these presuppositions takes on the appearance of the immediate reality of economic exchange. Reality appears, at the level of common sense, to be constituted in a way which makes work a mere means to the acquisition of objects produced by others who also labor for objects. All human production, work, action, is conceptualized as if they were mere means for sustaining life; all human production is constructed only for the utility of sustaining life.[15] To this extent, man is in bondage to his own products and must suffer the servitude of work in order to survive and ward off the terror of death.

The parallel can be clearly shown between Marx's reflections and Hegel's analysis of lordship and bondage in the *Phenomenology*. Just as Hegel showed that the slave could come to recognize his own potential from the world his servitude had produced, so Marx in his critique of the bourgeois concept of work shows that human production totally reorients the worker to the world produced by his work. Thus, Marx's early reflections anticipate the above definition of work in *Capital* by suggesting that if we presuppose *human* production, we would find the following presuppositions:

1. In productive work we express our own unique individuality and in seeing our product we enjoy our individual life and the sensuous power of our capacity to create;
2. In seeing the product of sensuous activity, we recognize our capacity to satisfy human needs and see that we can be the mediator

between the consumer and the collective potential of the human species. In so experiencing the fulfillment of need we come to realize that we are related to others in a way that enables each to be an affirmation and aid in the realization of the other;

3. We can therefore view human production as an end in itself which enables us to recognize the mutual reciprocity of human existence. Thereby we come to affirm each other in thought and in love to the extent that we realize that our production is a free expression and the ground for the enjoyment of social life.

By so contrasting the bourgeois concept of work and the transcendental conception of free human production, Marx moves us toward a recognition of the alienating consequences of work that proceeds under the conditions of private property. "Work" in the framework of property relations is activity whose meaning is reduced to its capacity to secure an economic equivalent; an income. Therefore, each sees his product only in terms of economic self-interest, and human interaction is understandable only in the sense of economic exchange. Social interaction becomes mutual pillage and systematic fraud in order to get the other's product. The common life world of man is perceived as a web of individual need and self-interest. This means a process in which work is wage labor; the market is perceived as a natural process which regulates this exchange and the state appears to be a disinterested "night-watchman" of this *natural* process. Marx argues, however, that the greater the class domination of market relations, the more egoistic and asocial human work appears.[16]

Proceeding in a phenomenological reconstruction, Marx shows that property relations are not transhistorical conditions of work but are mediated in each epoch by the social totality. In primitive society social existence does not involve property relations, since membership in the tribe is the only possible "property." Because there is no distinction between state and society, these conditions do not involve the alienation of work. Marx therefore concludes that property does not predate society but results from its evolution.[17]

In Oriental despotism, property is real only in that it belongs to the one ruler who symbolizes the social totality. In the classical *polis*, public and private property are interrelated in the public's mediation of all social relations. Feudal property consists of external objects whose reality is justified by political estates that regulate the movement of social wealth. This implies that the economic and the political are not yet separable; human labor under feudal relations remains tied to political estate structures in which there lies the status (*Stande*) mediation of production.

It is only as feudal relations deteriorate that labor and its products become separated and money (capital) increasingly takes over the mediating function of politics. As this process goes on, it is clear to the emerging bourgeoisie that the remaining political constraints upon production must be replaced by "movable" property relations. This makes the bourgeoisie the most revolutionary class in history; they force an emancipation of production from political constraints and, in so doing, they make all social relations subordinate to property relations. They thereby revolutionize production and force an increase in material output by making its end the creation of exchange value.

Having shown that private property is a historical social relation, Marx then argues that to overcome private property means the emancipation of all human senses and aptitudes, and that need and satisfaction lose their egoistic nature. Nature and society discard their appearance as mere utility and "use" becomes human use. By restoring the human meaning of objective work all products become reflexive symbols of man's actual capacities. Social wealth regains its reality as the development of human activity; the history of industry is revealed as the "open book of man's essential powers." Under these conditions Marx conceived man as unified by both the unity of his natural needs, which confronts all men as common needs, and by their collective response to these needs. Both as part of nature and as part of society man has a basic communality. This is the meaning of the concept of history as the humanization of nature (through industry) and the naturalization of man. An anthropological nature is therefore the culmination of human pre-history, after which all needs are sensuous needs which can be actualized in a sensuous praxis. In this way man achieves a unity of individual- and species-life and so attains a conscious life activity in which will and consciousness are an essential moment of personal and social development. Whereas under property relations man perceives nature and society as processes resulting from natural need, under the conscious self-positing of self-conscious praxis man learns to transcend and comprehend the historical processes of the human world. Under the conditions of alienated labor and reified consciousness man's activity is a mimesis or adaptation to natural processes. Under conditions of free human production man creates according to the laws of nature *and*, in comprehending this and the freedom to choose between ends, to the laws of *beauty*, too. The contradiction of freedom and necessity is reconciled at this level of human development.

The "natural" antagonisms between man and nature and man and man are reconciled in the fulfillment of the universal potential for individual development in a communal society. Here society does not stand over and against each individual but is an objective promise for the full development of all individuals. Communist society is thus the reconciliation of nature and history, the individual and society, the riddle of history solved.[18]

The Critique of Commodity Production: Capital as a Critique of Ideology

In a letter to Lassalle, Marx describes *Capital* as a "critique of economic categories or, if you like, the system of bourgeois economy exposed in a critical manner." *Capital* is thus at the same time a critique of the *categories* of political economy and a critique of the capitalist *economy* as a whole. By generating a critique of the categories, or forms of appearance, of capitalism Marx has produced a critique of bourgeois society as a whole and has restored a lost dimension to this reality.

The fundamental question that Marx poses, and then tries to answer in the projected work of *Capital* is: "Why, in the capitalist epoch, does labor appear under the guise of commodity worth?"[19] By reflecting upon the form of wage-labor, Marx generates a critique of the labor theory of value, as it is found in classical political economy, and at the same time achieves a critique of the central legitimation system of capitalist society: the equivalence of exchange between wage labor and capital.

Classical political economy had, according to Marx, become the most advanced form of bourgeois consciousness and was essential both for capitalist expansion and for the justification of capitalist social relations. By assuming that the "facts" of wage labor, capital, and monopolized land were natural forms, classical political economy begs the question of the relationship of labor and exchange value by simply quantifying these relations. The possibility that the value form is not natural but historical is not considered, and Marx's critique is essentially a phenomenological reconstruction of the historical constitution of the commodity form.

The classical labor theory of value was developed as an internal critique of feudal privilege and can be traced back to the long debate (thirteenth to sixteenth century) about the "just price." This discussion recognized the problems of legitimate reward and raised the general issue of what types of work deserved reward. These issues were the framework which informed the seventeenth-century value theorists and provided the basis for the labor theory of value. In the seventeenth century, however, the issue of price determination and traditional social norms were still interlocked because law and custom were also part of price determination.[20] This common matrice was broken by capitalist society.

Marx thus identified a turning point in world history, namely the institutionalization of economic growth, and the resulting social and cultural revolutions. He holds that an autonomous economic system undermined traditional cultural systems, or in a contemporary formulation, rational systems of economic action become freed from traditional social and political controls. For the first time in history systems of economic exchange force a questioning of traditional institutions and generate a legitimation system which justifies an autonomous extension of the material base of society. The economic sphere becomes a self-legitimation in the ideology of the equivalence of economic exchange and the logic of commodity form. These new types of cultural legitimation facilitate further development of economic activity and are most precisely expressed in the theory of classical political economy.

Marx holds classical political economy to be superior to all previous forms of social consciousness because it considered capital to be stored-up labor and thus realized that labor is the source of social wealth. It therefore exposes the mystifications of past phases of political economics and shows that the accumulation of capital and the division of labor together establish the macrodynamic of social reproduction. However, the value form is taken to be natural and the operations of capitalism make this an everyday reification with the constant extension of the commodification of social relations to more spheres of social life.

Marx therefore begins *Capital* with a discussion of the commodity form which he holds to be "the cell of capitalist production"— the form in which everyday experience appears to man. Beginning in a parallel with Hegel's critique of sense certainty, Marx reconstructs the historical presuppositions of the commodity form and demonstrates the abstractness of its false immediacy. He asserts that a commodity can be viewed in both a qualitative and a quantitative way; each commodity is an object that satisfies human needs (it has a use-value, and as such is intelligible at the level of everyday life) and it has a socially established exchange-value. Whereas the utility of an object makes it a use-value, the socially necessary labor to produce the object is its exchange-value in the market. Whereas use-value constitutes the "substance" of all wealth and in this sense all human production is the *material production* of use-values, under capitalist relations of production use-values assume the phenomenal form of exchange-value, and production is represented by the economic symbols of value production.

Marx shows that exchange-value is a historically specific equivalence between commodities and is in no sense a natural property. The "crystals" of exchange-value (e.g. the money form) are therefore value in the abstract and can be shown to differ according to the historically specific components that enter into value production. The social "substance" of value is constituted in the process of material production in which the socially necessary labor time needed to produce value is dependent upon historical changes in the productivity of labor. Hence, value is a social form created in the process of material production in which work is the synthesizing agent. Material production is a historical form of constitutive synthesis; man creates value under ever changing social forms.

The production of exchange-values proceeds then in such a way that the two-fold character of the commodity is itself (under capitalism) extended to the value-creating activity of labor. That is, the labor embodied in value is itself conceivable as use-value and exchange-value. As use-value labor is the living activity that alone can create value. As exchange value, labor is measured in terms of labor-power and is bought and sold like any other commodity. Yet Marx argues that living labor is not a usual commodity in that it is the active agent that creates all value, thereby making into ever-new forms the natural substratum of human society: nature. Despite the uniqueness of labor, its exchange-value is represented in the capitalist value production process only as the quantity of the labor time embodied in products.

Marx claims that he was the first to point out the two-fold nature of labor.[21] This distinction reveals the dualism of capitalist production and points to an internal antagonism between its material production (use-value) and value production (exchange-value) in that production for use is subordinated to the goal of production of more exchange-value. The bourgeois mode of production was revolutionary in its forcing of the material production process to produce more value. But it does so at the cost of separating the production process from the social processes of distribution and consumption. In reality, separation of these processes is overcome by their forcible unification in the market place thereby shaping the recurrent crisis of capitalist production.[22] Separation of production and distribution of value production and value realization results in the disjunction between the capacity for material production and the capacity to realize the produced values on the market (the classic capitalist tendency toward overproduction). This creates an objective conflict which forces the subservience of the sellers of labor power to the profit priorities of class-dominated commodity production.

Marx's analysis of the duality of commodity production culminates, then, in the claim that the universal value appearance of commodities (e.g., money) is not only unnatural but also unintelligible at the level of everyday life. Marx's Phenomenological method is again manifest when he argues that "we must trace the genesis of this money form . . . [by] developing the expression of value in the value relations of commodities from the simplest form to the dazzling money form."[23] Marx then proceeds to reconstruct the developmental phases of the value form through the elementary form, the relative to the equivalent form, and finally, to the total and general forms of value. These forms of value are constituted in the historical evolution of production and account for the genesis of value form up to the emergence of universal commodity production. Marx critically demonstrates why the exchange of use-values does not regulate the value of commodities and how it has happened that the magnitude of their exchange-value now controls the exchange of their material components. We are able to recognize that the general form of value (money) comes from the joint action of all commodity production and exchange and that value and its magnitude can be comprehended only in relation to the historically specific character of the labor process embodied in it. In this phenomenological reconstruction Marx shows why the products of human labor appear to be meaningful only in terms of their value relations. He suggests as the only parallel, the mystifications of religion which make the creations of the mind more real than everyday praxis. Similarly, the products of labor have become meaningful only in terms of the objective relations of their respective values.

To Marx, the critical analysis of the commodity form is a *"Schein,"* or showing forth, of the essence of human production. His analysis of the commodity form is really an attempt to make *transparent* the essential behind the appearance. At every point in *Capital* Marx tries to keep "the real" (use-value) in the foreground while dealing with the exchange-value system of capitalism. "Seeing" the commodity form is to reflexively understand its real nature. The moment of "show" is the moment of negation of appearance and the characteristic of a critical theory. Marx thus restores the historical dimension to an appearance which is simply false consciousness. Critique discloses the reality behind objective illusion and prevents the utilization of this illusion to conceal domination. Hence, in the form of wage labor, the appearance of equivalence not only mystifies the relation but conceals the domination of labor by capital.

In the volumes of *Capital* the author demonstrates the non-equivalence of the exchange between labor and capital by working out the developmental laws of capitalism. The practice of equivalence exchange was the basic legitimation of capitalist society, and at the same time, the source of the alienation of all labor.

> Thus, all the progress of civilization, or in other words, every increase in the production power of labor itself, does not enrich the worker, but capital, and thus increases the power that dominates labor.[24]

In the critique of the labor theory of value Marx unifies his early theory of alienation and his critique of political economy. Alienation is now conceptualized as the appropriation of living labor. In sacrificing the use-value of labor power the worker loses both his product and the control of his life activity. If accepted as legitimate, the ideology of equivalence exchange leads the worker to participate in the destruction of self and society.

The ideology of equivalence exchange embodied the principle of justice and the practice of domination. Reflection upon this fundamental contradiction of capitalist society liberated consciousness from the fetishisms of the "commodity form."

The Inadequate Dialectic of Domination and Emancipation in Marx

Throughout Marx's work is his critique of objective illusion that conceals domination, forming a continuous line from the early theory of alienation to the later theory of exploitation and crisis.

The ambiguity of Marx's work, however, can be posed as an unanswered question: How is recognition of domination possible and how does this relate to the analysis of accumulation of capital? How does Marx's *Capital*, in fact, relate the critique of the capitalist economy to possible class consciousness? There seem to be two possible interpretations: the first would imply that recognition of domination is itself determined by the socializing forces of production in the cooperation they force between workers, thereby making them more aware of the potential of free productive activity. This approach leads some Marxologists to argue that the objective forces themselves compel the workers to struggle for a shorter working day and that this is an immanently produced movement toward emancipation.[25] We will call this position "mechanical Marxism."[26]

The second interpretation involves Marx's analysis of the dialectics of accumulation, which also conceptualizes the consequences of this dynamic within the total community. Marx was highly critical of political economists who analytically separated the production processes from the totality of social institutions on the one hand, and, on the other, those who treated these as if they were natural processes that could not be mediated by the consciousness of man. For Marx, the capitalist accumulation system was increasingly costly for all in that it progressively exploited the worker and alienated him from the work process and the chances for representing his needs in society (political alienation). But despite the material constraints, the critical struggles of the working man to secure better working conditions and repudiate a social order that was unable to recognize or meet his needs was prepared *but not determined by the accumulation process.*

This position is a more dialectical one, in that it does not attempt to explain the class struggle by the objective dynamic of socio-economic processes. But again we can ask, *wherein lies the source of the need to struggle against domination?* Whereas there are many passages in Marx that imply an answer to this question, there is no systematic explanation of why man *needs* to overcome domination. For this reason the Hegelian notion of the "causality of fate"—the compulsion to overcome suffering inherent in the causality of reciprocal symbolic communication—remains an important supplement to Marx's critical theory. But this claim requires explication.

I: *The Category of Alienation and the Idea of Critique*

During the course of Marx's life his thinking about the relationship of critique and revolution changed several times. Stanley Moore has argued that Marx had three alternative models of the ways in which socialism could be won. These are: the pattern of permanent revolution, the pattern of increasing misery, the pattern of competing systems.[27] The concept of the permanent revolution envisions the ability of a small minority of professional revolutionaries to produce a political revolution that would then control the social revolution. This was Marx's early position prior to the 1848 turning point and was the climax in his relation to Blanqui, whose group and concept of permanent revolution he later termed the "alchemy of revolution." Later Marx presented the revolutionary transformation from capitalism to socialism as resulting from the dynamics of a system which created a greater and greater class polarization and increasing misery for the wage-workers. Hence, the pattern of increasing misery is the dominant theory, qualified only by the less frequent third pattern of competing systems which foresaw gradual changes within capitalism (e.g., the joint stock and cooperative movement, the successful use of the electoral system, the combined use of both by the labor movement for the education of the workers, etc.) as the beginnings of socialism without, or before, the political revolution. All three of these concepts involve the notion that a "political revolution," i.e., the seizing of state power, is the necessary component. But where the first pattern assumed that the social revolution (the re-structuring of the bourgeois institutions) would occur after and because of the political revolution, the second and third patterns are progressive upgradings of the significance of gradual social transformations as prerequisites for the political revolution. That is, the two latter patterns can be seen as modifications of the first in that *the social component*, i.e., the changes in the *forms* of economic, social, and political institutions may be more and more important as necessary aspects of a revolutionary situation.

The picture is more complex, however, due to changing events and Marx's reformulations. For example, in the speech to the Amsterdam branch of the First International in 1887, Marx asserted that a peaceful evolution to socialism might be possible in some countries, such as the United States and England. Starting from this analysis Engels further developed the competing systems pattern in the twelve years following Marx's death—but again, the relevance of this pattern depended upon time and place.[28] However, in all phases of this analysis the political remained uppermost in the Marxist theory of revolution.

The one event that challenged Marx's political principle (which clearly derives from his careful study of the French revolution) was the Paris Commune of 1871. In *The Civil War in France* and other writings on this event, he changed his previous insistence upon the primary importance of seizing the power of the political state. But eventually, after the Commune's fall, he became ambivalent about the affair. In the last year of his life he wrote that the Commune was no more than a single city uprising, that its majority were not even socialists and with a little sense would have made a "compromise with Versailles."[29] However, in *The Civil War in France* Marx had clearly been inspired by the Commune's concept of the "social republic" and described its decentralization and federation of the few necessary central administrations as the "de-stating" of administration and the emegence of a working-class-rule form for the first time. It was, to quote Marx: "the political form at last discovered under which to work out the economic emancipation of labor."[30] Although Marx had warned the French revolutionaries not to act while Paris was surrounded by the Prussian army and even though the form of the Commune was in no sense a fulfillment of his notion of the taking of political power, he was converted during its two-month existence and justified it, in his terms, as non-utopian. That is, "it has no ideals to realize . . ." and was not held to be premature. In later writings Marx's judgment changed and the concept of a centralist state power-taking as the *necessary* meaning of the political revolution resurfaces in his work. The only other exception to this was Marx's study of the significance of the Russian village community where he again recognized that liberated social forms may precede the political revolution. Again and again Marx returns to his initial framework in which the objective possibilities for political revolution are inherent in the economic processes and only a central power-seizing is sufficient for *the* revolution. Marx's pragmatism in these exceptions stands as evidence of a non-dogmatic orientation to unique situations and as a central theoretical ambiguity.

The documentation of Marx's tendency to a centralist, socialist statism and of his failure to appreciate fully the significance of social-cultural liberation has been made elsewhere.[31] It should be stressed here that this failure is related to Marx's ambiguous notion of the dialectic between domination and emancipation.[32] Marx's centralist tendency and his inability to recognize social-cultural claims for liberation as basic to revolutionary processes became a part of the received dogma of the socialist tradition. The socialist theory of the need for centralist political control of the social revolution was a material force in history: a tragically bloody one. To remember the Makhnovite Army, the Russian Soviets, Kronstadt, the anarchist-led federations in the Spanish Civil War, the Bavarian Räterepublik of 1919, the workers' councils in Hungary in 1956, is to realize that a centralist model of revolution can be a justification of the most brutal kind of genocide.

Today we can see that the inadequacy of Marx's conception of emancipation has resulted in a series of ad hoc explanations which have become ideologies in their own right. For example, Lenin's theory of the vanguard recognizes that within Marx's critique of capitalism there is no compelling reason for emancipatory struggle. The party therefore introduces the revolutionary project *from the outside*. Another example is Herbert Marcuse's return to Freud's libidinal theory which places the cause of emancipatory struggle in the revolt of the instincts themselves against the domination of industrial civilization. Both of these attempts to provide a need for emancipation introduces extra-social mechanisms: for Lenin the party organization, for Marcuse the inbuilt biological instincts. Neither of these theories is adequate, and herein lies the significance of Hegel's theory of the dialectical relatedness of "mutual-recognition" processes and the level of self-consciousness. Hegel's dialectical social theory shows that there is an objective need for social processes that enable man to achieve individuality. The distortion or rupture of open mutual-recognition sets up a dialectical reaction which is experienced as a pressure for emancipation from domination. Hegel's notion of "spiritual causality" can be developed into a theory of emancipation from social-cultural domination; this is the dimension of the lordship and bondage dialectic that Marxists usually overlook. The social-cultural interpretation of lordship and bondage has reappeared in contemporary formulations such as Fanon's *The Wretched of the Earth*. It can be seen as a contemporary reflection on the dialectics of domination which examines the social-psychological dynamics that the Marxist theory underemphasizes. It shows that there are needs within the human consciousness to overcome domination either symbolically or actually. But Hegel also knew that the types of emancipation sought might simply result in new alienated forms. His early undeveloped critical theory of society expressed this objective need for the dialectical relations of mutual recognition and self-consciousness. Hegel's later *Philosophy of Right*, however, held that the legal contract and the constitution are universal expressions of the need for mutual recognition in social-cultural processes and that these would ensure a non-alienated society and an ethical state. Marx's critique of the *Philosophy of Right* was the basis for his analysis of the economic restriction of the political. It is a lasting critique of Hegel's apologetic totalization. In its emphasis, however, that the relationship between self-consciousness and social-cultural process is objectively essential, Hegel's earlier theory is a moment that is needed for a more adequate critical theory. For example, if Marx had taken Hegel's analysis more seriously he would have given more thought to the cultural power of nationalism and would have anticipated this social-cultural block to the internationalization of the revolutionary movement.

The Need to Unify the Hegelian and Marxist Dialectics

To create a more adequate dialectical theory would necessitate a reconceptualization of the interrelated *needs* of human society and individual development. In this area both Hegel and Marx started with an interpretation of the classic ideal of the Greek *polis*. But Hegel saw the Greek *ethos* as the community of natural needs that made Greek culture possible. For him the Greek unity was "founded on nature and feeling," and was thus a higher unity "in which the individual unites himself freely and consciously with others into a community that in turn preserves his real essence."[33] The reciprocity of self-consciousness and symbolic systems embedded in humane institutions is crucial. As he expressed it in his later work, the concept of man involves the development of self-consciousness, or the capacity to be a self-reflective agent. This was put in a way that continued his constant logical concern that the universal is the "true being" through which the individual gains "reality." What is "essential" is the development of the self-consciousness of *all* individuals, which presupposes a sociocultural world that binds them together as a community—making universalization of systems of mutual recognition (i.e., social liberation) the central concern in Hegel's thoughts about the just society where freedom is possible.

For Hegel, work in the sense of making, producing, etc., is subordinate to the real essence of man—his intersubjectively developed self-consciousness. In the *Philosophy of Right* Hegel talks about the inalienable capacities of man as those of his "personality" (a subject aware of his *subjectivity*) and intelligence:

It is just in this concept of mind as that which is what it is only through its own free causality and through its endless return into itself out of the natural immediacy of its existence, that there lies the possibility of a clash: i.e., what it is potentially it may not be actually . . . and vice versa, what it is actually (e.g., evil in the case of will) may be other than what it is potentially. Herein lies the possibility of the alienation of personality and its substantive being, whether this alienation occurs unconsciously or intentionally. Examples of the alienation of personality are slavery, serfdom . . . , Alienation of intelligence and rationality of morality . . . is exemplified in superstition, in ceding to someone else full power and authority to fix and prescribe what actions are to be done. . . .[34]

Man may *will* alienation of labor insofar as this is a limited alienation—the criteria for limits of alienation of labor would be determined by requirements of the community's material needs and would be subordinated to the development of personality or the capacity to be in-*and-for*-oneself (social-cultural needs).

Marx's theory of alienation, in both his early and "mature" work, sees work, or "living labor," as the essential process whose disruption results in the fundamental alienation in the human world. Marx's view of man stresses his capacity for self-actualization through work. Alienation ultimately refers to a disruption of human praxis—but praxis is understood in the sense of poiesis[35] and is rooted in the economic base of society. This means that all alienation of mutual-recognition, or symbolic interaction systems, derive from the basic mode of production; in this sense the term "alienation" refers to the "rupturing of the process of production." All other modes of "alienation" (social-cultural alienation) or estrangements are reifications that result from the experience of alienated forms of productive praxis.

In this limitation of the concept of alienation the wide Hegelian use of it is narrowed radically. Hegel had conceived of praxis as "built" by a *socialized* actor, and not as "determined" by internal or external "forces." Disruptions of these "forming" processes are alienations of the recognition of self and others and hence suppress what we today would call open communication. Fundamental to Hegel's theory of alienation is an awareness of how distorted interaction patterns skew the use of language in everyday communication. In the section of the *Phenomenology* entitled "Spirit in Self-Estrangement—The Discipline of Culture," Hegel shows how the contradictions of human interaction related to wealth and state power are reflected in the language of "dumb service" or "flattery." As usual the analysis is an understanding of how persons shaped and functioning under specific cultural forms encounter the one-sidedness of the cultural perspective and become embroiled in the contradiction of a life style based on these alienating forms. Witness Hegel's description of the benefits of the French Revolution, demonstrating his sense of the alienating nature of outmoded social-cultural forms; in a letter written in 1807 he reflects:

I: *The Category of Alienation and the Idea of Critique*

> Through the bath of its revolution, the French nation has been liber-
> ated from many institutions which the human spirit had outgrown like
> baby shoes and which therefore weighed on it, as they still do on
> others, as fetters devoid of spirit; and the individual has taken off the
> fear of death and that life as usual which lacks all internal steadiness
> as soon as the scene is changed. This is what gives the French the
> great strength they are demonstrating against others . . .[36]

The Revolution had freed man from the fetters of "life as usual"
that constrained and perverted the human spirit and it thereby
confirmed for him the power implicit in man's release from social
symbols that distort and suppress human thought and emotion.
Today's Marxists who stress the necessity for a critique of "everyday life" have thus returned to the basic problem of social liberation.

For Hegel the natural unity of man and nature was rooted in
the generation of social cultural forms; for Marx it was linked to
the generation of production processes of all kinds. Whereas a
recognition of Hegel's concept of the natural unity of man and
nature in the social-cultural *needs* is enough to refute the claim
that Hegel is an "idealist," the Marxian stress on the primacy of
the material process of securing the capacity to meet needs is an
important critique and a more fundamental basis for a dialectical
theory of society. Both the material moment and the social-
cultural moment must be combined in a more adequate conception of the constitutive dialectic of human society. Such a theory
has been conceived already though it has not yet been realized;
this is Jürgen Habermas's critical reflection upon both Marx and
Hegel and his creation of a metatheory of "material synthesis."
However, the exposition of these ideas requires another mode of
presentation: that of a reflective philosophy of the method of
critical theory, to which we will turn now.

II: *A REFLEXIVE PHILOSOPHY OF CRITICAL THEORY*

*C*ritical theory derives from the methodological revolution of transcendental philosophy initiated by Kant, extended by Fichte and Hegel, and realized by Marx. Marx's one-sided critique of Hegel, however, while adopting the transcendental tradition, did so without making explicit the relation between this methodological framework and historical critique. For this reason, later Marxism degenerated into a mechanical materialism in which critique was justified methodologically by "the laws of history." This perspective was based on the assumption that history was determined by dynamic necessities impervious to the subjectivity of its constitutive elements. It reduces the dialectic of history to fixed relations between societal structures; and methodologically it is regressive in relation to the reflexivity of a critical science. From the very beginning, therefore, "scientific socialism" was unable to transcend its inherent tendency toward "objectivism"—the reduction of the subject's spontaneity to objective determinates.

A methodologically reflexive critical theory—as distinguished from the objectivism of the Marxist tradition—appeared only in the twentieth century. While other theorists, such as Simmel and Lukacs, are also important, the restoration of the reflective dimension to critical theory is, above all, the contribution of the Frankfurt school (e.g., Horkheimer, Adorno, Habermas, Wellmer). These theorists made explicit the methodology that Marx left unstated. The result was the systematic conception of a critical science which they used as the basis for a critique of the residual mechanical materialism in Marx—thereby completing the task begun by the early Lukacs. However, they restated the program-

matic of critical theory in their active engagement with the leading forms of twentieth century theoretical consciousness; neopositivism and the empirical-analytic methodology of social science.

In chapter three critical theory is presented on the one hand by a reconstruction of the evolution of transcendental philosophy from Kant to Marx, and on the other as an immanent critique of positivistic philosophy and social science methodology. Reconstruction of the development of dialectical theory shows that consciousness cannot be separated from the social-cultural world and, in this sense, science cannot proceed as indifferently to the social world as it has in the natural world. In the investigation of the social world, it is impossible to separate analytically the formation of concept and theory from the field of inquiry. In the understanding of the meaning of socio-cultural forms, one cannot reduce the problem of objectivity to the procedures of physical measurement since observation and interpretation are inseparable. To identify scientistic knowledge with the results of "the scientific method" does not adequately express the different subject-object relations. The objectivity of knowledge cannot be assured by the scientism of a "unity method" but must be referred to a unity of "the dialectical totality," which can be reconstructed only in the light of a reflective methodology.

Chapter four consists of an attempt to present Jürgen Habermas's categorical foundations of critical science. These constitute a new type of social theory that has absorbed the analytic philosophy of language into the tradition of critical theory. Habermas develops a non-scientistic philosophy of science in the form of a dialectical anthropology of knowledge. This is expressed in his theory of the cognitive interests of human evolution, which is a non-objectivist restatement of Marx's historical materialism. Habermas develops an entirely new type of critical analysis: the systematic study of distorted communication.

3

Transcendental Reflection and Positivism

A theme latent in German idealism, which later became the
motif and stimulus in Marxism, is the human agent's participation
in the construction of his world. Initially this took the form of
Kant's analysis of the receptivity and spontaneity of man's mental
activity. For Kant the theoretic subject constructs the world as a
meaningful whole in or upon which the moral or practical subject
can act. But in analyzing the ways in which the human agent is
active or passive in constructing the human world, Kant considers
only mental activity, not the activity of the person in his "practical" dealings. This separation of the theoretical and the practical
subject created a schism that later became the starting point for
numerous critics of Kant (e.g., Schiller, Fichte, Hegel) who saw
this division as an untenable abstraction. But nonetheless, Kant's
conception of the transcendental subject was fundamental to the
"Copernican revolution" in philosophy because it redirected epistemological inquiry to the sphere of the subject's a priori constitutive activity.

We begin from the perspective that views post-Kantian German
idealism as the tradition which restored the human dimension to
the critique of knowledge:

German idealism rescued philosophy from the attacks of British empiricism, and the struggle between the two became not merely a clash
of different philosophical schools, but a struggle for philosophy as
such.[1]

Yet despite the basic opposition of transcendental philosophy, empiricism—riding on the wave of scientific and technological success—became the dominant conception of knowledge. From the critical perspective, however, this "transcendence" of the tradition of German idealism was actually a regression in that "knowledge" became unrelated to the historical practice of man:

> The replacement of epistemology by the philosophy of science is visible in that the knowing subject is no longer the system of reference. From Kant through Marx the subject of cognition was comprehended as consciousness, ego, mind and species. Therefore, problems of the validity of statements could be decided only with reference to a synthesis no matter how much the concept of synthesis changed with that of the subject.[2]

It is important to show in detail how Kant's innovation of critical philosophy related philosophy and science in a way which extended the scope and significance of our understanding of scientific methodology.

Kant's Transcendental Critique of Knowledge

In the *Critique of Pure Reason*, Kant argued that though "knowledge begins with experience, it does not follow that it arises from experience." One source of human knowledge is independent of experience (a priori knowledge) insofar as it is logically necessary and universal and thus not derivable from particular sensations. A priori knowledge is therefore universal knowledge in that it is presupposed by all possible human experience. That is, the forms of the mind (e.g., the *intuitions* of space and time and the *categories* of the understanding) are the constitutive universals that logically, not temporally, precede and organize all experience.

In Kant's famous "Deduction of the Pure Concepts of Understanding" he shows that experience is possible only if:

1. a "synopsis" is given to the manifold of sense and there is a synthesis of apprehension;
2. a synthesis of imagination results in a reproduction;
3. a synthesis of recognition judges the object under a concept.

3: *Transcendental Reflection and Positivism*

In order to recognize an "object" as an object, therefore, it is logically necessary that we unify the sensible manifold which we have intuited in successive moments, reproduced in imagination, and recognized under a concept. The transcendental unity of apperception is the logically necessary constitutive "act" that makes possible the experience of a world of appearances. The theoretic subject can, on this analysis, know an object only via its capacity to logically unify the continuum of experience. This transcendental unity of apprehension is not the manifestation of a self, conceived as a substance, but is conceptualized by Kant as a spontaneous act that enables the subject to maintain its self-identity (*Ich-heit*). What is constituted is self-relation, or self-consciousness, making possible the unification of the successively given temporal and spatial manifold and the recognition of its relation to the past and future.

It is important to stress that Kant's transcendental analysis is not a temporal history of our coming to know; rather, it is a logical analysis of what is necessarily involved in knowing. The syntheses *are not empirical events*; nor are they the acts of the phenomenal self. The transcendental self has no content; it is pure logical identity: "I am I." We cannot be aware of our transcendental self as an object of knowledge; we can only reflexively recognize it as a presupposition of knowledge. Insofar as it is shown that the transcendental unity of apperception is presupposed by all empirical judgments, it is a logical principle that is necessary for all possible experience:

It must be possible for the "I think" to accompany all my representations; for otherwise something would be represented in me which could not be thought at all. . . . But this representation is an act of spontaneity, that is, it cannot be regarded as belonging to sensibility. I call it *pure apperception* to distinguish it from empirical apperception, or, again, original apperception, because it is that self-consciousness which cannot itself be accompanied by any further representation. The unity of this apperception I likewise entitle the *transcendental unity of self-consciousness,* in order to indicate the possibility of a priori knowledge arising from it. . . . Only insofar as I can unite a manifold of given representations in one consciousness, is it possible for me to represent to myself the identity of the consciousness in (i.e., throughout) these representations. In other words, the analytic unity of apperception is possible only under the presupposition of a certain synthetic unity.[3]

Kant is asserting here that all phenomena presuppose the self-identity, or unity, of consciousness. This is a proof that this principle (which is a presupposition of knowledge—it is *not* an object of knowledge) is necessary for all empirical judgments. It is therefore a proof of the necessity of synthetic unity for *all possible experience.*

We must remember that Kant's analysis of the transcendental level of cognition is not a psychological analysis but an analysis of the rules of synthesis that are *logically* necessary if there is to be any knowledge of objects at all. The goal of *The Critique of Pure Reason* is to establish the scientific limits of theoretical understanding in order to distinguish it from the speculative and metaphysical utilization of reason—a natural human tendency but one which goes beyond the limits of possible experience. By distinguishing between the transcendental conditions of possible experience (which Kant assumed were universal conditions for consciousness in general) and the utilization of these categories as ideas of speculative (non-confirmable) metaphysics, Kant at the same time created a new type of inquiry which resulted in a unique type of knowledge: "Critique." "Criticism" in the Kantian sense attempted to "deduce" (give a justification for) the general epistemological principles that are the logical presuppositions of our knowledge of "nature." "Nature," however, is scientifically known to the human consciousness only as it is organized by the understanding and re-presented as law-like phenomena under the categorical consciousness. We cannot know "things-in-themselves," or immediate reality. We can claim to know only what is mediated by the transcendental principles, rules, and representations of the human consciousness (the phenomenal world). Claims that go beyond possible experience cannot be validated. Kant's critical philosophy was based on the belief that both dogmatism (e.g., the rationalism of Leibniz and Wolff, and the empiricism of Locke) and skepticism (e.g., Hume) could be overcome by a mode of inquiry which could express the transcendental conditions for all possible knowledge and could thereby establish the logical rules for what Kant called "synthetic a priori judgments." Kant undermined Hume's skepticism, while not directly answering his argument, by establishing a transcendental epistemology whose function was to comprehend the sciences by a more general philosophical inquiry. To Kant, Hume's skeptical method could not be the basis for an adequate inquiry into the validity of knowledge because its results (e.g., the critique of causal inference) only restricted the understanding without defining its limits. Specifically, Hume did not make the logical distinction between analytic and synthetic judgments and therefore had no way of distinguishing between rules of psychological association and the a priori functioning of the human understanding.

In contradistinction to the Cartesian tradition, Kant's critical method did not attempt to pattern itself upon the model of certainty suggested by mathematics. Whereas the difference between necessary and contingent truths (e.g., Leibniz) is based upon definitions or axioms, Kant argued that transcendental philosophy cannot begin with either of these. In order to fulfill its purpose of exposing illusions of reason, transcendental philosophy must be able to clarify its concepts in a discursive manner; it cannot rest with an emulation of mathematical proof or method. Philosophical inquiry must, for Kant, comprehend the validity of mathematics (and of all scientific knowledge); it cannot simply assume the value of these spheres of knowledge and emulate their procedures as capable of guiding philosophical inquiry. There can be no scientific or mathematical demonstration in critical philosophy but only discursive proof which is conducted by the agency of language alone. A philosophical concept must be reached by an "exposition" (justification of its necessary and universal origin). Only through such a "deduction" can it be recognized as a formal condition of the phenomenal world; it can never be seen as a structure or atomic fact of the noumenal world. As such, a critical comprehension of the objectivity of scientific knowledge is in fact a self-understanding of the possibility of knowledge—it is not an application of tests of knowledge that have been generalized from the procedures of mathematics and science. (Such is the case with positivistic inquiry into validity.) Human knowledge is never a passive "picturing" of fact or an immediate grasp of the "real." It is always derived from the two-fold root of sensibility and the form-giving substratum of all experience derived fron the transcendental subject. However, it is not to be supposed that knowledge is "determined" by these two sources; the combination is "primordial." That is, the synthesis of knowledge is spontaneous insofar as the categorical organization of experience is not determined but creative, and form-giving. (This notion of spontaneity remains central to critical theory.)

The fundamental change brought by Kant can be expressed as a new type of relation between subject and object, one which, in a way, defines a new dualism in the midst of the old. Kant views the relation between subject and object not in terms of identity, as an absolute object, but as a phenomenal object in that it is built up by the forms of human understanding. It is hence consistent with a rational mediation of skepticism because the argument, on the one hand, denies that we can have any knowledge of the "thing-in-itself" and, on the other, grounds knowledge within the world of phenomenal objects. "Reality" is no longer seen as forced upon the subject by the object but as constructed by the spontaneity of the human spirit. The role of philosophy is now to make the subject aware that the object is a mediated construct. Philosophy is reflection.

Hegel's Phenomenological Radicalization of Reflective Critique

Hegel's unique departure from the German idealist tradition was a radicalization of its critical method. He argued that the specifications of the preconditions of knowledge (the transcendental mode of argument developed by Kant) cannot guarantee the validity of knowledge since it is not possible to absolutely justify the conditions that make the critique of knowledge possible.[4] That is, every epistemology, including the idealist attempt to specify the conditions under which knowledge is possible, falls into a circular argument if it claims that its criteria for valid, or possible, knowledge is itself knowledge.[5] How is it possible to claim knowledge for the status of the criteria by which one wants to test knowledge? Hegel thus perceives in all epistemological analysis another example of what he calls a "bad infinity." Epistemology cannot, for Hegel, be a first philosophy; it inevitably falls into a circularity which cannot be avoided.

Hegel takes the circle of epistemology to be but an instance of the universal experience of consciousness which reflects back upon its own constitution and its reflected objects. Reflection then is the experience consciousness has with itself: in reflecting about the status of knowledge, it starts with the knowledge it has itself acquired. Whatever knowledge is, it is reflexively known and derives from past conscious experience. Reflection upon the genesis of knowledge is therefore the beginning point for an epistemological analysis that is not a "bad infinity"; by linking the critique of knowledge with a *phenomenological reflection* upon the *formation of consciousness*, Hegel has added a dimension to philosophical analysis. Now the analysis of knowledge must begin with an analysis of the structure of awareness, as Kant (and Fichte) argued, but the circularity of the analysis is avoided by focusing upon the genesis of knowledge itself: to the traditional logical analysis of epistemology is added a "phenomenological," or historical-genetic, dimension. The development of the *Phenomenology of Mind* attempts to demonstrate the type of phenomenological reconstructive method which Hegel holds to be logically necessary to justify the objectivity of knowledge (and one which later defines Marx's unique method of critique).

Phenomenological reflection begins with its position of immediate consciousness which it takes for granted and utilizes uncritically; but in reconstructing the self-formation process of consciousness, at every stage the standards of the preceding one disintegrate and new ones arise. Such a radicalized self-critique of knowledge moves within a phenomenological framework. In this way, Hegel shows that transcendental critique is inconsistent, on the one hand, with Kant's presupposition that scientific knowledge is exemplified by mathematical physics, and on the other, with Kant's framework that presupposes a monadic ego. But most importantly, Hegel shows that the Kantian distinction between theoretical and practical reason is untenable because a phenomenological critique of knowledge is inseparable from a critique of rational action.[6] Critical reflection mediates not only the immediacy of sense certainty but also the dogmatic attitudes of habitual forms of life. At the same time, the Hegelian critique of knowledge involves a dissolution of reified norms that bind experience to alienated forms of life. It is a critique of successive stages in the self-formation of the subject; each new reflective reconstruction is a self-understanding of its past constitutive dynamic which breaks down the constraints of the old forms of consciousness. Continuity of the subject is maintained by the determinate negation of past forms of consciousness and yet the retention of these "stages" within a recomprehension of the totality. Thus, reflexive critique that has been radicalized as a phenomenological self-reflection of mind cannot stop with the recognition of a priori principles of the theoretical object; it must deal also with practical reason, or the binding of the subject to a moral community. Completion of the transcendental quest requires a phenomenological reconstruction of the constitutive experiences of the history of mankind.

So radicalized, critical philosophy demonstrates why all science can be grounded only phenomenologically and, ultimately, only as a reflection upon the self-formation of the human species (or the social totality). In the Phenomenology, Hegel transforms the phenomenological reflection into a reconstruction of the constitutive "stages" of reflection by a dialectical relating of:

1. the constitutive moments in the "socialization" (*Bildung*) of *the individual*
2. the constitutive moments in the *universal history of mankind*
3. the constitutive moments in the reflective reconstructions (historical forms of consciousness) of this historical development as it is expressed in the forms of absolute spirit

In this way Hegel initiates a mode of "dialectical" analysis which relates logical and experiential dimensions, or logical analysis and historical content. He further implies that the development and grounding of consciousness is always related to the development of the *Weltgeist* itself. In other terms, there is a dialectical relationship between the development of the individual human consciousness and the evolving consciousness of the social totality.

But in the end Hegel's dialectical analysis remains rooted in the traditional philosophical mold. His *Phenomenology* is a circle whose beginning presupposes the end: absolute knowledge. The validity of the whole is its status as a transcendental deduction in which each of the "stages" can be seen as developing immanently and engendering their own determinations. Thus, as Marx points out, Hegel's philosophy of absolute spirit contradicts its own radicalization of the critique of knowledge. If Hegel had remained within the framework of a self-consistent critical philosophy, he would have seen that "there can be no concept of knowledge that can be explicated independently of the subjective conditions of the objectivity of possible knowledge."[7] Hegel's doctrine of absolute spirit deflected critical theory into the idealistic path of absolute knowledge. Only Marx pursued the Hegelian critique of Kant without accepting the philosophy of identity; completion of the critical-transcendental quest was therefore up to Marx.

What results, however, from the Hegelian radicalization of Kant's critical method is a more totalizing method for reflection on the limits of knowledge. Rather than restricting critique to the presuppositions of scientific inquiry, he recognizes that theoretical and practical consciousness cannot be separated and the critiques of knowledge and of false consciousness are therefore continuous. Hegel's dialectical theory points to a method of sociocultural criticism[8] that reflectively conceptualizes the constraints placed upon human experience by rigid cultural traditions (e.g., Hegel's early critique of the positivity of religion). Marx continues this method, under materialist presuppositions, in his early reflections on socially unnecessary domination (e.g., the critique of capitalist exploitation).

Thus, beginning with Kant's attempts to comprehend the possibility of scientific knowledge by reflexively establishing limits of possible experience, transcendental critique furnishes the beginning point for a science of critique. In Hegel and in Marx this method is radicalized and takes as its focus the critique of false consciousness and illegitimate power relations that block spontaneous activity. Critical theory emerges, then, from the method of transcendental phenomenological critique as the scientific ideal suggested by this revolution in philosophical method. But the general recognition of the ideal of a critical science was blocked by the enormous success of the positivist perspective on knowledge, on the one hand, and the fact that Marx (as the genius who realized this ideal as a scientific method) was partisan to the forces that threatened the bourgeois world, on the other.

Positivism and the Empirical-Analytic Method

The method of critique clearly conflicts with the current positivistic conceptions of knowledge. Rather than simply identify "knowledge" with that which results from the procedures of science, the intent of Kantian philosophy was to comprehend the *meaning* of science from the perspective of a reflexive reconstruction of the transcendental principles that underlie the subject's constitutive activity. For Kant, knowledge is justified only by recognizing the framework of synthesis which was presupposed by the constitutive activity of the human subject. This unification of philosophic reflection and scientific method was for him the only way to ground the objectivity of human knowledge. The philosophical impetus to comprehend the meaning of knowledge was connected to the further goal of critically establishing the limits of scientific knowledge, thereby enabling man to recognize rational illusions. This method has always conflicted with the positivist traditions of philosophy despite a growing recognition by advanced positivists that they are beginning to confront the problems Kant was dealing with.[9]

Positivism is that conception of knowledge which denies the possibility of reflective reconstruction of the transcendental principles presupposed in human activity. In the positivistic perspective, the meaning of objectivity is not comprehended by reflection upon the subject-object relation but is given by the controlled processes of intersubjective observation. The procedures of science literally define the object domain of knowledge. The test of scientific meaningfulness is given by the method of empirical observation on the one hand and by analytic processes of analysis on the other. "Knowledge" is, therefore, that set of statements about the world which can be controlled by the intersubjective means of this empirical-analytic method.

Positivism begins with a rule of phenomenalism[10] that restricts the meaning of knowledge to that which is produced through the systematic application of the empirical-analytic method. If we consider the term *empirical-analytic* we see that, first, the stress on empirical observation rejects the necessity for critical reflection and, second, the analytic procedures of concept and theory formation are held not to change the domain of "reality." So conceived, conceptual abstractions of theoretical terms add nothing to the empirically-derived facts. (This is a nominalistic denial of the constitutive universals that Kant and Hegel considered logically essential to the processes of human cognition.)

Knowledge, in the positivistic sense, remains scientific only insofar as it is derived from the systematic application of the empiricial-analytic method. We can call this stipulation the postulate of *scientism*. However, the problems of a scientistic definition of knowledge, as synonymous with that which results from the practice of science, is how to justify this claim. That is, if all knowledge is derived from the empirical-analytic method, how can we establish the validity of the metatheoretical postulate of scientism? (Hegel's challenge to epistemology returns.) There is obviously a circularity involved in stating that knowledge derives from scientific procedure and then trying to prove this metatheoretical claim by pointing to the results of science. The scientistic restriction of the concept of knowledge is, of course, motivated by its positivistic, anti-metaphysical intent, and yet its very principle of scientific meaning is unjustified. It is precisely the need to justify the metatheoretical (epistemological) claims presupposed by scientific methodology that informs the method of transcendental reflection. Rather than permit ungrounded metatheoretical decisions in the construction of scientific theory, the program of transcendental critique has always attempted to show the rational necessity of these decisions. It is not enough to assert that there are "domain assumptions" behind each social theory.[11] Philosophy and methodology are inseparable in a critical theory approach.

Positivism therefore asserts its postulate of scientism in the belief that "the adequacy of our knowledge increases as it approximates the forms of explanation which have been achieved by the most advanced sciences."[12] This is, of course, a rejection of the need for a philosophical comprehension and grounding of the sciences—and yet the history of positivism could be reconstructed as pivoting precisely upon the relationship of philosophical analysis and scientific knowledge.

Note on the History of Positivism

While restricting the method of discovery to the empirical-analytic method, the postulate of scientism, as a philosophical metatheory has been defended in different ways. The difference can be illustrated by the manner in which the "unity of science" motif is understood. A critical positivism (e.g., that of J. S. Mill, E. Mach) stresses the sameness of the methods for acquiring valid knowledge in all spheres of inquiry, and that philosophical analysis functions as a metacritique of metaphysical assumptions in the concepts and theories of science. So conceived, philosophy is reduced to the role of an auxiliary or metascientific discipline that is useful for the clarification of knowledge but does not, in itself, add to the scope of knowledge.

Another form of positivism, that of A. Comte and H. Spencer, envisions a synthetic role for philosophy with a philosophical harmonization of the results of the sciences, e.g., Comte's law of the three stages, Spencer's law of evolution. These two versions of "systematic positivism"[13] asserted their scientism on both the principle of meaningful knowledge and the claim that human society itself advances to the extent that it produces more adequate knowledge in every sphere. Of course, there is a contradiction between the postulate of scientism and the derivation of a systematic law by philosophical synthesis, and the latter was rigorously rejected by later critical positivists. "Critical positivism" rejected the speculative program of systematic positivism but was just as adamant that the development of a positivist concept of knowledge was necessary for the advance of scientific inquiry. The impetus for this can be traced back to Hume, whose critique of the grounds of knowledge and causal inference provided the skeptical perspective that informed the development of late nineteenth- and twentieth-century critical positivism.

Twentieth-century critical positivism can be briefly described as deriving from two sources. First, from the Vienna Circle's conception of "Logical Positivism," a movement which originated *circa* 1922–38 around Morris Schlick and included G. Bergmann, R. Carnap, H. Feigl, P. Frank, O. Neurath and others. Second, critical positivism was stimulated by the Russell-Moore theory of logical empiricism which, in its early phase, was not so much concerned with science as it was with everyday events. Common to both of these traditions is a belief that philosophy is an analysis of experience, and is in no way a systematic account of the universe. They rejected both the program of systematic positivism and the monism of the German idealists, which they perceived to be hostile to science in general. For example, the early Wittgenstein, who was in neither group and yet influenced both, argued that philosophy is logical analysis and can be conceived only as a human activity; it is not a doctrine in itself.

For both of these schools, science is neutral and objectifies the neutral elements of intersubjective experience. The questions analyzed by philosophy are the relations between the neutral elements of experience and the logical elements of science. The relationship of philosophy to science remains throughout the later history of positivism one of elucidation of the method and language of science. But despite its rejection of the speculative use of the "philosophy of science," the implicit scientistic view of knowledge has retained its latent philosophy of history which sees the progress of human society tied to the advancement of science. This is as true for the critical positivists who reject the scientistic criterion of meaning (e.g., Karl Popper)[14] as for the direct followers of the tradition.

Karl Popper's "critical rationalism" may, in fact, be the most succinct formulation of the scientistic perspective of knowledge—one which is all the more important due to its critique of the remaining epistemological element of scientism: the distinction between meaningful and pseudoscientific propositions. Popper's formulation of a principle of scientific empiricism is a more direct advocacy of the scientific method as *the* method for the separation of the scientific interpretation of the world from the unscientific. By the method of systematic falsification, scientific theory can be developed into a more and more viable and technically useful theory. Popper's rejection of the empiricist criterion of meaning as the residual epistemological component in a scientistic philosophy of science brings clearly to the fore the latent positivist theory of the relation of knowledge and human action—that the function of scientific knowledge is to provide more effective technical recommendations for piecemeal social engineering.[15]

In all these formulations of the scientistic identification of knowledge with the results of science, there is, however, the same circularity which, from the perspective of transcendental critique, is never faced. Perhaps one of the most self-conscious attempts to deal with this circularity emerges in Carl G. Hempel's claim that the empiricist criterion of meaning

> . . . is therefore far from being an arbitrary definition; it is subject to revision if a violation of the requirements of adequacy, or even a way of satisfying those requirements more fully should be discovered.[16]

In short, the empiricist criterion of meaning, as the logical center of the postulate of scientism, is to be considered tentative too; if there are improvements in our ability to analyze the meaning of knowledge, or if we can more adequately achieve a "rational reconstruction" of the meaning of the explicandum, then we have a better formulation of this postulate. But is it adequate to ground the metatheoretical criterion of knowledge in a logical analysis which claims that the metatheory is itself as improvable as any other scientific proposition in the future of inquiry? Again the claim is being made that the metatheory is valid insofar as it is construed as an approximation of the process of confirmation inherent in the scientific method, thereby repeating the circularity of the relation of method and metatheory. Or, alternatively, as Wellmer and Habermas have shown, one could say the postulate is supported by the normative philosophy of history implied by scientism.[17] But this normative link between scientific knowledge and a belief in progress is a return to the metaphysical formulation which the program of critical positivism had rejected in idealism and systematic positivism. To repeat then, from the point of view of transcendental critique, positivism's postulate of scientism is indefensible.

But the validity of this reflexive critique or the need to guard against such illusions by reflection on the limits of possible knowledge is not recognized by positivism. The circularity of its latent concept of knowledge defends it against this recognition. Hence, positivism is further defined by a second postulate: the objectivistic image of knowledge.

Objectivism: The Positivist Concept of Knowledge

The circularity of scientism and the denial of the constitutive activity of the subject derive from the belief that knowledge in a sense copies reality. This belief, which can be called the postulate of objectivism, was always inherent in the empiricist perspective, but it was reintroduced in a number of ways in the latter half of the nineteenth century. For example, the development of a psychophysics (e.g., Helmholtz)[18] and the interpretation of the mind as an adaptive and order-creating mechanism (e.g., Mach) both reinforced the tendency to treat knowledge as if it were a map of reality whose "fit" was improved in the advances of scientific inquiry. While this conception of knowledge as a "picturing" of reality is itself the tacit epistemology of common sense, it reappeared in the philosophy of science as the assumption that the progress of knowledge improved the correspondence between facts and the world. "Facts" therefore became the essential reality[19] and, as such, were equivalent to an ontology. Facts were what is known by the ego and they copy the elements of things that were independent from the ego. The distinction between the subject and object of knowledge was, from the point of view of objectivistically conceived science, unnecessary for the testing of knowledge. The possibility that "facts" might be constructed in a synthesis that was not given in the fact-elements cannot be admitted by a method that holds that reality (including the mediating ego) is the totality of facts. The postulate of objectivism therefore negates the necessity for a reflective inquiry into the subjective conditions of possible knowledge.

Insofar as facts become the essential reality, it is impossible to question the procedures of science; the objectivity of knowledge can be derived only from its relation to the object domain of science. Mach can thus claim that natural scientific work "is the adaptation of thoughts to facts."[20] Science becomes the mimetic adaptation of thought to facts and, as such, the circularity of scientism is concealed by an ontology of the factual. As practiced, science adequately describes reality as it is and provides the basic framework to which all questions of objectivity and subjectivity can be referred. From this viewpoint, the methodological practice of science creates facts that are not affected by the modes of scientific praxis—objectivism thus conceals the distinction between the constitutive activity of scientific praxis and the facts constituted. That is, historically situated investigation results in empirical facts which exist in themselves independent from the activity that produced them. It is assumed that the given is transformed into fact without any interference from the subjectivity of a constituting agent, e.g., the community of scientists.

Concept and theory formation in an objectivistically conceived science forms its categories independent from the communicative experience of a historically situated community of scientists. So conceived, the categorical framework and factual content of science "represent" the structures of things-in-themselves. Positivistic science is, in this sense, a continuation of classical ontology, which claimed to disclose the very nature of being. Despite the antimetaphysical intent of the positivist tradition, the objectivistic image of knowledge has permitted contemporary science to regress to a scientistic ontology. In contrast, a reflexive methodology stresses that only the scientist's participation in the everyday world makes knowledge of social reality objectively possible; it cannot exist when the formation of concepts and theories is separated from the communication between the scientist and his "object."

This immanent critique of the positivistic conception of methodology is inherent in the foundations of critical theory, but there are numerous other antipositivist critiques which converge with it, such as phenomenology (A. Schutz), and linguistics (the later Wittgenstein). Perhaps the most direct challenge to the empirical-analytical model of social scientific inquiry is A. Cicourel's ethnomethodological critique of the justifiability of its theory of measurement when applied to symbolic meaning.[21]

Cicourel shows that in the natural sciences the categorical framework allows the operationalization of concepts, and the immediate specification of the measurement procedures. There is, however, no instant and rigorously justifiable way of moving from sociocultural concepts to the selection of social indicators for measurement. Interpretation of communicative interactions presupposes more than the theoretical constructs and protophysics (geometry, mechanics) of natural science measurements. It presupposes the normative structures of ordinary language communication. Therefore, to use Wittgenstein's terms, the language game of physical measurement differs from the language game of ordinary language communication, and the rules of the latter are not reducible to those of the former.

In this sense social science concept-formation is linked to the prescientific patterns of communication within the socio-cultural world, and measurement procedures must be adjusted to the tacit agreements that have already emerged in the self-understanding of socialized individuals. This problem has been recognized by all contemporary antipositivist schools of social theory (e.g., phenomenology, hermeneutics, etc.).

But the positivist dogmas of the necessary separation of science from philosophy, of scientific method from the problems of symbolic meaning and understanding, have been defended by a very one-sided American appropriation of Max Weber's methodology.[22] It is useful therefore to relate briefly Weber's Neo-Kantianism to the above contrast of positivism and transcendental reflection.

Is Max Weber a Positivist?

Transcendental reflection does not end with the general transcendental philosophies of Kant and Hegel, but makes a fundamental contribution to the history of social theory. This fact may be concealed by the current positivistic images of social theory. It is forgotten that social theorists, especially in the German tradition, have always asked how knowledge of social reality is possible. Often this took the form of reflecting on the possibility of a cultural science and it usually involved the claim that we must understand (*verstehen*) the meaning of our "data" thereby distinguishing the methodologies of the cultural and the natural sciences. The methodological reflections of Max Weber begin from this transcendental distinction between the two types of science.

Weber's famous claim that social science knowledge is transcendentally constituted with reference to value may be useful for delimiting moral philosophy from science, but it produces a systematic ambiguity for social theory. This confusion comes from the notion of "value" which, as used by Weber, is derived from Heinrich Rickert's neo-Kantian philosophy of science.[23] The status of value there is regarded as nonempirical. In Rickert's work the distinction between nature and culture was construed transcendentally as the difference between two areas of possible objects of knowledge, insofar as these "objects" were or were not constituted with reference to value. This is a transcendental-logical, not an empirical, distinction; the validity of value judgments is not referrable therefore to existential properties of the "object," but rather to the moral agent's acknowledgment of obligatory values. Because this obligation which exerts itself as moral necessity, *should not be regarded as an empirical fact* it shows the influence of Kant's distinction between obligation by virtue of practical reason and sensual inclination in the form of drives or needs.

The nonempirical status of value becomes deeply problematic for a social science which must objectify the meaning of preexisting human expressions (e.g., acts, events) from the standpoint of a preinterpreted position within a cultural horizon. Social science encounters its objects as fully constituted cultural items, created by the value-oriented action of historical subjects. Hence the understanding of symbolic meaning always departs from a situation which is logically an interpretive (or "hermeneutic") circle: the interpreter is situated within an actual value system and must engage in communicative interaction with his "object" in order to get access to the meaning of this "data." Weber's mode of reflection recognizes the circularity of interpretive understanding on the level of value-interpretation (act-meaning),[24] but on the level of motivational understanding (action-meaning) the difference between interpreter and "interpreted" seem to fade away, due to the controlled methods of scientific testing of the act-meaning. Thus, what Weber recognized as a special methodological problem in relation to act-meaning, becomes an unimportant issue in relation to action-meaning. Having recognized the special circularity of inquiry on one level, Weber's resolution of the conflicting methods of *Verstehen* and *Erklärung* on the level of action-meaning denies the survival of any special problem, thereby enabling him to claim that there is no reason not to conceive of the cultural sciences as methodologically consistent with the empirical-analytic method of the natural sciences.

There is apparently no reason why we should ultimately separate the cultural sciences from the natural sciences, at least on the level of methodology. However, this is not entirely true. Weber did suggest that because of the epistemological problem some techniques, such as ideal-typical concept formation and the comparative method, must be adopted by the social sciences. And yet, despite these special techniques, the final procedures of testing hypotheses are analogous to those of the empirical-analytic sciences. What results from this position is the tacit assumption, made more by "Weberians" than by Weber, that concept and theory formation are totally separable from the processes of interpretation and that we can therefore analytically define concepts and construct theories independent of the special processes of interpretation of meaning. This is a false assumption argued by the critique of scientism above. But the mode of transcendental reflection Weber used to define the epistemological problem led him to make this assumption and produced the aforementioned ambiguity, which becomes especially problematic in its implications for the universality of social theory.

An alternative analysis made by the late Dilthey defines the unique method of the cultural sciences as the "circle of interpretation" (or the hermeneutic circle)[25] and conceives as inseparable the relations between concept and theory formation and the process of inquiry.[26] Ultimately, this means that the logic-in-use (the actual practice of inquiry) of a science which understands meaning cannot be reconstructed as methodologically analogous to the systematic observation and measurement of an instrumentally controlled system. The objectivity of a science that understands human meaning requires an epistemological reflection upon the presuppositions of the hermeneutic circle; its objectivity cannot be grounded in a parallel to the instrumental praxis of strict scientific inquiry.

What is lacking in the Rickert-Weber transcendental reflections about the science of "culture" is an explicit recognition of the dialectical relation of self-conscious actors and historical development, as implied by the Hegelian concept of objective mind. For Rickert and at times for Weber the object domain of "culture" refers to all phenomena that can be constituted by the prevailing values. However, values are not once and for all deducible a priori from the postulates of practical reason, but are found in the content of historical cultures and, as such, change, fuse, regress. Values cannot be approached as analogous to natural data. They cannot be conceived as a closed system that can be measured in an analogous manner to knowledge about nature. Insofar as

3: *Transcendental Reflection and Positivism*

Weber's methodology is based upon a neo-Kantian transcendental philosophy of science, it produces a systematic ambiguity which implies that a social theory can be constructed with the same claim to universality as strict science theory. So construed, Weber's epistemological reflections fade away, leaving nature and culture standing as a continuous spectrum that can be adequately investigated by the empirical-analytic method without concern for the historical development of culture, or the unique problems posed by the hermeneutic circle.

Yet Weber's methodological reflections did point in a nonpositivistic direction which was not usually explored by his followers. That is, the nonempirical status of value did refer social science "observation" back to the transcendental principles presupposed by socio-cultural processes. Weber's methodology cannot be elaborated as a purely self-enclosed method whose validity depends solely upon controlled observation and rigorous analytic procedures. The very reflection of methodology refers the possibility of understanding back to the basic interests of the everyday world of socio-cultural processes. A cultural science is possible only because it is a self-conscious refinement of the procedures of understanding within the everyday world. This means that the procedures of a non-behavioristic science that objectifies the meaning of social action are rooted in the practical "cognitive interests"[27] of a cultural world; they cannot be explicated as deriving solely from the instrumentally controlled observations of sensory experience (presupposing only a technical cognitive interest). However, although Weber remained aware of the purely logical nature of the value criterion, it was precisely this that was misconstrued when the methodology was appropriated by Talcott Parsons.[28] Despite vacillations, Weber had at times recognized that the most general theories of human history are ultimately linked to the cultural values of their epoch, and that the purpose of nomological (i.e., lawlike) knowledge was finally linked to the practical cognitive interest of enlightenment.[29] Parsons never understood the transcendental form of Weber's argument, and reduced Weber's methodological reflections to a justification of a general theory of social action (or, finally, to the theory of the social system) which recognizes only the technical cognitive interest as a guide in the construction of social theory.[30]

Weber, however, never completely developed his recognition of the twofold interest of sociological theory. He remained ambivalent and failed to pursue the numerous indications for a sociological explanation combining the scientific models of *Erklärung* and *Verstehen*. He never clearly expressed the scientific ideal of sociology as an "explanatory-understanding."

This thesis, as expressed by Weber or as it was developed by Habermas as the logic of explanatory-understanding, is not a denial of the possibility of nomological generalizations, but rather a general statement about the relation of theory and life practice (including the practice of scientific inquiry). By admitting the epistemological presuppositions of meaning and understanding, Weber, and the recent Hegelian-Marxist proponents of the radicalized argument,[31] have admitted that neither the categorical framework of social theory, nor the conceptualization of the object domain, is independent of the communicative experience of inquiry.

We must conclude that Weber's actual scientific practice was more flexible than that of his positivistic followers: however, it is the ambiguity of Weber's neo-Kantian reflections that permits the latter interpretations. Weber's reflections become positivistic as soon as they are taken in a scientistic and objectivistic manner—as soon as his methodology is conceived as an empirical-analytic method which does not involve a necessary reflection upon the epistemological presuppositions of the understanding of symbolic meaning. By the same token, when Weber's theory of social action is generalized to a systems theory which can specify all possible action orientations, it presents a hypothesis of value-universalism which goes beyond that of his conception of science (*Wissenschaft*). Since establishment social theory has often based itself upon a positivistically interpreted Weberianism, the current methodological debate in Germany, in which neo-Marxists have played a leading role, has provided a public context for the revival of an academically effective critical theory.

Although Karl Popper's *The Open Society* (1945) may have

initiated the debate, the 1964 Heidelberg meeting of the German Sociological Association, which dealt with the significance of Max Weber's work, was surely the beginning of the wider discussion. The Heidelberg Conference reopened the *Methodenstreit* that Weber began at the turn of the century, but with the Marxist position regarding *Wissenschaftstheorie* forcibly represented by T. W. Adorno, Max Horkheimer, Herbert Marcuse, and Jürgen Habermas.[32]

In general, the debate has centered around the legitimacy of the separation of scientific knowledge and practical choice on both epistemological and societal levels. The neo-Marxists have attempted to show that Weber's value-free doctrine derived from an untenable (for social theory) Kantian distinction between theoretical and practical knowledge. While Weber's methodological reflections can be seen as relating knowledge to an interest broader than the purely technical, he nevertheless developed his historical sociology with emphasis on the increasing purposive rationality of the structures of society. This interpretive perspective suggests a concept of rationality, and a philosophy of history, which has been the subject of extensive criticism by K. Lowith, W. S. Mommsen, Herbert Marcuse, and Jürgen Habermas.[33]

The Notion of a Dialectical Social Theory

Insofar as social theory is conceived objectivistically, social reality is presented with a basic unchangeable structure to which human action can only adapt more or less effectively. Social theory thus approximates a type of geometry concerned with the basic natural processes that create social action. Basic to the objectivistic concept of social theory is a physicalistic bias that distorts and conceals the human constitution of social reality. This kind of social theory is refuted in a critical philosophy of science.

But if we cannot expect to find invariant "structures" in history —and this is what a non-objectivistic concept of knowledge implies—then we are again faced with the question: "What can we know?" German idealism provided an answer to this question which establishes the meaning of all modern dialectical thinking: we can reflexively discover the universal social forms that underlie the patterns of history, and they can guide our ongoing attempts to find past regularities, tendencies, and so forth. In other words, we can recognize that human activity is the chief "*formgiver*" of history and attempt to express the logical principles and/or historical rules that underlie this constitutive activity.

The positivistic approach to social theory has always involved what George Lukacs calls the bourgeois antinomy[34]—an organization of social phenomena as determined either primarily by the atoms of society (the individual) or by "social facts." This means that social reality is either reduced to a psychologism or reconstructed as a sociologism and an economism. Both extremes are partially true; the reciprocity of the self-forming processes of a social totality cannot be organized by a single generalized science such as sociology or economics. Dialectical theory is an adequate social theory that can express these reciprocal relations.

It is at this point that the theoretical significance of Hegel's radicalization of transcendental critique into a phenomenological reflection upon the self-formation of consciousness becomes clear. We can construct a critical theory only within a framework that expresses the dialectical relationships of the changing social totality to the cognitive interests of theoretical consciousness on the one hand, and the way in which these relationships predefine the self-forming praxis of the individual on the other. But as Marx showed, such a phenomenological reflection violates its own method if it culminates in a theory of absolute knowledge—it can be realized only as a dialectical theory of society with a critical intent.

In criticizing Hegel's philosophy of absolute knowledge, however, Marx went too far and made it appear that Hegel's entire logic of critique was "idealistic." Since Marx himself used this logic in his critique of capitalist development he obscured his own scientific framework. To restore the dialectical logic of the critical method we must return therefore to Hegel, without departing from Marx's critique, and recover the original method of critical theory.

Hegel had demonstrated that we can ground knowledge adequately only on a phenomenological radicalization of critical philosophy that reflects, not just on the process of science but on the general self-formation of consciousness. We must recognize that in establishing the limits of possible knowledge reflective critique will, at the same time, reveal the constraints of cultural norms that block the development of consciousness. Critique of the limits of theoretical knowledge and of practical choice cannot, therefore, be separated. We cannot comprehend the possibility of objective knowledge without at the same time reconstructing the cultural constraints that block the pursuit of truth and/or the "path of the soul." Thus at the root of the radicalization of critical philosophy is the unity of philosophical reflection and the critique of false consciousness.

It is obvious today that the failure to recognize the joint source of critical science in Hegel and Marx is rooted in the fact that this basic commonality was denied in the development of Marxism. The phenomenological framework and its anti-objectivist conception of the relation of theory and praxis have been lost in the evolution of Marxism, beginning with Engels. This became even more true later in the century when the dominance of Soviet Marxism forced a regression of critical theory to a mechanical, scientistic form of critique. In reaction against this theory an ontological type of critical theory has reappeared since World War II in a variety of forms that range from Sartre's early philosophy of freedom to the internal ontological tendency of Herbert Marcuse's critique.[35]

Recently, a more sophisticated form of "positivistic" Marxism has been developed by Louis Althusser, who denies precisely the reflective phenomenological framework (which he called "historicism") and the anti-objectivistic nature of dialectics (which he replaces with a structuralistically-conceived naturalism). As an apologist for Leninism, Althusser has identified precisely the authentically critical elements of Hegelian-Marxism and has attempted to remove them from the "scientific Marxist" method.[36]

The meaning of "dialectics" can, however, be elucidated only in a nonobjectivistic theory. Only by a transcendental reflection upon the ever-changing relationship of the individual and the universal can we conceptualize the self-forming processes of the human world without reducing them to the primacy of one set of determinants, e.g., the economic. Reflection upon the relationships of the individual to the constitutive universals remains the central logical concern of a dialectical theory and implies that the self-forming processes of the human world cannot be formally reconstructed from any one starting point or rooted in any invariant structure. A dialectical relationship is not reducible to a function of an independent variable but requires a nonformalizable reciprocal relation to other processes.[37] This does not mean, however, that one cannot gain knowledge about dialectical processes, although it does set limits to the range of generalization and the status of the knowledge itself.

Science, including critical science, cannot be taken as a self-enclosed method of fact production but must be rooted in a historical world. To be more precise, within dialectical social theory there is a need to continually recomprehend the possibility of science due to its *non*objectivistic conception of social reality. As social reality is constantly transforming itself, and the mediating capacity of human consciousness is no small component of this change, the relationship of scientific praxis to a changing social reality must also be reflexively reevaluated. Only in this way is it possible to avoid imputing to facts an objectivism that obliterates the active subject who constituted them from a contextual framework.

We can now generalize that in a dialectical theory of society we are objectifying the contexts of synthesis presupposed by the processes of society, the basic principles and rules of which we are attempting to reconstruct. The intent of such a theory is to objectify the self-formative dialectic of the human species conceived as an active subject, and in doing so to orient the active man to his world by breaking through the veil of objective illusion. In this sense dialectical theory is the foundation for a critical science which is a historically-generated and necessarily ongoing attempt to understand and transform the human world in accordance with the basic interest of human emancipation from domination. It is a restoration of the classic notion of the unity of theory and praxis in the context of contemporary society. Such a project is a unification of the method of critical philosophy and of the sciences that can interpret historical symbolic systems to identify modes of alienation and repression (or generally, domination). This means nothing less than the re-orientation of the goal of social theory to that of the critique of domination.

4

The Dialectical Foundations of Critical Theory: Jürgen Habermas's Metatheoretical Investigations

The Frankfurt School's Rediscovery of a Dialectical Critical Theory

*I*n the early formulations of the Frankfurt School it was assumed that the critique of political economy remained central to the theory. Critical theory was considered part of the ongoing class struggle that determined the relationship of positivist and critical science. Bourgeois science (i.e., positivism) was not regarded as a serious challenge since it was assumed it would be overcome in practice. The criterion of validity that critical theoreticians took seriously was the degree to which the theory could illuminate objective possibilities for dissolving class domination. The question is why there is so much concern with the critique of positivism on the part of Horkheimer, Adorno, Marcuse, and, more recently, Habermas. The answer to this question constitutes a record of the changing "politics" of the School.

In the context of both monopoly capitalism and a communist orthodoxy, Max Horkheimer had attempted to rediscover Marx-the-dialectician, thereby recovering the concept of reason, which could refute the instrumental end-means rationality that was being used increasingly to support the reproduction processes of both capitalism *and* bureaucratic socialism. In this way, the movement back to the philosophical dimension of Marx was not, as some critics have claimed,[1] to recover a philosophical concept of truth —for the relevant test was still political practice—but to develop a residual dimension of Marxism with which to combat the objectivist illusion of both bourgeois ideology and mechanical Marxism.

This objectivism is exemplified by the bourgeois scientific community, which has a naive image of the correspondence of knowledge and nature and is blind to the societal consequences of science. An objectivist understanding of science conceals the common interest the scientific community shares with mankind in the actualization of a rational society. Insofar as the meaning of knowledge is referred solely to methodological procedures for assessing factuality, the more fundamental anthropological interest in collective survival and intersubjective communication is disregarded. Horkheimer's attempt to show this link between cognition and emancipation must, therefore, be viewed as an attempt to reestablish a materialistic epistemology which places the logic of human cognition within the context of the self-formative processes of the human species.

Horkheimer's classic essay, "Traditionelle und Kritische Theorie,"[2] which appeared in 1937, formulates the basic Frankfurt analysis of the transcendental interests presupposed by knowledge-constitutive processes. (As we shall see, Jürgen Habermas's later [1968] theory of cognitive interests completes the dialectical theory suggested by Horkheimer's work.) Horkheimer shows that traditional theory is based on the assumption that there is no basic difference between the object of the natural sciences and of the humanities; they should therefore have an identical theory of science and a single methodology. Experience is organized on the basis of the reproduction of life within the framework of the existing society, for the purpose of gaining knowledge which can be used to control and manipulate natural and social processes. The social genesis of scientific knowledge, as well as the use made of it, is considered external to science. Traditional theory tries to construct conceptual frameworks of increasing generality; starting from the concrete, it hopes to develop general theories by continuous abstraction—a procedure which has proven successful in the natural sciences.

Critical theory, on the other hand, departs from the premise that every epoch has one or several constitutive principles for the reproduction of society and that these general concepts must be analyzed in a state of constant flux between the general and the particular. The "secret" of society will never become apparent in a blind accumulation of fragmented facts, hypotheses, short- and medium-range theories. Most significantly, critical theory does not exclude from scientific activity the question of the context in which knowledge is produced and used. It thereby reflects on the presuppositions of science as part of the analysis of the relation between theory and practice.

The Frankfurt School's critical reflections on science are thus primarily concerned with relating the object of knowledge to the constitutive activity of the subject within a historical context. They represent an attempt to combat the objectivist illusion that has become central to the ideology of the capitalist and "socialist" systems, and which is especially dangerous in the social sciences:

> . . . [it] leads to a misrepresentation of the object under scrutiny and to an accommodating conformism on the part of the scientists. Because they no longer see exactly how "in every act of perception" . . . they remain imprisoned in and take their bearings from a process of social life, *they misrepresent human history as a natural process* and willingly act out the role assigned them by the . . . system as useful and 'irresponsible' experts whose knowledge can be smoothly integrated in the system's utility structures. [italics mine][3]

Rejection of objectivism in the image of traditional theory is not intended as a displacement of critique to the level of metatheory but rather as a necessary supplement to a macrocritique. This "necessity" was imposed by the growing importance of the positivist self-image of neutrality in an industrial system which used this knowledge to mediate objective conflict and create new coercive controls. In this sense, the efforts of the Frankfurt theorists are an instance of the unity of theory and practice, in their generation of a metatheory to combat the objectivistic perception of history as a natural process. In the sphere of metatheory, as in the critique of political economy, what was held to be a simple matter of developmental processes is shown to contain a social contradiction with societal consequences. The critical theory of science itself is a critique of the ideology of positivism.

Whereas Horkheimer's early work still retained the hope that critique would be validated by revolutionary praxis, the later phases of the School held that the changing conditions had altered the relation of critique and praxis.[4] At this point the School brought critical theory to the level of the contemporary method- ological argument. There were two reasons for the shift of the level of discussion to a methodological one: the dogmatic solidification of the authoritarian-bureaucratic governments in the communist countries, and the involution of critical philosophy in Western capitalist society. *In the political as well as in the academic world critical theory has lost its impact,* and has, therefore, to turn against itself to *regain* the link with political practice. In the early thirties, this connection was given objectively; today it has to be created theoretically and practically.

But if we assume that the dogmatic reification of Marxist theory was not a historical accident, there must be elements in the theory itself which made this development possible. Albrecht Wellmer, a younger member of the School, discusses two of those elements: first, the speculative component in the interpretation of the transi- tion from capitalism to communism that is essentially an eschato- logical elevation of the proletarian's role; i.e., the fixed belief that the working class *must* make the revolution. Secondly, Marx's own objectivistic concept of labor, which becomes the basis for Frankfurt's self-reflective critique.[5]

This critique of Marxism in a post-World War II context led the School to break the traditional relationship of critique and the theory of revolution. The critique of positivism, beginning with Horkheimer's attempt to distinguish between traditional and criti- cal theory, was determined by the insight that any revolution in the advanced industrial world would have to *break through* a closed universe of technical rationality and reified relationships; a centralized political revolution could not simply execute a shift in these sociocultural constraints. The early Horkheimer recognized that the connection between the critique of political economy and the theory of revolution established by Marx had to be broken. And so, the famous *Dialektik der Aufklärung*, Horkheimer and Adorno attempt a critique of capitalist society which not only comes to terms with the liberal capitalism of Marx, but also with its state capitalist and state interventionist heirs. While Marx had related the cause of reification to a specific type of bourgeois property whose abolition would overcome it, Horkheimer and Adorno separate the critique of the exchange principle from the theory of surplus labor and transform it into a critique of instrumental reason. In this way, the critique of political economy is transformed into a more general critique of technical civilization.

However, the *Dialektik der Aufklärung* does not attempt a scientific continuation of Marx's ideas as an empirical theory with a practical intent. It analyzes the perversions of this society, but it neither shows the concrete social groups which could bring about change, nor does it identify the structural tendencies which signify the possibility of transformation. For the authors, critique has "become philosophical" as a necessary reaction to the bureaucratic solidification of socialism and the rise of communist orthodoxy. At the same time they believe that the Marxist labor theory of value has become inapplicable to late industrial societies. They have thus returned to the philosophical mode of critical theory.

The outcome of the work in Frankfurt is therefore paradoxical. While rethinking the foundations of critical theory, Horkheimer and Adorno have, in the end, returned to the philosophical (Hegelian) mode of the theory. They have given up, so it seems, the attempt made by Marx to create a critical science—that is, the concrete analysis of societal change. While Adorno, particularly, had produced a critique of the philosophy of identity in both its ontological and objectivistic forms, the work of Herbert Marcuse, supposedly allied with the other members, recreates an ontological mode of critical theory. Only Jürgen Habermas remained aware of the power of the self-critique of Marxism that the School's tradition had established. His work justly deserves the extremely high praise of George Lichtheim, who compares him favorably to Hegel.[6]

The Metatheoretical Analysis of Jürgen Habermas

Despite the vilification of the left, and to the dismay of the academy, Jürgen Habermas remains a Marxist. Yet he recognizes and publicly asserts that Marxism has lost its capacity both to defend its claims before the contemporary tribunal of rational discourse, and to release political liberation movements in the industrial world. He has also remained engaged in the struggle against the Western intellectual communities' division of knowledge and political decision, which has permitted social science to become so many varieties of social management theory. In his attempts to critically engage the academy while translating its achievements into an ongoing criticism of Marx, Habermas presents a model of theoretical praxis that contemporary Marxists could well emulate.

In general, Habermas's work is a major rethinking of the meaning of the unity of theory and practice.[7] Habermas has attempted to complete the basis for a critical theory that could become a material force for enlightenment, recognizing that such a theory must be both academically and politically effective. He has clarified the categorical framework of a critical-materialism in an attempt to justify the normative foundations of emancipatory critique. This has taken the form of a reflexive comprehension of the relation of knowledge to the cognitive interests of the human species, thereby yielding a metatheory. We will try to demonstrate that Habermas's synthesis is a major innovation in the history of Marxist theory in its formulation of a theory of the dialectical relationship between three action dialogics in which the unity of knowledge and action is grounded in a radically sociological concept of intersubjectivity. Rather than conceive critical theory naturalistically, or attempt to derive it from a Husserlian phenomenology[8] (whose monadic basis has been systematically exposed by the Frankfurt School), Habermas grounds it in a nonobjectivistic and nonscientific (that is, a dialectical) metatheory. He has, in fact, restored the meaning of "dialectics" in a critical sublation of a positivist philosophy, while simultaneously translating the meaning of emancipatory critique into a contemporary framework which attempts to justify its scientific status.

Marx's Notion of a Dialectical Social Theory

Marx rejected Hegel's belief that the notion (*Begriff*) is the ground of nature; he held, on the contrary, that nature is the absolute ground of Mind. In the first thesis on Feuerbach, however, we see that Marx is no crude materialist; nature becomes objective for us only through the mediation of human work. It is in this sense that the subject constitutes both an objective world and, through the synthesis of work, changes the social totality in a way that alters the transcendental presuppositions of human praxis. Work is both a basic mechanism in the social evolution of the human species and an element in the historical changes of the transcendental framework for experience. Habermas restores Marx's residual transcendentalism, stripped of its idealist meaning, to illuminate the way work establishes a process of material synthesis. So construed we can see that Marx has extended Hegel's critique of Kant and has effectively rewritten Hegel's *Phenomenology* by conceiving work—the "dialectic of negativity, as the moving and productive principle."[9] Marx's theory of society thus appears to be a materialization of Hegel's dialectic of *Geist*. But most important, it can be seen as a completion of the grounding of knowledge in the transcendentally conceived notion of "material synthesis." For Marx the synthesis of material production unites "subjective nature" (the historical subject) and the processes of nature into an objectivation whose "unity" is imposed by the form-giving character of human production. In contrast to an idealist notion, Marx's idea of synthesis through work creates neither a constitutive logical structure nor an absolute unity—but a historically specific unity. Material synthesis, however, does presuppose a logically invariant relation, that of the human instrumental orientation to nature. But this invariant moment is only one side of the concrete historical dialectic of material synthesis.

The notion of material synthesis more generally implies a twofold relation between man and nature (including subjective nature). On the one hand, man has an invariant relation in his instrumental orientation to nature, over the processes of which he must secure control to reproduce life. On the other hand, this basic and natural substratum is culturally mediated, thereby altering the relation between man and the system of productive forces. Whereas the invariant relation of man to nature (the instrumental orientation) is a Kantian moment and can be elaborated as an instrumentalist theory of knowledge (e.g., Peirce), man's alteration through critical reflection can be understood as a Fichtean moment. That is, the human subject, while produced by the preceding system of work, achieves identity of self by an active self-positing comprehension of its "production." For Marx, of course, the Fichtean moment of self-conscious positing is a historical struggle, not a logical relation between ego and non-ego.

The two moments of the dialectic of material synthesis are essentially different in their logical structure. The Kantian moment reveals that man is engaged in a step-by-step process of trial and error in his everyday encounters with nature (and, in its refined version, in scientific inquiry), resulting in the acquisition of technical knowledge that increases the range of his control over nature. (This is what Habermas calls the technical cognitive interest.)

In another formulation, the Kantian moment of material synthesis is the extension of the behavioral system of instrumental action, which is constituted historically by the unique configuration of existing productive apparatus and the living labor of man. The Fichtean moment of material synthesis reveals that man comes to self-consciousness through his comprehension of the self-formative processes of past generations which are constituted through his own self-positing struggles. The logical irreducibility of the Fichtean moment demonstrates that the mechanisms for self-understanding are not determined by the extension of technical control (by the work praxis itself), but involve a constitutive struggle to recover their identity. This is logically a comprehension of the historic-genetic process of self-formation (what Habermas calls the practical cognitive interest).

Habermas's reconstruction of Marx's critical-materialism as entailing two moments of material synthesis is a clarification of the dialectical foundations of Marxism, which is most explicit on the transhistorical level. The evolution of human society goes forward via the mechanism of human productive activity, on the one hand, and the reflexive self-formation of class struggle, on the other. Both mechanisms, constituted as active production and praxis, are essential to the emancipation of man. But the dialogic of productive processes and its constitutive world-building is not the same as the dialogic of class struggle which must break through sedimented constraints of power relations inherent in reified sociocultural controls. A comprehension of the historical relatedness of these two moments—or the dialectics of emancipation—is itself the focus of a science that takes as its object the interrelation between the material and ideological constraints on human development (what Habermas calls the emancipatory cognitive interest). Critical theory, as a materialistic radicalization of critical philosophy, proceeds then by an analysis of both the blockages on productive activity and the distortions of communicative praxis.

Habermas's Critique of Marx's Dialectical Theory

Habermas's reconstruction of Marx shows how the very perspective from which Marx criticizes Hegel prevents him from adequately comprehending the theoretical impact of his own work. Marx's identification of the forces of production as the mechanism for abolishing abstract, "positive," life forms encompasses both the Kantian and the Fichtean moment of the dialectic of history. In Marx's historical materialism both the coming to grips with nature through the development of productive forces and the reflexive comprehension of externalized and "naturalized" humanity are conceived as moments of the process of production. Thus, Fichte's concept of the independence of the self-constituting act of reflection is reduced, in Marx's theoretical presentation, to a feedback mechanism of the production process. This dialectical theory, and Marx's critique of Hegel's philosophy of absolute reflection, goes too far when it presents the production process as both the negative material activity (the dynamic that transforms historical life forms) and the "content" of that which is reintegrated into the subject's self-consciousness. In this reduction, the labor process is basic to both externalization and the reappropriation of an active subject—and, as such, production is the basic epistemological framework for both moments. The results are far-reaching and they prevent Marx from comprehending adequately his own more flexible analysis and intentions. Consequently, there are serious limitations in Marx's metatheoretical framework (which must be distinguished from his substantive analysis). Because of his concept of "reflection" as a feedback of production, Marx is unable to recognize the methodological status of his own work. For example, the distinction between the natural and human sciences is no longer important for him, since all of man's deeds can be conceptualized within the framework of feedback-controlled action. Since instrumental activity determines the scope of human action, for Marx, the logically distinct moment of comprehension can be expressed theoretically within the explanatory method of the natural sciences. Habermas argues that Marx was unable to distinguish theoretically between the natural history of socioeconomic formations and utilization of this reconstruction for the critique of ideological power relations—both of which are in his work. Marx transcends both the absolute philosophy of German idealism and the naturalism of classical economics, and yet he obscures the methodological status of critique by a one-sided development of the dialectic of material synthesis. In other words, Marx retained the phenomenological framework of reflection upon the self-constitutive dynamic of the human species, but he also denied it by understanding the second moment as analogous to productive feedback.

This is perhaps best demonstrated by showing that Marx has

two different conceptions of ideology, and of the relation of consciousness to work processes. In his defense, we can begin with Marx's more dialectical theory of ideology, which he develops in his critique of political economy. In discussing the classical theory of value, Marx shows that consciousness of the relationship between human activity and social wealth was a critique of feudal absolutism and represented a critical comprehension of the superior rationality of market society. Capitalist ideology resulted from the self-positing of the revolutionary bourgeois class; its self-comprehension became the ideological consciousness of the capitalist epoch. Implicit in the concepts of value and the market-secured equivalence of exchange between wage labor and capital were the ideas of justice, equality, and freedom—the utopian promises of the new epoch. This ideology thus identifies the utopian anticipations of bourgeois consciousness which are negated, Marx's *Capital* shows, by the structural tendencies (or "laws-of-motion") of capitalist development. Bourgeois consciousness is perverted into an ideological legitimation of the existing power relations, and utopian anticipations inherent in the bourgeois ideology become part of the appearance (the *Schein*) of capitalist reality and conceals the growing exploitation of capitalism. Marx's critique of political economy reconstructs the historical genesis of the bourgeois consciousness and demonstrates the gap between its utopian anticipations and its ideological distortion of alienation and exploitation.

In this sense, critical theory can enlighten the existing consciousness about its ideological content.

> The medium of this enlightenment is theory, whose destruction of ideology through the analysis of the context of social coercion must also be the disclosure of a concept of personal social freedom, which, as "real" utopian content of false social consciousness, it can obtain only in the course of this criticism.[10]

This concept of ideology implies the dissolution of false consciousness as an emancipatory process mediated by communication and reflection.

Marx develops a different ideology in his *historical materialism*, in which it becomes simply the mental expression of class domination. Ideologies are the thoughts of the ruling class, not any more in the sense that reason appears distorted by the interests of power, but in the "instrumental" sense of a superstructure which ensures domination. The superstructure appears as a direct function of the substructure, that is, a direct function of labor. The dialectic relationship between means of production and relations of production is reduced to a functional relationship; relations of production and ideologies become forces of production of a second degree. This is the basis of "positivistic Marxism," which Habermas and Wellmer have tried to separate from the more dialectical formulations of Marx.

Suppression of the dialectical independence of reflective comprehension from the theory of historical materialism has had unintended consequences. First, as mentioned above, the methodological nature of the human sciences has been misunderstood and the Marxist critique has been represented as a type of materialistic scientism. Consequently it has tended toward an economistic science which presents social evolution in a deterministic manner (i.e., the moment of productive activity is objectivistically conceived). Secondly, there has been an authoritarian use of critique by later Marxists which, in the organizational theory of Leninism, reduces the struggle for political emancipation to strategies for unquestioned instrumental ends. Marxism has evolved into an elitist paramilitary tradition which subordinates theoretical reflection and human liberation to the instrumental ends of "revolutionary" power acquisition. When reflective capacity is lost and authoritarian practice estranges its mobilizing potential, Marxism enters into the period of sectarianism and/or its current senility of keeping the faith and waiting for an economic cataclysm. Contemporary Marxism is in a serious crisis which, due to its objectivistic understanding of culture, it cannot transcend.

Marx's central theoretical deficiency is his misconception of the second moment of the dialectic of self-constitution, which extends into every area of his work. Even in his most flexible formulations, Marx sees conflict defined by the class appropriation of socially-created objects (exploitation) and the relations of men determined by their position in the production process. The reflexive comprehension (which is actualized as critical praxis of class struggle) of rigidified institutions is always linked therefore to blockages in this process. Although this is significant for a critique that will enable revolutionary struggle to remove the class constraints upon the productive forces, it is inadequate for the critique of repressed need-dispositions in a class-dominated society. Marx's concept of class consciousness is not really broad enough to represent the type of reflexive comprehension needed to objectify the constraints that are placed upon both productive forces and the self-positing subject by "social relations." Especially in late capitalism, where the capitalistic constraints upon full utilization of productive capacity have been supported by an "instrumental rationalization"[11] of all institutions, the classic critique of exploitation must be expanded to include the multifold repressions imposed upon the person by his privatized, yet bureaucratically controlled, existence.

While it is true that in his substantive analysis Marx clearly distinguished between productive forces and the powers that reacted upon man in the form of the strength of one social class over another, he did so in terms of the contradiction between the forces and relations of production. While production (instrumental action) extends control over natural forces and is aided or retarded by productive relations, it is not identical with the full range of the institutional relations that constrain self-realization of human potential. Institutionalization of power relations has a momentum of its own and coerces man by blocking self-comprehension on many fronts, not just at the point of production. Marx's critical theory could conceptualize the constraints upon communication possibilities only insofar as they were directed at the historical organization of the productive activity of society. Habermas's intent, therefore, is to develop that component of critical theory which was neglected by Marx's critique of political economy. Formulation of a communication theory supplements the theory of value, basic to Marx's theory of the historical evolution of modes of production. (However, we will argue below that the relation of these two theories has not been adequately expressed by Habermas.)

Whereas Marx wanted to criticize the exploitative character of capitalist production, Habermas seeks to extend critical theory in order to analyze the systematically distorted communication of all industrial organization. But most important, Habermas's work attempts to ground the normative justification of critical theory in his communication theory, which he believes is legitimated by the twentieth-century revolution in linguistic philosophy (to be discussed in section V). While this would invert the normative relation of work and class struggle, it would necessitate a retention of Marx's analysis of political economy. But these issues cannot be analyzed prior to a reconstruction of Habermas's notion of cognitive interest. The understanding and critique of Habermas must begin with an adequate grasp of this difficult concept.

A Phenomenologically Grounded Critical Theory

Habermas tries to show that critical philosophy attempts to grasp the self-formative process of an active subject, and is itself an *interest* in the comprehension and consequent liberation from dogmatic dependence upon habitual norms and the immediacy of human experience. Fichte's work, especially, analyzes the logical unity of theoretical and practical reason in the act of self-reflection. In Fichte's doctrine of knowledge the ego, through self-reflection, becomes transparent to itself in its self-positing, and thereby frees itself from dogmatism. Fichte comprehends Kant's distinction between the theoretical interest of pure reason and the moral interest of practical reason to be unified in the emancipatory act of self-reflection. Self-reflection mediates false consciousness analytically and practically; it both comprehends the source of error and frees consciousness from constraints. Therefore, for Fichte, self-reflective reason presupposes an interest in the emancipation and self-subsistence of reason.

If we place Fichte's analysis within the phenomenological framework of a self-constituting human species, it can be reinterpreted "materialistically." Hence, Habermas suggests that the conditions presupposed by emancipatory reflection must now be expanded into a theory of cognitive interests. We can develop a critical theory of society only if we first objectify the "basic orientations that are rooted in the specific fundamental conditions of the possible reproduction and self-constitution of the human species, that is, work and interaction."[12]

In other words, the Fichtean emancipatory act of self-reflection can be radicalized phenomenologically and comprehended materialistically only by conceptualizing the analytic and practical conditions that make mankind's active syntheses possible. Habermas tries to objectify the cognitive interests that are logically *and* historically presupposed in the syntheses of human evolution. The theory relates human cognition to subject-object dialectics as they are constituted in the moments of material synthesis and, as such, all knowledge creation is connected directly to the practical and technical processes of human society. Here, then, is a new concept of the relatedness of theory and practice in the form of a theory of the interests of cognition.

Yet, the technical and practical cognitive interests can themselves be comprehended only through phenomenological reflection, and are but moments in the more comprehensive emancipatory interest of the human species. In other words, a materialistic interpretation of the emancipatory interest in reason reveals that a self-positing subject (i.e., the human species) advances autonomously by reproducing the basic knowledge-constitutive interests, and in direct relation to the critical abolition of world views and social forms. Fichte's concept of self-reflection as an action that returns to itself to constitute knowledge and action is conceivable materialistically only as the result of a critical struggle against the constraints placed on the mechanisms of social evolution. Recognition of the emancipatory interest within social evolution prevents us from reducing human history to a naturalistic process, or from separating our concept of knowledge (and the standards for its objectivity and validity) from the processes of active synthesis.

This theory of cognitive interests cannot be developed by the scientistic materialism of orthodox Marxism, or by a positivistic perspective of the contemporary academy. Nor can it be conceived from within the framework of "phenomenological Marxism," which Habermas claims is as objectivistic as positivism, although this is a transcendental objectivism.

Given the extent to which objectivism has permeated contemporary consciousness, a return to reflective epistemology would seem regressive. Habermas believes, therefore, that the only viable strategy is to return to pragmatism (e.g., C. S. Peirce) and historicism (e.g., W. Dilthey), which begin from the positivist problematic but link the logic of inquiry to the objective processes of life. Habermas holds that these neglected investigations are actually more advanced than most contemporary philosophy of science because their analysis contains an assessment of the cognitive interests of these societal systems. Just as the natural or cultural sciences disclose and interpret reality from a specific transcendental framework (as predefined by the unique configuration of language and action in their methodological practice), so the "systems" of instrumental action and symbolic interaction, to which these scientific inquiries are linked, have transcendental functions. Habermas develops the notion of cognitive interest as a phenomenological radicalization of the transcendental reflections of Peirce and Dilthey.

Note on the Technical Cognitive Interest

The logical invariance of the human instrumental orientation to nature is not a pure transcendental relation but one that is always mediated by the historical configuration of technics and *lebenspraxis*. The basic orientation of man to nature remains an ever-transforming, yet logically invariant, relation of instrumental action. C. S. Peirce recognized this quasi-transcendental, quasi-empirical relationship in his attempt to articulate an instrumental logic of discovery. He showed that the synthetic modes of reasoning—induction and abduction—are chains of inference whose objectivity presupposes on the norms of procedure in the research practice of a community of investigators. In this sense, Peirce reflects on the synthetic a priori this collective subject presupposes and yet transforms in its active scientific praxis.

Within this frame of reference scientific reasoning consists of systems of *purposive rational* action that fixate belief, operate as guiding principles for the accumulation of new information, and accept revision when there are failures in anticipated results. Belief is secured when there is a successful enactment of a new recipe. This methodological framework is transcendental in that "reality" is the sum total of facts which a collective subject (the community of scientists) can possibly establish as true propositions. Valid beliefs are universal propositions (expressible in a formalized language) about reality which can lead, given initial conditions, to technical recommendations for the control of observed processes. The essential meaning, then, of any scientific statement is that it can be expressed as a prediction that an event will occur following upon another event which is itself produced by our manipulation of conditions. An explanatory hypothesis is basically the securing and extending of habits of efficient instrumental actions. The technical interest of strict science is that such inquiry presupposes a concern for certainty which is related to actions that can control objectified processes.

All behavioral orientations that are guided by a technical interest are involved with the modes of adaptation used by man to cope with and bring under control his environment. Such systems of action are called by Habermas *instrumental action systems* or, more generally, *purposive rational action systems*. They refer to all human activity that is guided by the following of technical *rules* based on empirical knowledge.

The conception of purposive rational action systems replaces the Marxian concept of the substructure of society. One advantage of this reconceptualization is its ability to grasp the scientific revolution of the twentieth century as part of the ongoing transformation of the system of work: the growth of the knowledge industry is recognized as a force of production; we don't have to produce a theory of "post-industrial" society!

Peirce's analysis is limited, however, by the impossibility of accounting for communication between scientific investigators.

The dialogue-like pattern of ordinary language communication depends upon a type of action different from that of instrumental manipulation. Habermas argues that there are two epistemological models presupposed by participants in the everyday world.

Note on the Practical Cognitive Interest

The capacity of man to understand the meaning of human expression is apparent in the symbolic processes of everyday life; any systematic inquiry into communicative experience assumes this in a way which is not clearly grasped by most current methodological reconstructions of the social sciences. The preinterpretation of symbolic meaning is taken by Dilthey to be the transcendental presupposition of all scientific inquiry into socio-cultural process. As such, the nature of induction in the cultural sciences enscribes a "hermeneutic circle" whose justifiability can only be elaborated as an epistemological reflection upon the relation of systematic interpretation and the cultural communality it presupposes. Dilthey considers the dialogic of interpretation to be the unique dialectic of grasping individuated meaning through a synthesis of three types of expression (verbal, emotive, and action) which nevertheless must utilize universal categories of language and cultural norms to achieve a *verstehen*. These acts of understanding are grounded in the objective structures of a socio-cultural world and cannot be logically reconstructed on a model of instrumental action or completely formalized in a context-free language. Understanding, and its reflexive self-understanding, constitutes a logically independent type of human action and, in that sense, it is a necessary and basic orientation of all societal reproduction and development.

However, the practical cognitive interest doesn't in itself make reality by extending our range of instrumental action; rather, it permits the grasping or "restoration" of reality through understanding under different historical conditions. It is a moment in a dialectic of material synthesis, and not an independent existential process, as able to constitute reality as is human work. Yet, without the symbolic mediation of work processes, the objective possibilities for human realization would not be realized and the instrumental activity of man would be perpetuated as a set of pseudo-necessities. Recovery of the practical moment of material synthesis is extremely significant in a global context in which the technocratic trends of both "socialism" and "capitalism" deny its basic importance.

All the symbolically mediated orientations guided by practical interest involve interaction patterns that secure a reliable basis for intersubjective communication and cooperation. Such systems are called *symbolic interaction systems* and refer to all human activity guided by social norms (reciprocal behavioral expectations that are shared by at least two persons). These norms cannot be reduced to technical rules; they are not true or false or testable by technical success, but are enforced by sanctions that depend upon mutual expectations and common recognition of obligations. Their meaning can be understood via ordinary language communication; their irreducibility to technical rules constitutes the logical criterion that distinguishes systems of symbolic interaction and of purposive rational action.

Habermas's theory of cognitive interests has given to the Marxist framework a twofold epistemological model which refers to the two moments of material synthesis. In this way, the history of mankind can be conceptualized as the ongoing mutual influence of two kinds of action systems: purposive rational action that secures man's capacity to satisfy his needs, and symbolic interaction systems which form the institutional framework of society based upon grammatical rules and social norms that enable man to engage in communication and interaction.

There is an analogy, then, between the way Peirce and Dilthey refer the validity of statements to the methodological presuppositions of science, and the way processes of learning and mutual understanding embodied in societal, instrumental, and symbolic interaction systems are referred to the reproduction dialectic of social evolution. Just as the meaning of a statement cannot be explicated solely by reference to methodological rules (as positivism implies), so the reproduction of society cannot be explicated within a biological or social systems theory framework. Humanity's self-formative processes are always mediated by the historical matrix of technical-cultural knowledge and cannot be reduced to naturalistic "needs," "drives," "functions," and so forth. The cognitive interests of the human species are neither natural determinants, nor pure transcendental principles; they refer to the logic of self-formative processes that are always linked to historical adaptive capacities and the cultural potential for self-positing comprehension.

Neither Peirce nor Dilthey recognized the concept of knowledge-constitutive interests, since they were rooted in the positivistic problematic, despite their respective analyses which referred methodological procedures back to their epistemological presuppositions. Neither recognized that the transcendental frameworks of instrumental action and communicative interaction underlie the methodological processes of the natural and cultural sciences, and were constitutive interests of the human species. They did not construe their analysis this way, since they were not reflecting upon the history of the species as a self-formative process.

It is only from the perspective of critique, therefore, that the self-reflection of knowledge becomes aware of its own interests and is able to recognize the objective context of its self-constitution. The rootedness of the constitution of knowledge in the objective structures of work and language entails a transcendental dimension, but comprehension of the subsistence of transcendental interests within man's history requires a recognition of the dimensions of *power* which constrains the actualization of cognitive interests. Only a critical theory can express the normative character of these cognitive interests and therefore can guide inquiry into historical power constraints that block emancipation. The notion of technical and practical cognitive interests can be recognized only when they are comprehended as moments of the dialectic of social evolution, and as such are seen as moments of the emancipatory struggle of the human species. Practical and technical interests can be comprehended only as moments in the emancipatory interest in reason. Habermas is very clear, however, that this interest cannot be taken in the idealistic sense:

... But if we comprehend the cognitive capacity and critical power of reason as deriving from the self-constitution of the human species under contingent natural conditions, then *it is reason that inheres in interest*.[13]

Materialistically conceived, the interest in reason is not apparent to itself and cannot provide its own foundation. Yet, we recognize within the "causality of fate" a compulsion to overcome suffering and thus to become emancipated.

In this way Hegel analyzed the dialogic of a moral community that constitutes its own causality by exerting moral "force" upon those who distort the moral relations of the community. The "causality of fate" is constituted in the dialogic relations of agents interacting within intersubjective norms that are accepted as legitimate. Suppression of these relations, whether through a single criminal act or, more generally, through class domination that restricts the freedom of another class, sets up a contradiction which exerts a compulsion to overcome this repression. The "causality of fate" can also be extended to the repressive class antagonisms that generate struggles culminating in revolution (although Marx did not conceive it this way). In this notion of dialectical synthesis, the reaction to repression is linked not to the processes of social labor, but to the "struggle for recognition" that reappears under the distortion of moral (communicative) relations. The dialectic of moral life (or communicative interaction) is therefore an irreducible mechanism for the constitution of humanity, though it is always interlocked with synthesis through labor.

Habermas interprets Freud's psychoanalytic theory as a science which, in its departure from positivistic foundations, discovers that self-reflection upon pathological compulsion involves an interest in its abolition. Reconstruction of Freud's work tries to exemplify a science which can proceed critically; Habermas's current attempts to construct a communication theory of society is another such attempt. He selects psychoanalysis as the only science which incorporates self-reflection in its method—precisely the dimension that positivism closes off. The interpretation reconstructs not only the remembered life history but in addition, it is guided by a theory and by an attempt to get behind the manifest memory and comprehend the distortions and self-deceptions of the subject. Internal disturbances, neurotic symptoms, distortions of everyday language games become incomprehensible symbols to the acting subject, since he has excluded the undesired motives from his awareness. The analyst's aid in reconstructing the subject's life history brings to consciousness the person's own self-formation process and results in the recollection and restoration of blocked parts of that life. The patient's self-reflection promotes a compensatory learning process that reunifies a self that has been in internal conflict. Suffering and desperation generate an interest in the critique of false consciousness which must be maintained if self-reflection is to be carried to the point of "working through" and eliminating dogmatic attitudes. This requires that the ego recognize and identify with itself in its alienated state and thereby return to itself in self-reflection. The reflexive comprehension of identifications, alienations, coerced actions, and past reflections are internal to the self-constitution of the subject who can theoretically release himself from the causality of "unconscious" motives.

Psychoanalysis is a prototype for emancipatory reflection in that its theoretical framework anticipates disturbed self-formation processes that are analogous to constraints upon the self-formation processes of the human species. Whereas the technical and practical "cognitive interests" are exemplified in the instrumental and communicative presuppositions of the methodologies of the natural and cultural sciences, the emancipatory "cognitive interest" can be illustrated by the connection between the language deformation and behavioral pathology that is presupposed by psychoanalysis. Habermas argues that due to his tendency toward an objectivistic grounding of his theory as a natural science of man, Freud did not develop an adequate methodological reflection upon the possibility of self-reflective knowledge. In this sense, Freud's theoretical constructions were more narrowly conceived than his description of the psychoanalytic technique.[14]

Reconstructed as a critical science, psychoanalysis grasps the causality of the deformation of language and of behavior with "split-off" (suppressed) symbols and repressed motives. In this sense, the "explanation" of behavioral deformations moves within the sphere of mind over mind, or within what Hegel calls the "causality of fate," and under special conditions it can lead to the dissolution of this causality. Because the explained empirical structures are at the same time intentional structures, their reconstruction and self-reflective internalization can result in the dissolution of this compulsively enacted causality.

Habermas asserts that Freud was ambivalent about the scientific status of his theory, describing it as if it were naturalistically rooted and yet insisting on the dimension of self-reflective enlightenment within the analytic situation. Habermas claims that if the communication preconditions of psychoanalysis were adequately developed in a metatheory it could only be conceived as a *general interpretation* of self-formative processes. However, this metapsychological interpretation differs from a naturalistic theory because it is generated within the field of psychoanalytic communication.[15] But when treated as a general interpretive scheme which anticipates common disturbed self-formation processes (e.g., the Oedipal conflict), it is clear that theory formation is itself inseparable from the analytic dialogue.

In these considerations Habermas attempts to elucidate the logic of an explanatory understanding. In contrast to the empirical analytic procedures of the natural sciences and the hermeneutic procedures of the cultural sciences, the methodological procedures of critical scientific inquiry can be reconstructed only within a logic of explanatory-understanding. While subject to falsification, the standards for verification and relationship of explanation to historical contexts differ (e.g., they are narrative explanations).[16]

Generalized as a metapsychological scheme of interpretation, Freud's theory permits a conceptualization of the origins of institutions and the function of power and ideology that Habermas claims is superior to Marx's parallel theory. Whereas Marx concentrates on the system of social labor and the organization that derives from it, Freud focuses on the motives of communication within the conflict between surplus impulses and the conditions of collective self-preservation. From this perspective the origin and function of historic institutions resemble individual acts of repression of the capacity to interpret needs. Institutions exercise power in the form of enforced substitute-gratifications whose character becomes fixed, opaque, and without the reciprocity of manifest compulsions. Institutional norms are suppressed symbols which have been removed from criticism to become legitimations of authority. *In this way, the institutions of a class society constitute the system of power which is imposed on all members of society and, as such, form a field of systematically distorted communication in which instinctual impulses are censored and directed toward "legitimate" ends.* Thus, the dynamics of power and ideology are more central to Freud's critical theory than to Marx's. For Freud, the movement of critical-revolutionary activity is directed against power and ideology, and although it also depends on the extension of objective possibilities by the productive forces, there is no certainty that emancipation will follow automatically from greater technical progress.

At every step, man is engaged in a struggle against the power constraints originating in scarcity, on the one hand, and institutional prohibitions and ideological legitimation of authority, on the other. For Freud, the critical comprehension of this dialectic leads not to a fixed theory of revolution, but to a "logic of justified hope and controlled experiment." The telos of this systematic critical struggle is:

. . . an organization of social relations according to the principle that the validity of every norm of political consequence be made dependent on a consensus arrived at in communication free of domination.[17]

Reason's emancipatory goal inherent in the interest structures of human history cannot be realized under all conditions; it is not a naturalistic imperative, but a constitutive "illusion" of humanity. The "illusion" of emancipation has been analyzed, however, to demonstrate that it is not a delusion but the objective and transcendental precondition of the conflicts by which humanity has been producing, struggling, and comprehending itself. The interest in reason can develop only through critique and the tentative, experimental realization of its interpreted consequences.

A Contemporary Interpretation of
the Meaning of "Critique"

Habermas has created a new synthesis that restores the meaning of critique through reconstruction of the dominant modes of contemporary consciousness. He understands contemporary philosophical and scientific thought in relation to their relevance for the critique of ideology (the reinterpretation of psychoanalysis as a critical hermeneutics or the extension of Wittgenstein's analysis of language games into a theory of universal pragmatics forming the framework for a new theory of ideology). In this sense Habermas has transcended contemporary consciousness in a way that is analogous to Marx's critical "sublation" (*Aufhebung*) of German idealism, French socialism, and British political economy. The result is a new synthesis of the critical Hegelian-Marxist tradition with the developments of contemporary consciousness.

This synthesis yields a reconceptualization of dialectical social theory which permits a critical analysis of the evolution and construction of world views; it rests upon the transcendentally-conceived theory of cognitive interests, but it is developed as a communication theory of society. Before discussing it we will show, by a review of the preceding, that Habermas's theory of cognitive interests involves a special way of conceptualizing the relationship of subject and object, theory and action. His formulations depend, specifically, upon the contemporary developments of a theory of language and communication that result in a new way of relating subject and object.

Habermas's work is radically sociological in its conception of the "subject's" constitution by the societal systems of instrumental action and the universal pragmatics of ordinary language usage. In this framework, "intersubjectivity" is not something that can be inferred from a generalized individual consciousness (Kant) or from the phenomenological observer who practices the *Epoche* (Husserl). Both Kant and Husserl *infer* the possibility of intersubjectivity from their respective reflections upon the monadic consciousness. In this sense constitutive activity is restricted to a self-referring, monologic framework. The problem remains how to account for the processes of work and communication that are constituted transindividually. The "subject" and "object" of the work and communication processes of society cannot be analyzed on the assumption that somehow the monadically-constituted worlds come together by a process of "preestablished harmony." The constitution of reality and the interpretation of social reality must be grounded in a reflective theory of intersubjectivity that can account for the "communality" of social reality.

Thus Habermas's interpretation of the dialogics of instrumental action and symbolic interaction is itself guided by a theory of the self-reflexivity of language, implying that it is the only symbolic medium that can be its own metalanguage.[18] Habermas refers to Wittgenstein's game in which symbols and action can interpret each other reciprocally, indicating that within communication the formal structures of the language are mediated by contextual, norm-guided actions and expressions. In a similar way, the distinction between an instrumental logic of discovery and the hermeneutic circle of interpretation is elaborated by Habermas in terms of the relations of language, action, and experience within their logic-in-use.[19]

In all these ways Habermas is reconstructing the link between subject and object, theory and practice as a dialogic relation between the generative rules of work and symbolic interaction as they are embodied in the activity of individuated participants. The linkage is conceptualized as the relations between the intersubjective grammar and pragmatics of ordinary language usage.

Habermas's recent writing begins with an interpretation of Wittgenstein's later work. The importance of linguistic philosophy for the categorical foundations of a critical theory lies in its capacity to express the idealizations (or counterfactual presuppositions) of symbolic action and rational discourse. Thus, the notion of an ideal speech situation, or nonrepressive communication, is the necessary condition for the simultaneous maintenance of communication and metacommunication.[20]

The Necessity for a Linguistic Theory of Communication[21]

Husserl's phenomenological theory of consciousness has, according to Habermas, an advantage over the Kantian mode of transcendental reflection. Husserl sees the life world (the *Lebenswelt*) as the primordial basis for the constitution of all knowledge of nature. He proceeds to show that Kant's transcendental reflections on the composition of our knowledge of nature itself presupposes a constitution theory of the life world. From the outset Husserl's reflections recognize the active construction of the world by subjects who are capable of synthetic activities. Instead of Kant's reflection upon the anonymous consciousness in general, Husserl recognizes the generative process of a life world in which a multitude of synthesizing subjects constitute an intersubjective social world.

Habermas finds two problems, however, that the Husserlian phenomenology cannot resolve, and that are necessary for the creation of a dialectical theory; the immanent relationship of society and truth, and the problem of intersubjectivity. The inadequacy of phenomenology to cope with these problems, he argues, necessitates the incorporation of a theory of linguistic communication into a contemporary dialectical social theory.

In relation to the first problem, Husserl's most important contribution was his elucidation of the structures of consciousness in the theory of intentionality. Consciousness is always consciousness of something, the possibility of which is given in our intentional consciousness. In his analysis of intentionality, Husserl claims that truth is simply the identifying thought-act that accompanies an experience of evidence. In this concept there is a phenomenological statement about the self-positing nature of consciousness which anticipates the factual givenness of its intentional object (the *noema*). Intentional consciousness is thus always pretending toward the fulfillment of its thought-acts and, in so doing, claims the validity of the to-be-completed object. Husserl suggests that this self-positing extends to the whole life world in which all claims come together. This is what Alfred Schutz called "the epoch of the natural attitude"; it is essentially the basic naive realism of the everyday world. In the *Lebenswelt* acts of willing and emotion are also intentional self-positings and are the products of transcendental subjectivity.

The basic problem of Husserl's truth-as-evidence theory is that it depends upon the concept of "categorical intuition," a vague and logically indefensible notion, according to Habermas, and one which Husserl himself rejects in some works (i.e., *Erfahrung und Urteil*). Husserl's reference of truth to the intuitive self-givenness of intentional experience is questionable. Habermas argues that this linkage is possible only in terms of a theory of linguistics. In this way, the categorical "objects" of intentional experience can be conceptualized as intersubjective rules for the construction and use of symbols. The thesis that there is a truth claim inherent in all meaningfully constituted acts can then be developed as a theory of language which conceives of the life world as a system of symbolic forms whose validity we can reason about discursively. Truth as evidence could be confirmed not by reference to intuitive intentions but by discourse within society about truth claims. Whereas Husserl considered the unfounded claims of the "natural attitude" to be a basic fact of the *Lebenswelt,* a critical theory of society would seek to comprehend the saturation of the everyday world with claims of unquestioned validity. A more adequate theory, therefore, of the relation of truth to the constitution of social reality would be concerned with the emergence and "sedimentation" of false consciousness.[22]

In reference to the second problem of his phenomenology, Husserl tries to infer intersubjectivity from the activity of the monadic consciousness. This results, Habermas argues, in a circular question-begging argument that can establish only that there is a "community for me" and "for others"; how they coincide is unclear.

Habermas claims that the problem of intersubjective meaning is much simpler for those theories of society that begin with shared rules for language games (Wittgenstein), or with roles that establish shared expectations (G. H. Mead). The concepts of "rule" and "role" can be defined from the outset in terms of the relation between subjects and can, therefore, express more adequately how symbolic expressions are constituted.

A Communication Theory of Society as a Contemporary Framework for Critical Theory

Habermas asserts that Wittgenstein's later preoccupation with the game model of natural language leads him to an insight into the communicative use of language which can be developed into a theory of universal pragmatics. Wittgenstein was interested in the status of rules in "language games" in which it seems that the use of words or sentences, rather than the words themselves, establish meaning; speaking and acting subjects are unified by a network of intersubjective rules presupposed in the generation of verbal, emotive, and action expressions. The "grammar" of a language game is rooted in the set of contextually specific generative rules assumed by all modes of communicative expression. In this way language competence goes beyond the scope of the cognitive and involves a capacity to perform.

Wittgenstein's concern, however, conceals the extent to which participation in a game is itself a self-positing of speakers and actors. Nor does Wittgenstein's analysis recognize the degree to which the constitutive games of language are rooted in the constraints of the societal context. Although Wittgenstein's language theory goes beyond the analysis of language, it recognizes neither its social-cultural significance nor the societal disruption of language communication.

Habermas builds upon Wittgenstein's game theory of language by comprehending it from a transcendental perspective, viewing the speech act as constituted from an intersubjective framework in which there is always a double level of communication. Communicative competence refers then to the capacity of the speaker to maintain communication on both the level of objects or circumstances and on the level of the individuated relation to objects. Wittgenstein's analysis shows that communicative competence presupposes the simultaneous maintenance of communication and metacommunication (or the individuated expression enabling the receiver to comprehend how the message is to be interpreted). From this point of view we are able to recognize that normal communication involves a self-reflexivity which makes human symbolic communication its own metalanguage. That is, the manifest message of every symbolic performance is accompanied by a metacommunication that expresses the individuatedness of that communication. Whereas the reflexivity of the "dialectic of communication" was developed by Fichte and Hegel, only in Habermas's critique of Wittgenstein's language games is it unfolded as the categorical basis for the systematic study of communication.

Habermas's development of the categorical foundations of a communication theory of society is difficult to grasp unless one understands that he is claiming this theory to be more like a linguistic science than a social theory based upon naturalistic science. The concepts Habermas is trying to form—communicative competence, the ideal speech situation—attempt to develop the fundamental presuppositions of speech and interaction processes in daily life. Habermas shows that reflection about communicative competence reveals the fundamental "idealizations" (counterfactual assumptions) of all human communication: the ideal speech situation.

We name a speaking-situation ideal where the communication is not only not hindered by external, contingent influences, but also not hindered by forces which result from the structure of communication itself. Only then does the peculiarly unforced compulsion of a better argument dominate.[23]

It is important to realize, however, that the ideal speech situation is a unique utopian concept. It is conceived as the basic idealization inherent in all human communication and therefore has no historical content. Habermas remains so much within the limits of rational reflection in his anticipation of emancipation that the application of the formal ideal of utopia requires systematic inquiry and political judgment in every historical situation. There can be no general theory of emancipation!

II: *A Reflexive Philosophy of Critical Theory*

The intent of this formalistic ideal parallels Marx's attempt to restore actual historical relations in the political economic analysis of capitalist production. Just as the use-value, exchange-value distinction enabled Marx to counterpose appearance and actuality, so Habermas's distinction of purposive rational action systems and symbolic interaction systems allow him to distinguish historical actualities that are concealed by the scientistic consciousness of our time. These distinctions, and the ideal speech situation, are based upon linguistic rules and idealizations that Habermas reconstructs as the basis of our everyday activity. The relationship of linguistic concepts and social reality is not as immediately apparent as more naturalistic concepts—they do not describe objectivistically, but express the generative rules and idealizations of social reality. The relevance of this type of theory construction lies in its capacity to express the normative character of social reality.

Habermas shows that the communicative use of language cannot in itself secure the validity of its truth claims. Again, the significance of the scientific community, as that unique institution investigating truth in modern society, is demonstrated. The inquiry into truth claims requires rational discourse that can distinguish between legitimate and illegitimate claims. In the cognitive conduct of discourse, there is consequently an "ideal speech situation" in which all claims to validity come together as a fundamental claim of reasonability.

Yet it is precisely this fundamental idealization which is contradicted by both the usual conduct of discourse (due to contextual and "internal" constraints) and in the everyday communicative use of language. Claims for validity cannot be resolved by transcendental intuition, as Husserl implied, but only by discourse that is freed from systematic distortion. Thus, the pre-tending of all human symbolic intention establishes an immanent claim to truth that cannot be represented by a correspondence theory of truth.

It is just this anticipated situation of ideal speech which can be used as a normative standard for the critique of distorted communication. The fundamental idealization made in every act of human speech assumes an ideal of reason which does not exist empirically but which every human assertion anticipates in practice.

4: *The Dialectical Foundations of Critical Theory*

In every communicative situation in which a consensus is established under coercion or under distorted conditions, we are confronting instances of illusory discourse. This is the contemporary form of the critique of ideology.

"Ideology" is, then, the compulsory suspension of doubt about its claim to validity. Ideologies are those belief systems which can maintain their legitimacy despite the fact that they could not be validated if subjected to rational discourse. The structures of the everyday world are saturated with counterfactual assumptions which could not sustain rational discussions. The question is not, as Berger and Luckmann suppose, what function these stabilized "reifications" serve (since that is essentially an objectivistic apology for ideological control) but rather what types of compulsions maintain these false claims. Thus, ideologies remove whole aggregates of social norms from public questioning and discourse. Constraints impairing the recognition of ideological beliefs that only appear legitimate are rooted in power norms that usually promise certain gratifications (e.g., equivalence for wage labor in the market place) for the nonquestioning acceptance of the legitimacy of other norms (e.g., the capitalist mode of production as the most rational form for industrial society).

Whereas most ideological masking of domination takes the form of historical narratives which legitimate the existing order (e.g., the utopian components of the bourgeois ideology which justify the destruction of feudal controls), Habermas claims this is no longer true. The ideological structures of contemporary industrial society no longer justify the present in terms of a critique of the ideology of a previous epoch (and thus refer to utopian anticipations) but refer increasingly to the "neutral" authority of science. Despite this transformation of the content of ideology, its dynamics remain tied to the structures of communication. In this way, power relations enter into the symbolic rules and roles which are part of the structure of everyday life. Insofar as need dispositions can be interpreted only in terms of the existing values which actually justify unequal access to opportunities, we have entered into an institutionalization of power relations.

A suppressed dimension of Marx's work can be illuminated

from this perspective. The appropriation of surplus requires that those who restrict the freedom of others render it "just" in the language of exchange relations. Hence, the fetishism of commodities is a deformation of symbolic communications; neither the wage laborer nor the capitalist can communicate about the material conditions of society. However, despite the claims of just exchange, the actual meaning of human production becomes a repressed ideal which weighs like a fateful causality on the mind of the active man.

Like the specter whose reappearance to Macbeth changes the meaning of kingship, the meaning of human activity is impossible to suppress. Man's ability to express reflexively the difference between being and pretense, essence and appearance, "to be" and "ought to be," contains a self-reflexive potential for the statement of contradictions. Language is the medium that allows man to combine his intellectual capacities and to organize his interactionist systems. It is only by using intersubjective symbols that man is able to cope with an elaborate status system and yet retain a personal identity, to create adequate self-representations in novel situations, and to maintain a flexible interpretation of internalized norms. In the unique causality of an open system of linguistic communication there is a potential reflection process which can emancipate man from cultural reifications.

Has Habermas Transcended Marx's Critical Theory?

Habermas's present work formulates the metatheoretical principles that guide the formation of a dialectical social theory and can critically comprehend the dialectic of social evolution. These metatheoretical reflections are also a critique of an objectivistically-conceived social theory and point toward the construction of a communication theory of society. But the working out of the substantive theory itself is still proceeding. It begins with Habermas's interpretation of the relation of his work to Marx's critique.

Habermas's reconception of Marx implies that increasing restrictions on communicative interactions have sustained the material constraints placed on the development of the forces of production by capitalism. This is manifest in the progressive adjustment of all institutions to the innovating private economic sector. Capitalistic power and privilege is thus maintained on the one hand by the degree to which the truth of capitalist ideology is beyond doubt, and on the other the extent to which socialization processes are reified in a technological milieu. Habermas further points out the extent to which scientism has provided a model of institutionalized rationality which facilitates acceptance of the existing structure as legitimate.

Despite these advances, Habermas has not demonstrated their relation to Marx's critique of political economy. Is the communication theory, which achieves a normative foundation in the rational idealizations of human communication (thereby grounding a cultural Marxist critique in a manner different from other members of the Frankfurt School), presented by Habermas as the new conceptual basis for critical theory? An affirmative answer would imply that Marx's value theory has been superseded and that the economic criticisms of it are viable.[24] Although Habermas claims that the quantitative formulations of Marx's work cannot express the surplus created by the unique potentials of a scientistic production system, he does not really refute Marx. A demonstration of this point is developed in the following chapter, in which an attempt is made to reconstruct Marx's theory of the inbuilt *limits* of capitalist reproduction.[25]

Insofar as Habermas has replaced one normative foundation with another he has completed a moment of critical theory which has never been developed.[26] Both Marx and Habermas have formulated normative foundations for one moment of the dialectic of social evolution. We are confronted therefore not by a sublation but by Habermas's dialectical completion of the basis for a critical theory of society. It is not either Marx or Habermas but Marx *and* Habermas that make possible a critical dialectical theory.

Another area in which Habermas could be said to transcend Marx is in his conception of the relation of science to social liberation. Habermas, and other cultural Marxists, have shown how the reproduction dynamic of late industrial society in general (i.e. both advanced capitalist and "socialist" societies) necessitates the scientific-technical strata that generates the new rationales and techniques which both stimulate economic growth and make further ideological control possible. These groups, while not constituting a necessary and sufficient "class" for the activation of change, are increasingly in a pivotal strategic position within the dynamic of late industrial society. Embedded in the social norms that bind the scientific community to its projects, and in their basic *telos* of the discovery of truth, there is a revolutionary potential for the recognition of domination. The need for rational discourse about the objectivistic and scientistic dogma of established science is legitimated by the norms of open scientific communication. The turning around of a small part of the scientific community to recognize the ideology of amorality and the pseudo-neutrality of state use of science would release new types of research and could create new alignments between science and society.

The consequences of the scientific community's consciousness of domination cannot be anticipated, but a possible result is the creation of models of liberated social development that would enable other institutions and/or groups to emancipate themselves from unnecessary domination.[27] Habermas's work reveals that liberation from the contraints of block utilization of productive forces for social needs is not enough. Emancipatory struggle must be broader than Marx imagined and it must increasingly involve the self-liberation of persons from the "ego-identities" that are emerging from a scientized civilization. Social emancipation requires self-emancipation from the social costs of late industrial society, not only in the overproduction and underutilization of societal potentials, but also the transformation of life styles into so many types of adjustment to rationales which foreclose communicative interaction. Habermas's reconceptualization of the relation of critique to communicative practice adds to the interpretive scope of critical theory and to the realization of a theory of emancipation.

In the end, however, there is something very muted about Habermas's utopian ideal that suggests why Marx remains essential. The ideal speech situation is a purely formalistic concept.

Whereas Marx conceived of the use-value concept (an essential component of the utopian ideal of communism) as a historical actuality, Habermas's formalistically derived ideal has no components that express historical relations. There is no part of this utopian ideal which can express the mode of realization that Marx's ideal of use-value did in its ideal of an "organic" relation between production, distribution, and the mediation between universal and individual needs. Habermas's ideal depends upon the community of scientists to measure and assess the historical specifics of distorted communication and this seems to imply that no other function need be performed by critical theorists. No doubt Habermas would use this difference in defense of his ideal by pointing to the objectivism of such notions as use-value and he would then be able to show the totally non-objectivistic nature of the ideal speech situation. There is a sense in which the utopian moment of critical theory requires a recognition of the emancipatory potentials of reconstructed histories. This doesn't entail the working out of detailed plans of strategic action but only the identification of the potentialities inherent in a given historical configuration and those aggregates of people who seem to be most directly associated with these objective possibilities. To put this another way, Habermas's concept of the dialectic between domination and emancipation stops short of an adequate realization of its utopian moment. While trying to maintain critique strictly within the limits of reason, Habermas also fails to include the needs of people who are able to see the possibility of enlightenment only in everyday activity.

Habermas's theory of enlightenment is therefore too Hegelian. Like Hegel, he makes the assumption that the logic of historical development is moving toward greater actualization of freedom, or non-repressive communication. Human consciousness is extended as the scope of world history widens; like Hegel the development of human enlightenment moves ever forward. Perhaps Habermas's passion for reason is here, like Hegel's, the result of a life of reason that sees all existence as the manifestation of a comprehensive system.

Until we have completed a reconstruction of the social evolution of mankind along the lines suggested by Habermas's theory of cognitive interests, we are still dependent upon the most comprehensive theory of the historical tendencies that we have—that of Karl Marx. Perhaps this will remain so. But it does not stop us from reconstructing the objectivistic aspects of Marx's work along the lines established by Habermas's metatheory.

III: *TOWARD A REUNIFICATION OF CRITICAL THEORY*

The most general theoretical framework for critical theory can be called "the crisis theory." It is expressed as a critique of the basic categories of the culture of an epoch but it refers to the internal constraints of the societal tendencies of that epoch. In this sense Marx regarded Capital *as a critique of the categories of political economy and of the capitalist economy as a whole. He constructed a theory of capitalist development in which he shows structural tendencies ("laws of motion") recurrently intensifying the inbuilt barriers that lead to economic stagnation, overproduction, and increased alienation. In the twentieth century, the cultural Marxists have developed a crisis theory which reconstructs the societal process of "rationalization" as a force for the systematic reification of social-cultural processes and the undermining of the individual's autonomy.*

Whereas these two crisis theories were developed for different stages of capitalism and in this sense express different levels of its mushrooming domination, the relation between them is often overlooked. While actually two moments of a more general crisis theory, they also contradict each other in important areas and require a unified reformulation. At this point we will ignore the contradictions and stress the unity. Marx showed that development of the forces of production are increasingly constrained by capitalist social relations; the cultural Marxists maintain that the society rationalizing for an extension of economic growth forces social-cultural processes to adapt to this dynamic. Marx demonstrated that capitalism blocks the optimal utilization of technological potential for liberation from unnecessary toil; the cultural Marxists show that these power relations are further institutionalized in a scientific civilization and, mystified by a technocratic strategy that blocks the extension of public discussion about social needs and personal liberation. Only the unification of these two theories can serve adequately both as an explanatory hypothesis and an interpretive principle for the analysis of domination. But their combination also (potentially) restores the political aspects of critical theory by relating it to the higher level of capitalist development.

Until this unified framework can stimulate empirical analysis of contemporary domination, the idea of a critical theory will remain an abstract utopian ideal for estranged intellectuals. It cannot, as Marcuse assumes, remain a platform for the grand gesture of "the great refusal," but must become a serious effort within the scientific community itself. Because science and technology are now a major mode of ideological mystification of power relations, critical theory must extend to the community of men who are its living embodiment. It must restore to scientists the actual relation between science and society and expose the deepening contradictions of the scientistic ideology and the objective containment of science for the purpose of extending exploitation and domination throughout the world. Development of critical theory within the scientific community can contribute to the creation of alternative programs for research and development. In this way, knowledge can be generated that relates to the needs of peoples who are trying to build social community, resist cultural manipulation, facilitate decentralization movements, and in general contribute to the actualization of human needs that are otherwise ignored. By reorienting the scientific community, or at least a significant sector of it, critical theory can become a material force for change by counteracting the current drift of science toward the formation and implementation of state policy.

The following exegesis of the crisis theories of Marx and the cultural Marxists constitutes the bones of a more systematically unified framework. In the former an effort is made to explicate both the suppressed methodological assumptions and the sociological dimension of Marx's crisis theory; it also attempts to express the more dialectical aspects. In the discussion of cultural Marxism the work of Herbert Marcuse is stressed both because of its sug-

gestiveness and its methodological problems, which demonstrate why a more contemporary framework is needed.

The final chapter is a first approximation of the application of a unified critical theory to the dynamics of American capitalism. That chapter is the beginning of a more concrete application of critical theory, submitted to the reader as an example of a broader and more scientifically relevant form of critique.

5

Marx's Crisis Theory: The Contradictions of Capital Accumulation

*M*arx's work is unique in the nineteenth century because of its conceptualization of the inherently contradictory character of capitalism. It is a revolutionizing force in world history through its release of the economic forces from traditional political or social controls, and it also produces a separation of societal processes (e.g., distribution and production) that result in violent contradiction for the reproduction of society:

Crisis is nothing but the forcible assertion of the unity of phases of the production process which have become independent from each other. . . .

Crisis is the forcible establishment of unity between elements that have become independent and the enforced separation from one another of the elements which are essentially one.[1]

Where other political economists analyzed the phenomena of economic crises as the accidental result of the "formal possibilities" for economic crisis, Marx insisted that crisis is the "manifestation of all the contradictions of bourgeois economy." The very social relations that make the revolutionary innovations of commodity production possible also make possible and necessary the recurrence of the overproduction of capital and therefore the overproduction of commodities that cannot be sold. In precapitalist societies economic crisis emerged only by the underproduction of use-values which resulted from natural calamities such as floods, famines, war, plagues, etc. Capitalistic economic crisis is unique in that it is characterized by the overproduction of exchange-values which cannot be bought or sold. Only under the economic conditions of universal commodity production can the capacity to sell and the power to buy be so completely separated that normal reproduction of the economy can be blocked economically.

In his analysis, Marx demonstrates that under capitalist social relations the material production process, producing use-values, is constrained by the need to produce exchange-values. Therefore, added to the natural constraints upon productive activity, such as the scarcity of resources and the level of the social productivity of labor, is the additional imperative (which also becomes a block) of using and expanding the productive apparatus for the single goal of creating more exchange-values. The productive capacities of society are separated from the man whose labor activates them; material production is transformed into value production, and the capitalist and the wage laborer stand opposed by their position within the production process. The contradiction between means and relations of production, between material production and a production which proceeds under value imperatives, correlates with the class division of labor and the recurrent "formal possibility" for a crisis of overproduction.

Marx generated a critique of the categories of classical political economy and developed his crisis theory by keeping the *totality* of material production and the specific relations of value production together. He refused to analyze the economics of production independently from the institutional framework in which exchange and distribution proceeds.[2] For Marx, production begins the process from which distribution, exchange, and consumption are inseparable. On the one hand, the social relations that establish the division between wage labor and capital also separate the processes of distribution from production; and yet, on the other hand, they are unified because a definite historical level of production determines the forms and relations of all components. In this way, Marx's criticism of political economy proceeded to reconstruct the fundamental societal components (and economic categories) and their dynamic relations as an analytic framework for the systematic analysis of capitalism. By reuniting within a critique of the social totality the processes that classical political economists had separated, and by comprehending the economic categories as referring to the historically emergent social forms of value, commodity, money, etc., he created a new type of theory. The impossibility of treating Marx as just another political economist can be illustrated by pointing to the difference between the economic categories—which always must be related to the genesis of economic social forms—and the logical categories which make the critical comprehension of economic categories possible, e.g., quantity, quality, essence, appearance. While rejecting Hegel's form of "spiritual" phenomenology, Marx has effectively reconstructed a genetic-historical phenomenology of the basic forms that make capitalist production possible. However, at the end of this "phenomenology of capital" is a return to the immediacy of "capitalist production as a whole" (Vol. 3), in which the "natural" appearance (*Schein*) of the forms of value—commodity and money—is penetrated and the essential relation between material production and historical man restored. The result is a critical theory whose synthetic scope has often eluded critics and disciples alike. The interpretation of Marx that conceives of the "laws of motion" as "predictions" is incorrect; but this view is held by most contemporary Western social scientists as well as by many mechanical Marxists. Ironically, the social scientists who assume that Marx's analysis isolates the economic as the determinant of the social are the same theorists who separate analytically social organization from the economy.[3]

Even if Marx's crisis theory is reconstructed as I will attempt to do here in the most sympathetic manner, its incompleteness becomes clear. Marx was unable to finish the critique that his 1857–8 project promised and it is precisely the omissions that have become more relevant to the dynamic of late capitalism. So to the framework developed by Marx must be added another dimension that reconceptualizes the relations of the political and economic processes for late capitalism.

It is necessary to add that no uncritical revival of Marx is suggested here. Marx's method of "critique," as well as the general formulation of the contradiction of the capitalist epoch, remain relevant for today's critical analysis. But Marx postulated a theory of revolutionary consciousness from his critique too rapidly. He based it upon the two-sidedness of the social developments under capitalism and upon the misleading analogy of the enforced "emancipation" of the serfs and the proletariat. In *Capital* he argues that the growing cooperativeness of the proletariat would itself force a greater consciousness of the necessity for public (socialist) control of production. This connection between the critique of the capitalist epoch and the theory of revolutionary consciousness is too mechanical and contradicts the most central ideas of Marx's own theory.[4] His attempt to ground the hope for revolution in an objectivistic critique is now a past revolutionary dream that all too easily returns to distort contemporary political possibilities. A new politics remains to be conceived and realized.

The Epoch of Capitalism

The main corpus of Marx's work—especially *Capital*—makes one central point: capitalism is a transitional phase of human history, it is not the final social form. Marx's work pivots on his theory of the inevitable recurrent crisis of capitalism that makes it an antithetical societal form for further "rational" development. Capitalism established a new set of social relations of production that irreversibly destroyed the feudal system of its local control, while creating two new classes, each one possessing an essential factor of production: capital-land (bourgeoisie) and labor-power (proletariat). The emergence of capitalist production proceeded with the institutionalization of private property relations by turning all factors of production into commodities subject to market controls. These new relations aimed at overturning absolutist relations of privilege but they also broke the "organic" links between human needs and the production process. An economic market rationality increased the quantitative output but it also forced changes in the social organization that transformed the qualitative dimensions of human life, as, for example, in the "emancipation" of the serf who is forced to define his own relation to the productive forces which had been separated from communal control.

Marx's crisis theory was an attempt to reconstruct the constitutive dynamic of capitalist accumulation and the social consequences of this dynamic. Marx viewed the emancipation of the economic system from the restraints of traditional social norms as the revolutionary innovation of the capitalist epoch and the driving force that progressively replaced social relations (traditional normative controls) by relations of production.[5] As the absolutist control of production collapsed before a growing market economy, so too did the institutional protections for everyday life; man was literally reduced to an appendage of a production process.[6] As a "self-regulating market" emerged, all traditional ways of life were disrupted and finally reestablished as so many adjustments to the primacy of the market. Numerous strategies, such as the Speenhamland system, were adopted to alleviate the dislocations wrought by a market economy; but the transformation was irreversible and all attempts to reintroduce paternalism only resulted in more inadequate adjustments to the accelerating dynamic of society. In the end the market dominated and the nineteenth century became an era during which the economic system "determined" social change; economic gain for the first time in history replaced all other life motives.

Marx's theory of capitalist crisis tried to grasp the whole dynamic of the capitalist epoch. Its intention was to show how this dynamic recurrently generates intensified constraints upon societal and human development. The difficulty is perhaps that no other social theory attempts such a broad scope of reference. Not only does Marx try to express the central epochal innovation (market rationality) and its dynamic, or structural tendencies (laws of motion of capitalist development), but he also makes an effort to interpret the consequences of these changes for the quality of everyday life. Rather than assume that man must passively adjust to the "objective necessities" of historical development, Marx attempted to critically comprehend the quantitative nature of this "necessity," to assess its qualitative results and thus contribute to the emancipation of man from the grim determinism of early capitalism.

Skeptics may ask what was so unique about Marx's analysis of capitalism to warrant our return to his work today? How is it relevant for the ongoing analysis of contemporary western society? We can reply that Marx was not misled by the seemingly automatic character of the "self-regulating market." While expressing its epochal significance, Marx claimed that market rationality is not an adequate model for social development and that within the released productive forces there resides a potential for another goal for history: communism. Marx's critical theory is of the greatest significance today since we are again in a period when there is seemingly a self-regulating character to social change; and, again, it is being elevated to an ideology. Where once economic liberalism perceived self-regulation in the laws of the market, today's technocrats perceive it in the "imperatives of technical development." Both ideological viewpoints stress the adaptive function of man to objective dynamics beyond his control. As Marx generated a critique of the earlier ideology, so we now must comprehend the current one. Marx's crisis theory can be reformulated for the critique of the ideology of late capitalism.

Marx anticipated the crisis of late capitalism by showing that when production is guided for private ends (a surplus that accrues to that aggregate of persons who control the means of production), its social costs will grow as the crisis of overproduction returns on ever higher levels of societal development. Where commodity production proceeds by means of factors of production that have become commodities, only quantitative economic criteria are considered relevant for production decisions.

The following chapter will show that in such a society public discussion and reordering of value production priorities recede below the horizon of political possibility. Capitalist production restricts political alternatives by making economic growth appear to be the first priority of all societies. Alternative types of investment policy and the social consequences of capitalist policy are issues no one represents effectively in a capitalistic context. Where it has recently become fashionable for social critics and "planners" to question the rationality of the profit motive, it is precisely the unmodifiability of this motive that is the cynosure of Western capitalistic societies, especially the United States.[7] Where "private enterprise" has been institutionalized and protected from critique by legal and cultural systems, the basic contradiction of capitalist society is not recognized or confronted. Today the significance of capitalist society seems to have been lost in the euphoria of the post-war boom. It is only now reemerging as the ecological costs and societal consequences of the profit motive are rediscovered.[8]

Marx's Crisis Theory: Structural Tendencies of an Irrational Social System

Marx showed how the dynamic of capitalist society ends periodically in crisis which devalues existing capital and blocks the realization of profit; but he never suggested that "a breakdown" would occur.[9] The economic crisis is a means by which capitalist economy restores favorable conditions for further expansion. "Crisis" is built into societal development wherever capital constitutes the generative criteria; but the advent of crisis is merely the mechanism by which the system can be reactivated. One could say that the point of crisis is a feedback which permits readjustment to changed reproduction conditions. The crisis feedback gradually restores favorable conditions for profit realization and capitalist expansion is reactivated. For Marx the recurrence of crisis is an index to the irrationality of capitalism's structural dynamic. Formulation of the crisis theory provides a map of the restrictive conditions internal to and recreated by the reproduction of the capitalist system. A theory of crisis is in this sense a critique of internal constraints that block rational development.

There are, then, two aspects to Marx's theory of capitalist crisis. On the one hand, he shows that economic crisis is a rational mechanism for the reactivation of the economy, and, on the other hand, that it is a manifestation of the basically irrational contradiction of capitalism. The crisis theory is, therefore, a theory of economic (value) rationalization that proceeds in an objective context of social irrationality (i.e., the value imperative superimposed upon material production). The theory assesses the growing potential for human emancipation, as the forces of production are expanded, while demonstrating the historical constraints placed upon human freedom by the confining capitalist relations of production. *Critique* restores the memory of blocked potential and so anticipates the emancipation of man from these constraints.

Having discussed its intent, it is now necessary to outline the scope and "contents" of the crisis theory. We must distinguish between the economic manifestation of crisis (an empirical phenomenon) and the structural tendencies (laws-of-motion) which are conceived analytically. It is these tendencies which shape the constraints of the system thereby reproducing the conditions that drive to historical crises. Whereas the immediate causes of economic crisis are open to empirical analysis, the structural contradictions which tend to reproduce *the conditions* promoting crisis are on a general theoretical level of abstraction and cannot be treated as empirical predictions. All who think Marx's "predictions" are directly falsified by history have not understood his work.[10] This is not to say that the crisis theory cannot be tested, but only to indicate that it is on a theoretical level and must be interpreted before a hypothesis can be formed. Especially since the laws-of-motion are conceived within a generative reconstruction of the social totality, any attempt to interpret them as naturalistic "laws" will result simply in the separation of components that were created in mutually reciprocal (dialectical) relations.

Before discussing these "laws" it is important to stress again that they are not formulated with reference to immediate social-economic reality but as structural tendencies of the totality of the processes of capitalist production. As such, they are interpretations of the analytic scheme outlined in Volume 1 of *Capital*. They are not refuted or "falsified" by the short run empirical performance of the capitalist system(s). Refutation of the "laws" requires reinterpretation or an internal critique of the variables that make up the analytic scheme.[11] Once clearly expressed, however, these laws do anticipate that capitalism has to slow down; it cannot continue to expand. If indeed it continues to do so without repeated crises whose social cost increases, then the Marxian analysis of capitalism must be discarded into the museum of theories that cannot express historical reality.

To recapitulate: the economic crisis is not the end of capitalist expansion and, in more contemporary terms, it is merely one phase of the business cycle. Discussion of the specific empirical causes of business cycles constitutes an ongoing debate; the crucial point here is that the conditions that produce such a cycle are, for Marx, emergent from the contradictions of the capitalist system and are moved forward by the laws-of-motion.

Law of the Tendential Fall of the Rate of Profit

This law is the central structural tendency of capitalist development; it can be reconstructed with the following interrelated components:

1. The Profit-Maximization Motive

The accumulation of capital in which the capitalist attempts constantly to lower the cost of the factors of production (i.e., the cost of labor, of raw materials, of the instruments of production) in order to increase the production of exchange values and therefore of surplus value (the unpaid labor);

2. The Duality of Capitalist Production: Material and Value Production[12]

The rate of surplus value $\dfrac{S}{V} = \dfrac{\text{surplus value}}{\text{cost of variable capital}}$ can be increased by the introduction of labor-saving machinery (which lowers the wage cost [V]) or by other technical innovations that either lower the cost of materials or increase labor productivity. In any case, the composition of the means of production is transformed insofar as the mass of these means increases in proportion to the mass of labor employed. This is what Marx calls the "technical composition of capital" and it refers to the changes that occur in the process of material production (the production process considered qualitatively apart from its historical context in the midst of capitalist social relations). At the same time, these relations have a quantitative side in the fluctuations of the value of the means of production (constant capital) and the value of the living labor (variable capital) that activates them. When considered from the value side the change of the ratio of constant and variable capital (C/V) is called by Marx the "value composition of capital."

The importance of distinguishing between the technical and value composition is that the rise in the technical composition of capital usually also involves a rise in the productivity of labor, because of the increase in the mass of use-values produced. But at the same time there is a decrease in the exchange-value of commodities because it takes less socially necessary labor time to produce these use-values and the exchange-values of the products is therefore lower. *Consequently, the value composition of capital rises more slowly than the technical composition*—that is, to the extent that the social productivity of labor goes up with the absorption of new capital.[13] This point has been missed by most critics of this "law."[14] Between the technical and value composition of capital there is a relation which Marx calls the organic composition of capital;[15] by this he wanted to point out that the rates of change of composition have two sides (a material and value side) that can be expressed by the single indicator of the organic composition. Here, as always, the word "organic" refers to a two-sided relationship; namely, that of the production process as it evolves its capacity for greater material production and the same process that is controlled by the capitalist imperative to produce value. Whereas normally there is a "strict correlation" between the technical and value composition of capital (expressed as the organic composition), it is precisely these phases of the production process that are always in formal contradiction and, under permissive conditions, in actual contradiction during a crisis.

3. The Tendency for the Organic Composition of Capital to Rise

Given the ever-present motive of producing more surplus, the tendency is toward the introduction of labor-saving machinery and techniques that reduce the cost of variable capital while maintaining or increasing value production. The long-run trend when averaged for each economic sector is toward a productive system in which the total value of constant capital is increasingly higher in proportion to the value of variable capital. This means a progressive introduction of technology and/or instrumental strategies that alter the organic relations between the factors of production.

What Weber would call "rationalization" can now be seen as specifically that which can increase value production.[16] Marx's concept of the rise of the organic composition of capital seems much clearer about the process of rationalization, although its sociological meaning is not immediately apparent. By recalling the distinction between material and value production, we can distinguish between a material rationalization that increases the productive capacity in general and a value rationalization that would have the specific effect of increasing the production of value. A Marxist critique of Weber would show that though a correlation exists between the material and value rationalization of capitalism (i.e., due to the crisis there is a periodic destruction of the less productive units in every economic sector) these two types of rationalization do not, in fact, coincide. What Weber and contemporary social scientists take to be the neutral adaptive character of the capitalist economy and the rationalizing consequences it has for the entire society are not able to distinguish between value or material rationalization of society. For example, a material rationalization of industrial society need not, as recent studies suggest, reproduce the automotive-oil complex that now dominates the transportation sector of society.[17] The road building programs, oil depletion allowance, and so forth, are components of a value rationalization which, if questioned, could be publically discussed and posed as a problem of material rationalization of society. At the moment, the impossibility of distinguishing between value and material rationalization is an index of the ideological function of pluralistic democracy.

In any case, the tendency for the organic composition of capital to rise means that the amount of productive labor necessary for production decreases in proportion to the dead labor embodied in the increasingly value rationalized apparatus. In another formation, the amount of living labor required to activate production decreases proportionally, in mass and in value, to that of constant capital.

4. The Tendential Fall of the Rate of Profit

The usual reading of this "law" is that a long-term trend toward a rise in the organic composition of capital will involve less and less living labor and eventually the available surplus will permit less and less profit. However, the "law" must be interpreted before it can be used for empirical analysis. A usual misconception treats the law as if it referred only to the value production process and not to the two-sided relation between material and value production. This results in the failure to see that insofar as the organic composition of capital rises, the material capacity of production also rises (not just its value-production capacity) and, in that case, there is a tendency for both the social productivity of labor and the amount of surplus to increase. While on the contrary, the usual critiques of the "law" assert that Marx formulates it with the assumption of a constant rate of surplus and in this way avoids the offsetting consequences of the rising productivity of labor.[18] Marx is quite clear that a rise in the technical composition of capital increases the productiviy of labor and tends to raise the amount of surplus.[19] (Hence Baran and Sweezy's law of rising surplus[20] is anticipated by Marx.)

Even though this interpretation takes the wind out of the usual criticisms of the law, there remain several ambiguities in it which prevent a totally explicit formulation.[21] The least problematic is Marx's language which seems to imply that the rate of profit will fall continuously in line with the rise of the organic composition of capital. This facile formulation contradicts Marx's analysis of the counteracting influences which maintain the rate of profit despite the rise of the organic composition.

Otherwise, the remaining problems are expressed in this recent reassessment of the law:

> The main criticism which can properly be made of Marx's treatment of the problem is that nowhere does he precisely define the conditions under which the rate of profit will fall with a rising organic composition of capital, if we assume that this rising organic composition is associated with a lowering of the value of elements not only of variable but also of constant capital. As his argument stands, all he really says is (a) that there are certain "insurmountable limits" to the extent to which the cheapening of elements of variable capital can offset the effect of a rising organic composition upon the rate of profit; and (b) that cases where the cheapening of elements of constant capital causes the rate of profit to rise or remain constant, although "abstractly" possible, are very unlikely to be met with in practice.[22]

In the end, the major problems of the law are that it attempts to relate too many complex processes, and its capacity to be interpreted and used for prediction depends upon the correspondence between the assumptions of the model and historical reality. In cases where some of Marx's assumptions are not valid, the law cannot be used for prediction and has only a suggestive theoretical use. In this case:

> We should not be too disappointed, then, if the statistics we gather do not, in fact, show a "falling tendency of the rate of profit." The main value of Marx's model in the present-day world is two-fold. In the first place, it provides us with a conceptual framework within which certain problems relating to the long-term behaviour of the rate of profit may perhaps be usefully considered. And in the second place, it keeps before our eyes the extremely important fact that changes in the rate of profit depend not on technical factors alone but rather on the interaction of these with sociological factors.[23]

5. The Law of Increasing Misery

Capitalist development recurrently exerts a downward pressure on wage costs in the production process. Marx assumed that the industrial reserve army would always reappear in times of crisis and that this would cause the wage cost to be held near or at subsistence level. He realized, however, that the wage cost could be sustained by other mediating processes, despite the more typical stress on those forces which kept it low.[24] If we reconstruct the formulation of this "law" from all parts of *Capital* together, we can see that Marx effectively conceived a maximum-minimum function for the cost of wages. That is, the wage cost could be both a cause and an effect of the accumulation of capital. Marx's theory attempted to formulate this dialectical relation by establishing the range of the wage bill for any capitalist society.

A rising rate of mechanization can theoretically drive the wage rate down to the cost of reproducing the laborer (e.g., "subsistence" as that is understood in terms of *historical* human needs). On the other hand, expansion of the labor market by the establishment of new job categories can proceed to the point where the number of people involved in non-productive activities renders it impossible to maintain profits, at which time the labor-cost factor will be the first to be cut back. Between these two extremes the level of wages will depend upon the "respective power of the combatants"[25] (i.e., labor and capital). That is, upon the "class struggle," which is not determined by the process of accumulation of capital. (This expression of the relation of the wage theory to the laws of capitalist development is more consistent with a recognition of the dialectical relatedness of class struggle to the developing "forces" of production: it admits that "emancipation" is not determined by, but depends upon, the capacity of the "working class" to form itself as a political force.)

In his later work Marx does not claim that real wages will decline, but only that *relative* wages will fall in relation to the improvements in productivity. Or, alternatively, if real wages rise, this would mean that there was a rapid growth of productive capital. But the law is formulated qualitatively, in addition to the quantitative indicator, in that relative social position is related to the same dynamic that forced the relative wage rate down. It was just as basic and as clearly stated by Marx that the consequences of capitalist accumulation were the strengthening of the capitalist's power to control the production process and a weakening of the political leverage of the working class. The power of the capitalist and of the working class is contradictory; the increase of economic power in the hands of the first involves the weakening of the societal capacity of the working class to resist this power. "Proletarianization" is a broader category than the designation of where one stands in an income scale, and its dynamics entail much more than the probability that real wages will fall. It is also a reduction in the capacity to *represent* one's interests in society and an increase of the obstacles to overcome in order to arrive at a critical consciousness about society.[26]

Marx's class analysis has been distorted by the attempts to force it into the narrower framework of a social stratification analysis (which proceeds objectivistically by assuming that rank ordering of indicators to income, education, prestige, etc., establish "class"). His class analysis is much more complex and internally connected to his entire discussion of capitalist accumulation. For Marx no single socio-economic indicator can yield information about power and class position. All such approaches (social stratification, elite analysis, etc.)[27] are themselves fraught with assumptions that he would not accept. For example, the attempt to measure class position always involves a set of assumptions about the relationship of the political and economic processes of capitalist society and it was with just this that Marx wanted to include in a theory of the development of the social totality. Thus, when Dahrendorf claims that Marx's analysis is limited because of its claim that property is the single class determinant, he is not interpreting Marx, but justifying his own brand of Weberian analysis.[28] Similarly, C. Wright Mills' "power elite" thesis involves a polarization between an all-powerful elite and the apathetic mass in a way that denies entirely a dialectical attempt to relate objective class position, within a transforming context of conflict, to the possible development of class-conscious struggle against power relations.[29] What Dahrendorf, Mills, and numerous mechanical Marxists have not recognized is that Marxist class analysis is not separable from an analysis of the context of objective conflict (as determined by the dialectics of accumulation), and the possibilities for a self-positing class struggle. In this way, Marx's more dialectical economic analysis was at the same time an endeavor to see how this development established limits to the political expression of objective interests; in other words, how the economic processes also established constraints upon the political ones.

For a critical theory, social stratification and elite class analysis are caught in the false immediacy of asking "Who governs?" and "Who has power?" They fail to recognize that these questions are linked to the more fundamental ones of "How is power created?" or "How can the relations between economic and political processes establish limits on each?"[30]

It is from this narrower view of class analysis that Marx's law of increasing misery has been so easily dismissed as historically incorrect. While it is true that real wages have risen, it is also true that overall income distribution has not changed for the past seventy years in the United States.[31] Marx anticipated the possibility of a rise in wages, but he did not assume that this would mean the end of "misery," since structurally the power to control wages (e.g., the 1972 wage-price controls) still resides within the scope of the political power of the capitalist class. Under conditions of economic recession, the wage cost was and remains one of the first "reforms" of a capitalist society. However, any attempt to control wage costs cannot proceed too far since that would undermine the source of a wide consumer demand which contradicts the goal of continued accumulation. Growth of capitalist power, therefore, also involves an undermining of the sources of effective demand, thereby generating the need for new administrative systems to mediate deprivations that can no longer be represented politically (e.g., poverty, technological obsolescence of occupations, regional underdevelopment, etc.). Hence, value rationalization also entails rationalization of what Weber calls "the means of administration." The dialectical consequence of the structural tendency toward increasing misery is the necessity for the capitalist state to take on more and more interventionist functions which themselves react and indirectly undermine the profitability of capitalist society, thus creating new intra-capitalist conflicts.[32]

The Law of Concentration and Centralization of Capital

Value rationalization, or the growth of the capacity to create value, is at the same time the growth of the capacity to extract surplus ($\frac{\text{surplus value}}{\text{cost of constant capital}}$ grows). This means that the wealth of society grows in such a way that the proportion of wealth created each year is less and less of the total wealth accumulated. Whereas this is generally viewed as the beneficial consequence of steady economic growth, under the conditions of capitalist production it means the development of monopolies in each productive sector as well as the tendency toward greater and greater centralization of economic power. This happens through the process of competition for profits, which in each economic sector enables the best-equipped enterprise to reduce the costs of production and achieve a higher degree of productivity, securing its capacity to get a larger part of the market and a higher probability for surviving an economic crisis. In capital-intensive sectors where new technology is needed for growth, larger firms are more likely to have the resources to develop advanced technical processes, but they usually stimulate only those investments necessary for expansion and development. Hence size, capital, skilled labor, planning and internal functional rationalization, and so forth, all contribute to the chances for further centralization and concentration of capital.

Despite the diminishing of price competition in the oligopolistic markets of late capitalism, this ongoing structural tendency of capitalism is the most apparent of all the "laws-of-motion." Every day the collapse or merger of small firms fills the financial pages of the newspapers. For example, a recent *Wall Street Journal* article stated that "A record of 3,000 companies were involved in mergers last year, up 25% from 1966. . . ."[33] But perhaps more substantial are the five volumes of hearings on *Economic Concentration* given before the Senate Subcommittee on Antitrust and Monopoly in 1964–65. These hearings are a record of both the extraordinary rate of economic concentration in the United States and, at the same time, the impotence, or rather the myth of federal monopoly regulation. One datum may illustrate this point:

The approximate 2041 corporations with assets of 10 million dollars or more earned 89.3 percent of all corporate profits, whereas the about 178,000 remaining corporations earned 10.7 percent.[34]

The awesomeness of contemporary capitalist economic concentration has been the focus of much study and need not concern us here.[35] Yet, this all too obvious tendency has dialectical consequences: greater economic concentration means greater potential for financing large-scale transformations in society (e.g., the development of new forms of energy which requires huge expenditures for instruments, training, and sustained research). Despite this potential, the massive domination of huge firms restricts the application of these new social innovations by suppressing or concealing such emergent possibilities for the benefit of the systems' goal of private economic gain.[36] Thus, the development of economic wealth under the conditions of capitalism means at the same time the necessity to control all new objective possibilities and subordinate them to the priority of reproducing private economic power and privilege. For example, scientific development releases ever new possibilities which must be "internalized" (contained) by the capitalist relations of production.[37]

The Law of Increasing Severity of Cyclical Crisis

Whereas this "law" is seen erroneously as leading to a breakdown theory of capitalism, it is best interpreted as the overall consequence of all the other structural tendencies. Here, too, the sociological implications can be enlarged upon as well as the purely economic. Returning to the basic contradiction of capitalist development, we can see that Marx believed it tended toward increasing socialization of the means of production through the process of capital accumulation which at the same time increased the social power of capital over labor:

We have seen that the growing accumulation of capital implies its growing concentration. Thus grows the power of capital, the alienation of the conditions of social production personified in the capitalist from the real producers. Capital comes more and more to the fore as a social power, whose agent is the capitalist. This social power no longer stands in any possible relation to that which the labor of a single individual can create, it becomes an alienated, independent, social power, which stands opposed to society as an object, and as an object that is the capitalist's source of power. The contradiction between the general social power into which capital develops, on the one hand, and the private power of the individual capitalists over these social conditions of production, on the other, becomes ever more irreconcilable, and yet contains the solution of the problem, because it implies at the same time the transformation of the conditions of production into general, common, social, conditions. This transformation stems from the development of the productive forces under capitalist production, and from the ways and means by which this development takes place.[38]

The general direction of capitalist development is, therefore, toward continuation and intensification of capital's domination over society *in general—not simply over labor or the production process.* The power of the social relations of capital (e.g., legal and state structures, etc.) becomes not only the source of the power of individual capitalists over labor but at the same time the source of a common set of alienated social conditions. The basic contradiction establishes trends (analyzed as specifically the above structural tendencies) which create ever new forms of social domination to secure the social priority of capital accumulation and profit maximization. Marx's crisis theory, and the fourth law particularly, can be seen as a thesis which conceives all further social development as so many adjustments to the ever-renewed power of the social relations of capital. While the crisis theory is ostensibly concerned with the constant tendency toward economic crisis, at the same time it expresses a structural tendency toward a deepening domination of capital over "common social conditions" (that is, over social organization).

The theory refers to the combined crisis of economic prosperity and social conditions of life for every individual in society, and as such it can be interpreted both economically and sociologically. Although Marx's formulation clearly involved both aspects, the history of Marxist analysis has overemphasized the solely economic. This economic stress is, of course, related to the hope that the socialization of the forces of production would force the emergence of a revolutionary class consciousness.[39] Into the void of this mechanical connection between the forces of production and the nonemergence of a decisive class struggle rushed Lenin with his reformation of the necessary conditions for a successful class struggle. Given Lenin's success in Russia, two generations of Marxists have subordinated their critical capacities to the harness of a much more mechanical form of Marxism than that held by Marx, who described himself as "not a Marxist."

The Unfinished State of Marx's Crisis Theory

While it is generally recognized by some of Marx's sympathetic critics that the crisis theory is the center of his work, it is also argued (e.g., by Schumpeter) that this theory is his "great unwritten chapter."[40] The theory is, in fact, unfinished and *Capital* is only a preliminary form of it. If we take Marx's 1857–58 projections as definitive of the total plan, we must conclude that he simply was unable to complete his critique of capitalism before his death.[41] In 1857–58 the general analysis that Marx projected included several major topics (e.g., the state, the world market) which he never finished. From this plan the four volumes of *Capital* were only a sixth of the total scheme! The abbreviated plan for *Capital* came in 1863 when Marx decided to deal with surplus value as a whole rather than the specific forms in which it appears.[42] Yet, despite—and because of—this shorter procedure, the crisis theory was not completed; particularly the analysis of the state as a reciprocal moment of accumulation remained undeveloped.

While perceiving its incompleteness, Schumpeter and others have failed to recognize the logic of Marx's concept of an antagonistic system which repeatedly, even if on higher levels of development, leads to crisis. There are two differences between Marx's crisis theory and later theorists of the business cycles. First, Marx's theory attempts to assess the consequences of a dynamic contradiction (it is "dialectical"). Secondly, it links up an economic theory of capitalist accumulation to an institutional analysis of the social consequences of this ongoing process.[43] While identifying the sources of economic growth, Marx's crisis theory also shows that there are no independent variables in society; all societal components are step-by-step affected and pulled into the "cyclo-dynamic feedback mechanism . . . [in which] the 'knowns' as well as the 'unknowns' . . ." are involved.[44] Rather than focus on the circular notion of business cycles, Marx's primary concern with production is an attempt to relate the *totality* of human activity to the revolutionary innovation of capitalist economic development. No institutional sphere is unaffected by the new generative logic of commodity production; economic rationality gradually penetrates all normative systems and reconstructs them upon the new model of rationality. The lasting genius of Marx's concept is his recognition of the structurally-induced transformation of the socio-cultural process while at the same time attempting to assess its inherent limits.

Later Marxists and economists working with Marx's theory have lost the idea of the social totality and have often made the crisis theory one-sided, either placing the source of crisis in the reproduction processes of capitalism (the disproportionality theorists) or in the circulation process (the underconsumption theorists). While these interpretations may have economic significance as later developments of Marx's work, neither version seems really to continue what Marx's crisis theory was attempting to do. His concept was formulated at a higher level of abstraction and it did not locate the recurrent source of crisis in either the reproduction or circulation processes, but rather in the ensemble of restrictive limits that are constantly recreated because of the basic contradiction of capital itself. Marx expressed this central contradiction of the capitalistic system as follows:

The real barrier of capitalist production is *capital itself*. It is that capital and its self-expansion appear as the starting and the closing point, the motive and the purpose of production; that production is only production for *capital* and not vice versa, the means of production are not mere means for constant expansion of the living process of the society of producers . . . The means—unconditional development of society—comes continually into conflict with the limited purpose, the self-expansion of the existing capital. The capitalist mode of production is, for this reason, a historical means of developing the material forces of production and creating an appropriate world-market and is, at the same time, a continual conflict between this, its historical task and its own corresponding relations of social production.[45]

Crisis, therefore, cannot be traced to the primacy of one component of the process of capitalist accumulation but rather to the impossibility of avoiding the internally reproduced barriers of capital against itself. Contemporary criticism of the disproportionality theory of crisis has been based on this broader conception.[46] On the other hand, the underconsumption formulation of crisis has generally been accepted more sympathetically, e.g., by Rosa Luxembourg, Paul Sweezy, Joan Robinson and other left-Keynesians. But here, too, it isolates the circulation process as the basic limit placed upon production and, by doing so, reduces Marx's generative, or dialectical, theory, to a static theory of the limits of economic growth.[47] Whereas a theory of economic growth is entailed in Marx's concept of accumulation, the scope of the crisis theory goes beyond this and tries to reflexively show that indefinitely continued economic growth is impossible due to the basic contradiction of the capitalist epoch.

In many ways, the completed parts of *Capital* are not as comprehensive as the series of monographs and fragments now known as the *Grundrisse* (written 1857–58). It is possible to take from these essays additional formulations of the crisis theory which have not been considered by later theorists. Perhaps most instructive is one specific restatement of the basic contradictions of the capitalist epoch which reveals a great deal about the logical structure of the crisis theory. At this point in the *Grundrisse* Marx suggested that capitalist production was based upon capital in such a way that it was impossible to continuously extract surplus value and convert it into exchange value without the recurrent prospects of overproduction and stagnation. This formulation is chiefly an attempt to define the restrictive (self-limiting) conditions that are established by the internal contradiction of capital. The passage is as follows:

These inherent limits necessarily coincide with the nature of capital, *with its essential determinants.* The necessary limits are:

1. *Necessary labor* as the limit to the exchange value of living labor power, of the wages of the industrial population.

2. *Surplus value* as limit to surplus labor time; and, in relation to relative surplus labor time, as limit to the development of the productive forces.

3. What is the same thing, the *transformation of money* into exchange-value, as such, as a limit to production; or, exchange based on value, or value based on exchange, as limit to production. This is again

4. The same thing as *restriction of the production of use-values* by exchange-value; or the fact that real wealth must take on a specific form distinct from itself, absolutely not identical with it, in order to become an object of production at all.[48]

These four self-limits of capital are the internal negations of capitalist production; they represent the dialectical patterns which manifest the destructive inner necessities of the system. Through the *Grundrisse* (1857–58) the philosophical exposition returns again and again to the Spinozistic and Hegelian concepts of determinate negation.[49] It is precisely these logical forms which are central to the crisis theory and which establish the meaning of "limit," "barrier," and "contradiction."

But it will be easier to illustrate the logic of the theory by expanding the above quote. These four limits constitute the self-produced boundary conditions of capitalist development:

1. Necessary Labor:

It is possible to lower the wage cost only so far—at its minimum it would be the cost of the necessary labor for reproducing society. Approaching this limit also tends to undermine effective demand to the extent that the consumption process would be critically lowered. When this barrier is reached, there must be a creation of effective demand by one means or another. But there are other limits that exert pressure upon how this demand is created.

2. & 3. Surplus Value and Transformation into Money:

Where there already exists a mass of commodities they must first be sold in order to realize the surplus value that has already been appropriated. (As Marx puts it elsewhere, "the conditions of direct exploitation and those of realizing it [surplus] are not identical.")[50] Such a mass of commodities (or unrealized surplus value) is, in itself, a twofold barrier to the expansion of capital. First, it sets a limit to the further appropriation of surplus value in the form of the pressures of expanded inventories and reduction of liquidity (number 3). Secondly, the existence of such a disproportionality also reduces the acceleration of the extraction of relative surplus value. The latter is a feedback restriction of the entire production process because new innovations which increase productivity (and that also absorb capital) may not be adopted because of the unrealized surplus. In the same manner, any disproportionality between extracted surplus value and existing consumption capacity creates a crisis of circulation and blocks distribution of necessary commodities to stagnated sectors. Thus, the social relations of capital restrict production by making it impossible to distribute goods and services without constant concern for immediate transformation into exchange-value.

4. Restriction of the Production of Use-Values:

If any of the above limits are manifest, the "real wealth" of society is correspondingly diminished. By forcing use-values to assume the form of commodities in order to be produced, distributed, or consumed, the capitalist class imposes growing social costs upon society to make itself secure. This is for Marx the logic of capitalist development (value rationalization) and is exemplified in the constant willingness of capitalists to underutilize available productive capacities to ensure profitability. This strategy can only be adopted in certain situations however; if the production of exchange-values is too severely limited, the above cycles of disproportionalities and dynamic contradictions are reactivated. Expansion is therefore necessary to restore profitability—*but* the wage cost cannot be too high or too low, the mass of surplus must be realizable; and the capacity to transform values into money must be present, *or* the tendency to overproduction and stagnation reappears. Under the conditions of a continually expanding process of production, capitalism becomes more involuted and the scope that must be controlled becomes wider. There can be no final game plan since the changing conditions of social expansion make realization of the private goal more difficult.

The inherent limits must be reactivated due to the cyclical motion of economic growth and its basic contradictions. No matter how many more significant variables emerge in the process the system is subject to recurrent and increasing crisis.

This is the legacy of Marx's crisis theory. Its applicability to the dynamic of late capitalism remains to be shown.

6

Cultural-Marxism: The Contradictions of Industrial "Rationality"

> It is not ideology in itself which is untrue but rather its pretension to correspond to reality.
>
> * * *
>
> All reification is a forgetting: objects become thinglike at the moment when they are grasped without being fully present in all their parts, where something of them is forgotten.
>
> —T. Adorno

*I*n the twentieth century a new form of crisis theory was gradually developed that could be extended to both capitalist and "socialist" industrial societies. Suggested by George Lukacs and developed by the Frankfurt School, this theory forecast both a unique crisis of advanced industrial development and the danger to human subjectivity which this implied: As advanced industrial societies developed, the individual was more integrated into and dependent upon the collectivity and yet less able to utilize society for active self-expression. Although in Lukacs' early work the focus remained upon capitalist development, the Frankfurt School members later conceptualized the tendencies of all industrial systems as shaping a crisis of human subjectivity. Since historical studies of the Frankfurt School and the libertarian communist tradition have recently appeared[1] it is not necessary to repeat them here. What is important are the main ideas of this tradition which may form a new foundation for critical theory.

In general, the central thesis of the new theory is that industrial production, guided by the motive of economic growth, can generate a new type of crisis—one which is embodied in both late capitalism and socialism—to mediate its internal contradiction and stimulate continued expansion. In this way the nature of production, the direction of social and personal development, all become dependent upon the "needs" of economic development. Thus, the qualitative dimension of Marx's theory of the structural tendencies of capitalist growth is manifested as coerced economic development, on the one hand, and increasing indirect controls upon life styles, on the other.

Contemporary neo-Marxism seems to have gradually converged on this thesis of a new level and mode of domination. Theorists such as Lukacs, Marcuse, Habermas, Lefebvre, and others, have all emphasized the combination of enforced dependence, cultural manipulation and growing political powerlessness that derives from the dynamics of late industrial society. By reconstructing the main points of these contemporary critiques it may be possible to show the communality of their conception and to demonstrate the continuity of this critique with Marx's crisis theory.

George Lukacs's Critique of "Rationalization" as the Dynamic of Reification[2]

Lukacs's early work (circa 1923) began with a Hegelianized Marxism which stressed that the abstract immediacy of human experience under capitalism was derived from the objective and subjective dynamics of commodity fetishism. In the objective sphere fetishism manifests itself as the invisible laws of market forces that operate behind or beneath the consciousness of historical man. This fetishism is reflexively experienced as the enforced formalism of purely economic imperatives that establish equivalents between human activity and measured units of space and time. Through this two-fold dynamic all qualitative social relations are increasingly redefined into abstract relations that permit specialization of tasks, increased calculability, and efficiency for organizations. Where the "natural unity of producing" is reconstructed by the "needs" of profit-guided production, and the laborer's activity is controlled by these requirements, the organic unity of production for human use is concealed by a veil of quantitative criteria. The principle of commodity fetishism, which derives from the logic of commodity production, is the reification of the human world. Both objective laws of capitalist development and the subjective experience of man in these contexts are mystified by the reification of "quantitative meanings" (e.g., wage labor and money) that conceal the historical nature of productive activity and its relation to the gratification of human needs. The result is a type of social change that reifies all human reality into a new appearance which substitutes the abstractions of commodity production for social relations.

Throughout his early writings Lukacs was engaged in a debate with his teachers, George Simmel and Max Weber. The most significant thesis of this encounter is Lukacs's depiction of the principle of rationalization as fundamental to the processes of capitalist reification. Rather than view the process of rationalization as a neutral extension and progressive institutionalization of Western rationalism, Lukacs links it to the capitalist class division of labor and thus to the process of reification. The process of bureaucratization is, for Lukacs, especially illuminated from this perspective in that it can be explained as the *adjustment* of all ways of life, work, and consciousness to the demands of the socio-economic premises of the capitalist economy. Bureaucratization is the mode of organizational change which permits expansion of the capitalist economy by promoting a formal standardization of justice, the emergence of an interventionist state, and the growth of civil service. It also increases its own remoteness from the qualitative relations of a humanly produced and understood world. Whereas Lukacs acknowledges Simmel's influence in recognizing phenomena of reification, Lukacs shows how he—and Weber—have divorced these processes from their foundation in capitalist development.

For Lukacs, an adequate analysis of modern capitalism consists of a return to Marx's method of immanent critique beginning with the illusory immediacy of capitalist appearance and its reified laws. By grasping the inherent dynamic of this development, the one-sidedness of it is manifested as the processes of objective and subjective reification. Lukacs, following Marx, believes that it is possible to recognize the internal limitations of capitalist development. He maintains that the nature of a capitalist type of rationalization generates its own internal negation; its very *formalism* renders it more and more vulnerable. All capitalist rationalization is only partial, since the particularistic social relations (the guiding criteria of profit and private control of production) cannot themselves be subject to rational transformation. By retaining private hegemony over production decisions, capitalist society reveals that its unmodifiable end is its own internal negation. The internal constraint of capitalist rationalization originates in its incapacity to rationalize the whole of society; it is restricted to the subsystems of society which do not affect the greater irrationality of the whole. Insofar as there is a main drift of society, it must remain an unconscious "law" of "mutually interacting coincidences." Consequently, there exists a tension between the unknown directional law of the whole and highly formalized rationalizations of societal subsystems. This is the central contradiction of modern capitalism; it represents a reformulation of Marx's concept. The vocabulary has been shifted to absorb the Weberian analysis of rationality in much the same manner in which Marx adopted the categories of political economy in order to demonstrate their historical reification of human productivity.

Lukacs claims there is an inherent tendency of all formally rationalized subsystems to become increasingly autonomous. This recurrently reproduces crisis by the emergence of a disequilibrium between the internally rationalized subsystems which cannot, once the crisis is overt, autonomously readjust to a dynamic whose logic remains unclear. (To take a current example, the highly rationalized semi-public aerospace industry has suffered an economic shock unanticipated by its planners—the unrecognized priority of corporate capitalism's right to control production for profit.) In periods of crisis the incoherence of the whole is exposed by the subsystems' inability to respond to externally-triggered crisis. The very formalism of rationalized subsystems destroys any objective image of the whole and promotes instead an internal incapacity to grasp it. The index to crisis is here the degree of blindness to the source of crisis that permeates a rationalization process. For example, the great depression of the 1930s and the utter inability of businessmen or social scientists to objectify the crisis is a case in point.

During periods of crisis the unrecognized human needs of society reassert themselves as the most decisive issues. The ideological pretense of "natural laws" of objective development are, at these times, exposed. When the basic reality of human needs reappears, the capacity of the capitalist system to survive depends upon either meeting them and/or blocking a mass recognition of the contradiction between these needs and the logic of capitalism.

The Frankfurt School and the Critique of Culture

The closing of the horizons of the industrial world by a dynamic principle of reification is well charted in the cultural criticism of the Frankfurt School. The studies of Horkheimer, Benjamin, Fromm, Adorno, Neumann, et al., have documented the reifications in the currents of philosophy, social theory, art, music, literature, and its institutionalization into the family, the state, and the sphere of human subjectivity. Much of the criticism is devoted to the analysis of the "culture industry" of late industrial society and shows how the individual is enslaved by the suppressions and denials of modern mass culture. The Frankfurt School's philosophical modes of cultural criticism were supplemented by empirical research such as *Studien über Autorität und Familie* (1936) and *The Authoritarian Personality* (1950). However, the seminal work of this series was Horkheimer and Adorno's *Dialektik der Aufklärung* (1947) which suggests that the Enlightenment introduced a notion of reason which reinforced the objective processes of reification. In this book, and in Max Horkheimer's *The Eclipse of Reason* (1947), this notion of reason was viewed as a uni-lateral concept which treated knowledge as an instrumental control over nature. However, this conception of reason legitimated an atomized sociocultural process which reflexively increased the domination of man. That is, the progress of instrumental ration-ality involved the constitution of structures of domination which did not release eros but its opposite. There is, however, a "revolt of nature" in the "instinctual" rebellions of advanced industrial society. Fascism and authoritarian communism are both seen as the irrational consequences of a civilization that worshipped in-strumental reason. Having lost a critical dialectical notion of rea-son, modern man is left without a guide for emancipatory praxis. While Adorno and Horkheimer conceived of a reconciliation with nature as the goal for liberation, they also came to believe that there was no way that man could achieve this in a reified universe of domination. Only in the *memory* of nature could there be a reflective opposition to the false identity between man and nature in modern industrial systems.[3] The Enlightenment concept of rea-son was a dynamic principle of reification because it overlooked the dialectic of nature and spirit in history. What Weber had called the disenchantment of the modern rationalizing world was actually the concealment of the critical dialectic between man and nature— now reified by scientized domination.

Reconciliation between man and nature requires not the false immediacy of fascistic identity of the "natural hierarchy of soci-ety," but a reflective recognition of the constraints now operative within man's experience. And yet the critical theory developed by the Frankfurt School could not suggest any objective praxis which could break through the reified universe; it concluded with an affirmation of the self-liberating practice of the individual, thereby suggesting that the restoration of the individual to himself had to be achieved as a prerequisite for a more collective praxis.[4]

The entire tradition of the Frankfurt School has been given its most systematic theoretical presentation in the work of Herbert Marcuse. While most representative in some ways, Marcuse also deviates from the School most radically in his retention of an ontological framework and his continued solidarity with left organizations. The essential components of the Frankfurt School's crisis theory can be presented by reconstructing Marcuse's work. Here, too, the main focus is the category of "rationality" which seems to correspond to the earlier debate about the labor theory of value which had become central to Marx's critical theory.

Herbert Marcuse's Critique of "One-Dimensional Rationality"

Marcuse's analysis of the political content of the contemporary concept of rationality extends Lukacs's analysis while retaining his strategy of reformulating critique in the categories of contemporary social science. Marcuse's work stresses the new type of political domination which develops in late industrial society under the seemingly neutral guise of "technological rationality." The central meaning of "one-dimensionality" is the repressiveness of technological rationality which, however, posits itself as societally and normatively neutral. Marcuse tries to show that the extension of science and technology is, in advanced industrial society, at the same time an extension of social control and domination. Under these conditions, the greater capacity to control nature turns into a deeper control of man, although this remains unrecognized in the universal celebration of the power of science and technology.

The inability to critically comprehend the actuality of domination is the focus of much of Marcuse's analysis. Yet, he seems to deal with the question on different levels: first, he makes a claim about the inherent instrumental nature of modern scientific rationality; then, he maintains that there is a social dynamic which produces the tendency toward the reification of sociocultural and cognitive processes. Although these approaches should supplement each other, there is a certain conflict between them. The notion of technical reason at times seems to have usurped the need for any historical analysis of the social mechanisms that transform science and technology into modes of domination. By stressing that a subjective instrumental orientation is basic to the objective process of human society, Marcuse implies that the development of one-dimensionality is inevitable. There is no need for an analysis of the social interests that skew the process of technical reason into a snowballing of sociocultural and cognitive reification. Marcuse's analysis is flawed by its lack of methodological self-understanding; it is at one and the same time a type of "phenomenological" Marxism with an internal tendency toward ontology, and a very general type of macroempirical analysis which tries to reconstruct the dynamic of reification. This dual character of the analysis does not seem to be recognized by Marcuse, who moves from one level to the other without any hesitation. If we examine the arguments of Marcuse's sympathetic critics (e.g., Offe, Bergman, Leiss, Shapiro, Habermas, etc.)[5] we discover that they all stress the confusions that emerge from the scope of generalization and the vague and contradictory connection between the notion of technical reason and the new level of social domination. The result is that Marcuse's analysis is brilliantly suggestive, but inadequately expressed or systematized. In many ways, it is distorted by its isolation from the contemporary methodological debate currently going on between philosophical consciousness and established methods of scientific inquiry.

The Project of Technical Reason: The Phenomenological Presentation

Due to this internal ambiguity, it is necessary to briefly reconstruct both sides of the argument. The essentially "phenomenological" approach (i.e., an attempt to recognize the principle that is logically presupposed by all productive activity) is partly inspired by the Frankfurt School tradition and partly a residue of Marcuse's earlier philosophical inclinations.[6] It is a critique of the modern concept of reason as having severed the human subject and the natural object without recognizing their intermediations. By conceiving of reason as a property of the subjective consciousness, the realm of nature was separated from man and viewed as a sphere to be controlled and dominated. The bifurcation of subject and object resulted in a denial or masking of the extent to which history transformed "nature" (as experienced by man) and the modes in which man is himself part of nature and integrated into natural processes. By failing to recognize that the historical constitution of the human world is, as Marx put it, ". . . a humanization of nature and naturalization of man," modern philosophy (with some exceptions, such as Hegel) and science produced a pseudopolarization between man and nature. Nature became an external object to be conquered and controlled by the development of "neutral" techniques emergent from the progress of science and technology. By failing to recognize the mediation of history and nature and by developing society instrumentally in order to secure the domination of nature, a historical reversal increases the control over man. Instead of fulfilling the Enlightenment vision of man's emancipation through the mastery of nature, the growth of a technical civilization has increased the layers of man's domination.

This endeavor to demonstrate the instrumental character of the modern concept of reason is Marcuse's way of presenting a highly influential convergence of Hegelian-Marxism (especially the works of Max Horkheimer), Husserl's later conception of the crisis of Western science and philosophy, and Heidegger's notion of technical reason.[7] Marcuse's "synthesis" pivots, however, upon his early categorization of human existence in terms of "modes of being" (*Gegenwärtigkeit* and *Gewesenheit*—presentness and having-been-ness) suggesting that only reflection can mediate the immediacy of a reified existence.[8] In this way, the closing of the horizons of consciousness in a scientized civilization is not simply a crisis of economic development or social organization; it is a crisis of human existence in general. Without the capacity for reflection to restore the connections between a mere appearance and the constitutive dynamic of historical development, there seems to be no way, within Marcuse's framework, for liberation from one-dimensionality. On the one hand, the possibilities for an emancipatory mass movement are blocked by a one-dimensional totality and yet, on the other, Marcuse is concerned with showing how a critical theory can be conceived that will recognize possibilities for political praxis. This internal contradiction drove Marcuse to the most extreme ontological formulations to legitimate the project of emancipation itself. That is, the very scope of Marcuse's phenomenological presentation undermined the rooting of "interest" in emancipation in a reconstruction of the dynamic of history—the project had to be justified *ontologically*.

The possibility for reflective mediation is grounded, for Marcuse, in the category of *remembrance* which is, both on the level of the individual and of the universal, the mechanism for the restoration of wholeness and the impetus to liberation. While one-dimensionality conceals the distinctions between essence and appearance, potentiality and actuality, the social and the natural, it is through "remembrance" that these essential dualities are restored. It reasserts the realm of essence by reflecting upon the present (perceived under capitalist conditions as an ahistorical realm of mere appearance) and by a rational reconstruction of the constitutive dynamics of history. This restoration is not a mere theoretical intuition of "essence," it is a critical comprehension annulling or negating that which exists via a critique of ideological structures. The intent is to realize (in the double sense of come to know and produce) the objective possibilities that are concealed by the immediacy of the present. Critical remembrance is a process of man becoming-for-himself and the step-by-step realization that productive relations are social relations and provide a field for human actualization. Even in its theoretical moment, the process is one of individuation, of the mediation of the givenness of self by a reflexive comprehension of the self-formative dynamic. This means that critique conceived as critical remembrance has ultimately the "practical intention" of emancipating man.

To make the mediation of one-dimensionality appear tenable, Marcuse integrates Freud's psychoanalytic theory into the foundations of a Marxian critical theory. In finding a parallel concern with memory in the psychodynamic of psychoanalytic reflection, Marcuse believes he can justify critical remembrance in an objective situation in which the consciousness of history is suppressed. By linking remembrance to the universal situation of human psychosexual development, Marcuse hopes to ground the possibility of transcending one-dimensionality. Given the extent to which critical remembrance is blocked by a pregiven continuum of means-ends rationality, Marcuse is unable to return to Marx's mode of grounding the promise of liberation. That is, Marcuse's analysis of one-dimensionality makes it impossible to point to mass movements based on a recognition of the class basis of society—these have been closed off by a horizon of reified institutions and consciousness. The "hope" for liberation must be rooted in a more general and a deeper level of existence. Marcuse must thus overcome the loss of historical existence by locating the impetus for liberation in a depth layer of the human condition itself. The solution to this seemed to be in a transhistorical reinterpretation of Freud's theory—Freud's metapsychology.

Marcuse's metapsychology is based on a Hegelianized Freud. The latter's developmental concept is interpreted as a dialectical theory of the reassertion of domination of the universal in and through the *Bildung* of the individual, which consists, according to Hegel, "in his acquiring what is thus given to him; he must digest his inorganic nature and take possession of it for himself."[9] Marcuse argues analogously that individual development is "the living process of mediation in which all repression and all liberty are 'internalized,' made the individual's own doing and undoing."[10] Or, again, on the individual's relation to society:

By 'dissolving' the idea of the ego-personality into its primary components, psychology now bares the sub-individual and pre-individual factors which (largely unconscious to the ego) actually *make* the individual: it reveals the power of the universal in and over the individual.[11]

Marcuse seems to have found in Freud's metapsychology the modern "empirical" equivalent of Hegel's analysis of the movement of *Geist*. Although he considers Freud's formulation to remain in a "reified form in which historical processes appear as natural (biological) processes"[12] its relevance lies in its ability to deal with both the horizontal (present) and vertical (having-been-ness) dimensions of the human world in a single dynamic theory. It can dialectically relate individual and universal in a given societal setting, as well as in the dimension of historical development.

. . . we have argued that Freud's psychology reaches into a dimension of the mental apparatus where the individual is still the genus, the present still the past. Freud's theory reveals the biological de-individualization beneath the sociological one—the former proceeding under the pleasure and Nirvana principles, the latter under the reality principle. By virtue of this generic conception, Freud's psychology of the individual is *per se* psychology of the genus. And his generic psychology unfolds the vicissitudes of the instincts on historical vicissitudes: the recurrent dynamic of the struggle between Eros and death instinct, of building and destruction of culture, of repression and return of the repressed, is released and organized by the historical conditions under which man develops.[13]

But Marcuse's reconstruction of Freud's metapsychology pivots upon his retention of Freud's instinct (*Trieb*) theory, as its fundamentally *critical* aspect and its "dialectical" relatedness with Freud's later metapsychology. By stressing Freud's most naturalistic dimension while claiming that it is "dialectical," Marcuse's use transcends empirical referents and becomes essentially ontological.

The Historical Presentation of One-Dimensionality

Marcuse's theory of *One-Dimensional Man* had already been anticipated by Marx in the *Grundrisse* where he points out that production begins to control human needs themselves:

Production thus creates the consumer. Production not only furnishes the object of a need, but it also furnishes the need for an object.[14] [italics mine]

Marcuse's key point is that systems of technics in advanced industrial society have become:

. . . totalitarian to the extent to which it determines not only the socially needed occupations, skills, and attitudes, but also individual needs and aspirations. It thus obliterates the opposition between the private and public existence, between individual and social needs. Technology serves to institute new, more effective, and more pleasant forms of social control and social cohesion.[15]

Technology is not a neutral element in social change; it is now a means to control both political and personal "projects." Choice of societal and individual ends and means are manipulated by the internal logic of an economic-technical coordination which remains attached to a given structure of privilege and power. Marcuse's central thesis is but a reformulation of Marx's model of capitalist society but which goes on to point out that the productive forces of advanced industrial society have become so powerful that a qualitatively different form of domination has emerged. However, the difference ushered in by the development of a higher technological rationality is not visible, but has been mystified by the seeming "rationality" of the whole. Social conflicts appear as "social problems," to be dealt with by instrumental techniques. Administrative pluralism functions in a cooperative "rational" manner which acts jointly against those who reject the logic of domination inherent in the whole. The contradictions of a capitalist society cannot develop in a society which has the technological capacity to contain them and to negate all oppositional potentialities. Marx's theory of the development of internal agencies of social resolution is therefore contradicted by the capacity of the system to "deliver the goods." All potential opponents, or agents of social change, are absorbed by the *Schein* of rationality.

Marcuse has produced a twentieth-century theory of the alienation of work, which stresses that the work praxis has been changed due to the qualitative alteration of the technological process. Labor is not the brutalizing and deforming drudgery which characterized its alienation in the middle of the nineteenth century. Under the conditions of advanced capitalism work takes on an increased degree of integration; the machine process has now become a "technical ensemble" which approximates more and more a self-regulating system (which, if realized, is potentially the emancipation of man from the alienation of nature; but it is deflected by capitalist social relations toward built-in obsolescence and semiautomation). The work process now has the following characteristics:

1. Individual "work" becomes integrated into a technical "rhythm" which replaces individual praxis. Workers get into the

"swing of things," i.e., they imitate the automatic process and, in this way, replace the reflexive work praxis by a *mimetic adjustment to a technical process.*

2. The extension of the machine process undermines the "professional autonomy" of the worker which was his power to oppose the work process. Now automation alters *qualitatively* the relations between dead and living labor; it tends toward a point where productivity is determined "by the machines and not by the individual output."

3. The result of the "technicalization" of work in advanced industrial society is the social and cultural integration of the worker with the production system.

Assimilation in needs and aspirations, in the standard of living, in leisure activities, in politics derives from an integration *in the plant* itself, in the material process of production.[16]

This process is related to the unique requirements of the technicalization of work itself: higher job training, faster rate of technological obsolescence, greater power of management over these factors. All contribute to a tighter integration of the worker with the plant, its prospects and its future. The private life and consciousness is polarized by the work life.

4. All these factors weaken the negative position of the working class, which no longer seems to stand as the living contradiction of capitalist society. At the same time, the management and owners are also "losing their identity as responsible agents," assuming the function of bureaucrats in a corporate machine. All are thus subservient to the superiority of technical administration and production. The universality of the technicalization of the work process has therefore become a form of universal domination in which the dialectical relation between master and slave has been broken and has become a vicious circle:

A vicious circle seems indeed the proper image of a society which is self-expanding and self-perpetuating in its own preestablished direction —driven by the growing needs which it generates and, at the same time, contains.[17]

6: Cultural-Marxism: Contradictions of "Rationality"

Whereas Marcuse at times seems more of a Hegelian, or even a Freudian, than a Marxist, his theory of alienation is, nevertheless, based on the material "negativity" of the production process. It is ultimately the continuation of Marx's materialization of Hegel's "Cunning of Reason":

. . . expanding automation is more than quantitative growth of mechanization—that it is a change in the character of the basic productive forces. It seems that automation to the limits of technical possibility is incompatible with a society based on the private exploitation of human labor power in the productive forces.[18]

But Marcuse is very explicit about the link between technical alienation and reification:

. . . Technology has become the great vehicle of *reification*—reification in its more mature and effective form. The social position of the individual and his relation to others appear not only to be determined by objective qualities and laws, but these qualities and laws seem to lose their mysterious and uncontrollable character; they appear as calculable manifestations of scientific rationality. The world tends to become the stuff of total administration, which absorbs even the administrators. The web of domination has become the web of Reason.[19]

Marcuse has several parallel analyses of the reification of consciousness. The first utilizes the above-mentioned Freudian metapsychology to point out how the critical functions of the ego are weakened in a technological milieu. The central thesis of this theory is that, due to a radically different socialization process in advanced industrial society, there is a "pre-formation of the ego" that results in a weakening of its autonomous functioning. Marcuse argues that there is a (pseudo) pre-socialization of the person in a technological milieu. It is a pseudosocialization in that it is an external conditioning, a mode of adjustment which is an immediate identification of the individual with *his* society—a mimesis:

This immediate, automatic identification (which may have been characteristic of primitive forms of association) reappears in high industrial civilization: its new 'immediacy,' however, is the product of a sophisticated, scientific management and organization.[20]

Marcuse is concerned now with showing that the "mechanisms" of socialization have been altered in this qualitatively different kind of milieu. First, the socializing agents have changed from the father-oriented family to a situation where "others" such as peer groups, mass media, etc., become more important at an earlier age. The crucial oedipal situation in which the child comes to acquire a relative autonomy by a process of rebellion and attainment of maturity is undermined by changes in the social configuration. Marcuse's reconstruction of the new dynamic of socialization can be summarized as follows:

1. The classical, psychoanalytic model, in which the father-dominated family was the agent of mental socialization, is being invalidated by society's direct management of the nascent ego through the mass media, school and sport teams, gangs, and so forth.

2. This decline in the role of the father follows the decline of the role of private and family enterprise: the son and daughter are increasingly less dependent on the father and the family. . . . The socially necessary repressions and behavior are no longer learned and internalized in the long struggle with the father—the ego ideal is rather brought to bear on the ego directly and "from outside" before the ego is actually formed as the personal and (relatively) autonomous subject of mediation between the self and others.[21]

In classic Freudian terms this means that socialization in advanced industrial society (capitalist *and* socialist) is an *adjustment* to social prohibitions which entails a regression of the ego. More than this, "ego-libido" is itself used to identify with the external ego ideal. Socialization is thus not an internalization of collective norms and values, but an immediate identification, an "acting-out," a mimesis, which involves a loss of reflective capacity.[22]

To the extent to which this interpretation is valid, we can see how socialization can be replaced by an externally conditioned adjustment process which does not require the dialogic of communicative praxis. Man can be conditioned to respond automatically to an artificial "necessity" which is the state of total reification of reflection that A. Huxley depicts in his *Brave New World*.

Marcuse thus attempts to show the self-limits of a rationalizing industrial society. The costs of one-dimensionality are visible in a loss of self-consciousness, in the unrecognized deterioration of the quality of life, and a blocking of the objective possibilities for political transformation. These self-limits of rationalization have been given a related reconstruction by Marcuse and must be mentioned briefly.

He argues that the capacity for sublimation in a "higher culture" is negated by a technological milieu. In Marcuse's unnecessarily obscure phrasing, this is summarized as:

. . . what is happening now is not the deterioration of higher culture into mass culture but the refutation of this culture by reality . . .[23]

This absorption of ideology into reality does not, however, signify the "end of ideology." On the contrary, in a specific sense advanced industrial culture is *more* ideological than its predecessor, inasmuch as today the ideology is in the process of production itself.[24]

When decoded, Marcuse's argument becomes a variation of mass society theory which stresses the "massification of privacy": control and management of "free time" in advanced industrial society can now only be described as "cultural manipulation." While parallel to C. Wright Mills's analysis of "technological illiteracy" and the commercial control of the cultural apparatus,[25] Marcuse's construction unites the psychoanalytic, sociological, and political dimensions of the social totality into one unified theory. In this way a theory of mass society becomes a metapsychological hypothesis of "repressive desublimation."

In a technological milieu, the ideals of consciousness undergo a materialization process which makes them seem realizable by self-production or consumption. The result is a reduction of erotic sublimation and an intensification of social control at a "depth" level of consciousness:

Thus diminishing erotic and intensifying sexual energy, the technological reality *limits the scope of sublimation.* It also reduces the *need* for sublimation. In the mental apparatus, the tension between that which is desired and that which is permitted seems considerably lowered, and the Reality principle no longer seems to require a sweeping and painful transformation of instinctual needs. . . . The organism is thus being preconditioned for the spontaneous acceptance of what is offered.

III: *Toward a Reunification of Critical Theory*

Inasmuch as the greater liberty involves a contradiction rather than extension and development of instinctual needs, it works *for* rather than *against* the status quo of general repression—one might speak of 'institutionalized desublimation'.[26]

Under the conditions of functionally rationalized institutions, performance of work merges with the individual's self-rationalization process and there seems to be little irreconcilability between the self and the functioning of the apparatus. Since societal development and self-development are considered to be mutually reinforcing, there is no objective conflict between them!

Habermas's Notion of Instrumental Rationalization[27]

Habermas agrees with Marcuse on the existence of a new interpenetration of technology and power, but he argues that Marcuse is unable to show on a categorical level precisely what he means by the double function of the scientific-technological progress (as a force of production *and* of domination). Marcuse cannot be stating that science and technology are *inherently* ideological because he would then have to demonstrate that an alternative science and technology are conceivable. On the other hand, his various formulations often suggest that he considers science and technology to be neutral forces which only in their usage become tools of domination. Habermas sees the solution of this dilemma in a reformulation of Weber's concept of rationalization.

As a categorical framework Habermas proposes the distinction between "work," i.e., purposive rational or instrumental action, and "interaction," i.e., communicative action. The former takes place according to *technical* rules which are based on empirical knowledge, the latter according to social *norms* which define mutual expectations of behavior. We can distinguish social systems by the type of action which predominates in them: the institutional structure of society consists of social norms, such as the family, which is based primarily on normative rules of interaction, while the economy and the state are subsystems organized mainly according to standards of purposive rational action. Thus, we arrive at the distinction between (1) the institutional framework of a society, or the sociocultural life world (or symbolic interaction systems) and (2) the subsystems of purposive rational action, which are "embedded" in the institutional framework (or instrumental action systems).

These categories can be developed as a historical metatheory, by conceptualizing the history of mankind as constituted by the ongoing interrelation of two action systems. Purposive rational action secures the human capacity to satisfy human needs, and symbolic interaction systems form the institutional framework of society based upon grammatical rules and social norms that enable man to engage in communication and interaction.

From this perspective, we can speculate about human evolution. Up to neolithic times there is a total dependence of instrumental activity on certain types of symbolic interaction. That is, all instrumental activity had to be enacted as if it were an interaction between personalized agents. In the period between neolithic man and high cultures the purposive rational action systems began to be emancipated from the mediation of symbolic interaction systems.

In pre-modern "traditional" societies the development of instrumental action systems takes place within the limits of the cultural tradition. The normative-institutional framework is of primary importance and social developments have to be legitimated in accordance with it. The threshold of modern societies is crossed in the moment when the expansion of subsystems of purposive rational action do not depend any more on legitimation by cultural tradition. This historically new phenomenon, which appears for the first time with the development of capitalism, is one which Weber tries to grasp with his concept of rationalization: the continuous institutionalized expansion of subsystems of purposive rational action which is guided to a growing extent by the standards of scientific and technological progress.

Until the present time, the main drift of industrial societies has been the growing dominance of purposive rational action. The emergence of advanced capitalism is based on the extension of purposive rational action systems in the forms of bureaucratization, urbanization, and the growth of science-stimulated technologies of every conceivable sort. In short, we have entered a period of instrumental rationalization in which a historical reversal has been set up and the model of purposive rational action becomes prescriptive for more and more spheres of symbolic interaction. This is the crisis that Habermas sees as internal to the dynamic of all advanced industrial society.

This development brings about a change in the form of legitimation of power. Traditionally, the existing power relations were legitimized by a cultural normative system—an ideology. In the moment where the traditional relationship between the institutional framework and the subsystems of purposive rational action is destroyed, this form of legitimizing power becomes obsolete. It is replaced by a "technocratic consciousness," a new ideology which has gained wide support among social scientists (such as Parsons).

The new ideology hides the dualism between work and interaction, between the institutional framework (which still is defined by particularistic interest, e.g., the private ownership means of production) and the subsystems of purposive rational action. It appears as if the logic of scientific-technological progress determines the development of the social system. Practical questions, or questions about societal goals, are reduced in public discussion to technical questions: problems which can only be solved according to the objective standards of science and technology.

The technocratic strategy is, for Habermas, a contemporary delusion that holds it is possible to use science to reconstruct interactional systems and replace them more effectively with purposive rational behavior systems modeled upon cybernetic self-regulating systems. If this project were actualized, it would not only be a total inversion of the original "primitive unity" where all techniques were tied to social norms, it would also imply the end of historical reasoning. The only valid framework for understanding would be the strict science approach and self-understanding would involve apprehending oneself from the viewpoint of an interest in technical control. In this way, the categories of history and the autonomous individual would be eliminated as Skinner and Levi-Strauss are already trying to do in their work.

6: Cultural-Marxism: Contradictions of "Rationality"

If we analyze the sociological meaning of instrumental rationalization, it means:

1. a passive adaptation of all institutions to the leading innovative economic sector and associated state controls;
2. a coerced acceptance by all social groups of the system goals of conflict avoidance in economic and international systems;
3. cultural acceptance of the principle of efficiency and calculability, the "upgrading" of role requirements, etc. These establish the boundary conditions for admissible social action and therefore constitute a structural constraint upon the type of issues that can be represented politically to the "public."

Thus, instrumental rationalization constitutes a tendency to create ever new forms of instrumental action in all spheres in a way which permits more and more conflict avoidances through centralized decision-making processes.

Extending Habermas's argument we need not accept the widespread Parsonian view that the societal trend is toward greater and greater structural differentiation. Instead what is actually taking place is a two-fold process of de-institutionalization, where traditional institutions are deteriorating under the onslaught of functional rationalizing forces and dedifferentiation,[28] where institutional spheres are being fused by technical programs and strategies which are generated and advanced by private corporations and governmental agencies. (It is not accidental that the past president of IBM Corporation was a chief advocate of "planning" for the entire society, or that the Litton Industries has become a major management consultant for local, state, federal, and foreign groups.)[29]

Insofar as the technocratic consciousness becomes the general form under which society appears, we have a general background model of "rationality" which permeates all institutions and styles of life. Thus the propagandistic reference to the role of technology and science can explain and legitimate why in modern societies a democratic decision-making process about practical questions "must" lose its function and "must" be replaced by plebiscitary decisions about alternate sets of leaders for the administrative personnel. Habermas argues that the technocratic consciousness now

219

functions as a societal *a priori* which uncritically contributes to the generation of decision-making whose "rationality" is instrumental effectiveness and efficiency. Such mechanisms work against a broader mode of rationalization which would maximize the participation and individuation of persons affected by societal decisions. Scientism has become a powerful ideology which masks the difference between instrumental action and communicative interaction. In the technocratic consciousness, models of instrumental rationality have become a self-fulfilling and self-reinforcing prescriptive matrice which guides social policy and reconstruction. A technocratic self-understanding of contemporary society—specifically, the ideal of rationally managed social change—now functions as both the principle of justice and the practice of domination.

Our contemporary crisis is rooted precisely in this growing trend toward an instrumental rationalization; it is exploitative to the degree to which the growing dominance of purposive rational action systems absorb systems of communicative interaction. In a "rationally managed" society, communicative action which is oriented to meaning articulated in language and presupposes the internalization of norms, is supplanted to an increasing extent by conditioned modes of behavior. "An increase of adaptive behavior is, however, only the obverse side of a sphere of a linguistically mediated interaction which dissolves under the structure of a purposeful rational action."[30]

Socialization is increasingly an accumulation of technical rules that guide adaptation and less and less the internalization of social norms on the basis of communicative interaction. Insofar as the institutions of advanced capitalism have become polarized and rationalized toward the end of crisis management, the acquisition of private needs has already been structured *a priori* by their technical decision-matrice. The overall consequence of the new structural tendency of state intervention is, therefore, the progressive alienation of socio-cultural processes.

The Crisis of "Everydayness"

Jeremy Shapiro has constructed an extremely interesting and original investigation of the meaning of one-dimensionality. By interpreting Marcuse's concept within the theoretical framework of Jürgen Habermas's reconceptualization of critical theory and by utilizing the work of Henri Lefèbvre on the crisis of everydayness, Shapiro presents a concise and historically specific theory of the emergence of one-dimensionality.

Shapiro maintains that it is "the perfection of technology that makes possible the mediation of art and industry and the integration of the language of information with that of the senses."

One-dimensionality operates as a universal semiotic of technological experience in which all of the oppositions of two-dimensional civilization are irreversibly homogenized and subjected to self-regulating laws of a synchronic system in which the traditional distinctions of form and matter, subject and object, the conscious and unconscious and the beautiful and the necessary are overcome. This universal semiotic is the ground of all future political and social development.[31]

Transition to the one-dimensional world was forced by the acceleration of two historical processes related to the emergence and development of capitalism. First, the institutionalization of exchange relations and, second, technological change—both conceptualized as systems of purposive rational action. These systems progressively forced a step-by-step replacement of symbolic interaction systems.

This latter phase of advanced industrial development is accelerating the reduction of symbolic interaction to purposive rational action and has, Shapiro argues, fundamentally transformed human experience and the manner in which its "meaning" is bestowed. Whereas Marx analyzed the reification of sociocultural systems as a result of their quantification and translation, or reduction, into the language of commodities, Shapiro argues that the later phase of this process brought about a qualitative change in social and perceptual experience. He illustrates his argument by an analysis of the "fetishism of images" and "the technical object." Just as commodity fetishism reduced socially dependent "use-value" to an economic sign (referring to exchange value "symbols") so later modes of fetishism transfer the meaning of the sign to the object itself; objects became lifelike, "symbolic" in themselves.

In the very act of everyday perception the fetishism of images and technical objects integrates the person into the technical ensemble. The trends of modern design can be understood as facilitating the operationalization of experience and the reduction of symbolic interaction to an instrumental adjustment to functional systems. Communicative dialogue is more and more replaced by perceptual inputs from technical objects whose "understanding" requires that crucial transindividual information—not understanding of social needs and values. The prototypical form of technological experience is "the gaze at the technical object."

To the degree to which the individual is absorbed into the technical ensemble, there is a sense in which the crisis of advanced industrial civilization is a crisis of subjectivity itself. Man's relation to one another and to himself is increasingly mediated by technical systems and therefore less and less subject to the spontaneity of his subjectivity. The technical ensemble surrounds him as an ever-ready definition of the situation; a permanent spectacle to which he can "tune in" with a flip of a switch. We can "watch the world with the world-watchers," or participate in "the revolution" at an acid rock concert—all by responding to the "vibrations" of the moment. While flooded with messages, we are, at the same time, passive agents of the technical ensemble.

To the extent that our lives become dependent upon technical operations, it can be argued that we are less able to recognize the limits of nature (e.g., our own bodies becoming apperceived as technical objects) or the social obligations of novel situations (human responsibility is replaced by "functional responsibility"). These tendencies are sometimes placed under the rubric of the "crisis in morality": though this is true, it explains nothing. We are confronting a radical break with the cultural traditions of the past due to the growing technical mediation of life praxis. If we are unaware of this tendency, moralizing about its consequences only reinforces the new totemic identification with the machine.

In the recovery of individual *needs*, there is potentially a restoration of the *social*, intersubjective aspects of everyday life. The critique of everyday life has produced some interesting conceptions of new forms of liberatory praxis.[32] But the development of the background to the technically transformed process of cultural change requires more work than is possible here. Such critique would involve a reconstruction of the modes of *translation* from perceptual and behavioral "imputs" that predated and succeeded the "technotronic revolution."[33]

The immediate result of these cultural critiques has been a reorientation of emancipatory praxis, making individual praxis necessarily simultaneous with collective praxis. But again the question emerges: How is recognition of domination possible? The analysis of the microdynamics of everyday life has an advantage in this area, since it is concerned primarily with the restoration of meanings that otherwise are unrecognized.

For example, Shapiro claims that the key to this question is that the "new sensibility" increases instances of a new kind of "negative experience." In "absurdity, nausea, . . . meaninglessness and schizophrenia" are the sources of need for reflection and the awareness of freedom. One strategy for the development of radical practice is a translation of the meaning of "the total semiotic system" into the language of a social group that wants to extend its limits of comprehension and choice and thus reconstitute *the individual* and his *differentiation from the group*. This is in direct opposition to older modes of radical organization which held that suppression of individuality was a prerequisite for political praxis. This type of praxis will produce a politics of individuation which is the only way in which *choice* can be regained by communicative processes. Only in this kind of politics can personal experience be raised to the level of interpersonal expressions and become the beginning point of political organization. This has already begun in the numerous movements that resist the cultural hegemony of late capitalist society, as, for example, black liberation, women's liberation, and the many types of communal "enclosures," such as free schools.

7

The Crisis of American Capitalism: a Preliminary Conceptualization

*I*t is widely claimed that the socialist and capitalist worlds are "converging" since the former is experimenting with the "market mechanism" and the latter has taken to new forms of "national planning." This convergence thesis is ideological insofar as it ignores historically unique social configurations that shape the internal and "external" barriers to development. To recognize that all "industrial societies" face more and more problems issuing from the limits of economic nationalism should not confuse these common issues with the basic differences between "industrial systems." Nor should the idea of similarity conceal the presence of the dominant international capitalist system which continues to determine global chances for economic development. If the converging aspects of industrial processes are stressed, there is a tendency to mystify the historical realities that block the creation of wider forms of unification.

In defense of a nonconvergence of industrial processes we can point to the unique barriers emerging within "socialist" and "capitalist" states that illustrate the continued relevance of these concepts. While centralized "socialist" states grapple with the problems of consumption, the "capitalist" states try to control private enterprise and meet the needs of people not integrated into the "affluent society." While socialist nations continue to fail to plan for mutual development, capitalist nations find it increasingly difficult to stimulate economies by state expenditures. Hence social change in each of these industrial processes is still determined by unique configurations of internal barriers to development and external constraints to expansion. Only by retaining both the common and unique components of specific "systems" can we describe the contemporary global system and its dynamics.

While industrial systems and their evolutions are unique, they share a common form of crisis. That is, all advanced industrial societies are committed to the stimulation of economic growth (indicated by GNP, per capita income, and levels of investment) which creates social dislocations that increase the need for social amelioration. Societal planning and organization to increase economic growth has conflicting consequences because the revolutionizing of production deepens the collectivizing trends that uproot communities, individuals, and the environment. In this general sense, the dynamic of all advanced industrial societies recurrently results in a contradiction between the priority of economic growth and its social costs and consequences. It is this contradictory tendency that promotes the extension of bureaucratic organizations to deliver goods and services to those groups that suffer from rapid economic development, e.g., occupational or regional obsolescence. This generally results in the increasing integration of the individual into the web of bureaucratized organizations, concerned with work, education, government services, and so forth, and the resultant growth of "dependent participation"[1] and manipulated consumerism. This trend has led the cultural Marxists (Lukacs, Marcuse, Habermas, et al.) to reconceptualize the objective crisis as a crisis of reified rationalization, "one-dimensionality," and "instrumental rationalization." These reformulations stress the sociocultural consequences of stimulated economic growth that make the work experience and everyday life less intelligible, transforms the human milieu into a technologically determined system, and systematically blocks symbolic communication by the superimposition of more and more technical rules and constraints deriving from rationalizing processes. These new interpretations of Marx's crisis theory are based on the general belief that the economic and the sociopolitical have fused and are no longer conceptualizable within Marx's substructure-superstructure model. The cultural Marxists have accepted the convergence thesis to the extent to which they see the common sociocultural crisis that is moved forward by economically rationalizing capitalist and socialist systems. The critical scope of their analysis is thereby increased and the common constraints that block human development have been illuminated by their penetrating critiques. And yet their formulations may be premature and ungrounded in that they have not attempted to show the specifics of economic development that are unique to capitalism(s) and to socialism(s), and to that extent they have failed to relate their crisis theory to the macrodynamic of societal reproduction.

Capitalist economic growth represents a more severe form of economic rationalization in its tendency toward a greater inequity in the distribution of income which ultimately undermines the relation between demand and real needs. To quote Oskar Lange:

Under Capitalism the distribution of ownership of the ultimate productive resources is a very unusual one, a large part of the population owning only their labor power. Under such conditions demand price does not reflect the relative urgency of the needs of different persons, and the allocation of resources determined by the demand price offered for consumers' goods is far from attaining the maximum of social welfare. While some are starving, others are allowed to indulge in luxury. In a socialist society the incomes of the consumers could be determined so as to maximize the total welfare of the whole population.[2]

A second reason for the severity of capitalist economic growth is the fact that capitalist firms do not calculate the social costs of the "externalities" used in their processes, thereby creating social problems that demand state mediation. Consequently, there is a built-in tendency to misallocate resources and maximize social waste and dislocations in the capitalist mode of economic development. These tendencies are increasingly recognized by contemporary ecological analyses:

. . . the institutionalized system of decision-making in a system of business enterprise has a built-in tendency to disregard those negative effects on the environment that are external to the decision-making unit. . . . Hence, a system of decision-making operating in accordance with the principle of investment for profit cannot be expected to proceed in any way other than by trying to reduce its costs wherever possible and by ignoring those losses that can be shifted to third persons or to society at large.[3]

To the extent that the inequitable distribution of income and capitalist profit-oriented cost-accounting intensifies the conflict between the needs of economic expansion and the needs of the people, there is a tendency for capitalist economic growth to be more severe than other systems in its social costs.

Any analysis of contemporary social reality must begin from this context of objective crisis. Americans in general—and social analysts in particular—appear to have deluded themselves about the basic dynamics of their society for the past two decades. In the years following the Second World War, American society became committed to two interrelated state interventionist mechanisms which, until recently, have effectively concealed the inherent tendency toward crisis within the dynamics of capitalist development. These mechanisms are the growth of state intervention into the private economy to create the necessary conditions for economic growth, on the one hand, and the extension of an administration rationalization of both economic intervention and welfare and income functions of the state on the other. These two phases of state interventionism are both needed more and more to reproduce late capitalism and yet they are increasingly in contradiction with each other. This is the emergent structural tendency of late capitalism, recurrently activating a deeper sociocultural crisis than that of early capitalism.

We will attempt to show here that the crisis theory Marx developed for early capitalism can be supplemented and a deeper structural and sociocultural crisis reconceptualized. In this sense, our analysis tries to show the correlation of Marx's crisis theory with that of the contemporary "cultural" Marxists (Lukacs, Marcuse, Habermas, Lefebvre, etc.). But the cultural Marxist theory must be linked to the unique dynamics of late capitalist development. Whereas we are concerned here with American capitalism, it is also necessary to ground the cultural crisis theory in the macro-dynamics of socialist development. In failing to relate it to the specific macrodynamics of late industrial societies, the cultural Marxist critique is abstract and incomplete. And yet it points the way toward a new critical theory that could conceptualize the socially unnecessary domination of all modern societies.

The Origins of the American Interventionist State

Marx, more than any other social theorist, believed that men *learned* how to control natural and historical processes, including the "economic," but he also argued that the "economic" was inextricably tied into the social totality throughout which certain controls over its processes had unanticipated consequences. For Marx, human consciousness could not only learn to control more effectively, but man could also recognize and struggle to realize new possibilities emergent in higher levels of development. He believed that a comprehension of the self-forming social processes would result in a self-positing class struggle in which social domination would be overcome.

As American capitalism entered the twentieth century, however, it was the leading entrepreneurial elites that were conscious of their objective class position and who struggled to secure their interests in the midst of the general euphoria and false consciousness of the antimonopoly politics of the "progressive" era. It was the *class* conscious sector of American capitalists who saw that the clash of capitalist interests among themselves and against labor endangered sociopolitical stability. The response of this sector involved laying the foundations for systematic corporate-state coordination of political and economic policy making. The dynamics of this process have been reconstructed by William A. Williams in *Contours of American History*. Weinstein and Kolko have fleshed out the process in greater detail. Martin Sklar's thesis of "disaccumulation" has provisionally attempted to place it within the framework of a general theory of capitalist development.

Unfortunately, Kolko takes his analysis as establishing the "exceptionalism" of American capitalism to the social theories of either Marx or Weber. He labels American society a "political capitalism," meaning by this "the utilization of political outlets to attain conditions of stability, predictability, and security—to attain rationalization—in the economy."[4] But Kolko's thesis cannot really yield such a theoretical conclusion. The capacity of corporate capitalists to create and utilize the state for economic advantage is not, in itself, a refutation of Marx. Marx's crisis theory claims only that capitalism cannot resolve recurrent crises and Kolko's analysis merely submits that a new variable has emerged in the history of capitalism—not that the state has decisively resolved the crisis of capitalism. The question pivots, then, on the way in which the emergence and evolution of an interventionist state has mediated the crisis that Marx claimed was ever-renewed by the constitutive dynamic of capitalism.

In the 1907–29 period U.S. capitalism, as interpreted by Sklar, entered a new phase in which expansion of production capacity proceeded increasingly as a function of absolutely declining employment of labor time in goods production. This represented a transition from accumulation to disaccumulation in the real processes of goods production. For Sklar, the growth of state regulation is the result of "the corporate-bourgeoisie's class-determined response to *disaccumulation*." The disaccumulation concept expresses the declining requirement of living labor-time in the immediate production process and hence the development of productive forces beyond social relations determined by the exchange-value (commodity) form of labor power and its products. Where Kolko's analysis of the origins of twentieth-century state interventionism claimed the irrelevance of Marx, Sklar's analysis restores it.

Sklar claims that 1899–1914 was the last great period of accumulationist capitalism.[5] After World War I the absolute number of production workers in farming, manufacture, and railroads declined in the midst of rising production for the first time in American history. As the 1920s proceeded, the growing capacity for material production matched consistent underutilization of this capacity. Rates of investment, as a proportion of the National Income, were lower during the twenties than in the post-Civil War industrializing period. Sklar suggests that the twenties were the turning point in the development of American capitalism. The growth of productivity, the decline of workers and investment rates in the goods production sector, the tendency toward the development of manipulated consumer needs—all are an index to the emergence of the disaccumulation phase of American capitalism. The growing role of the state to "regulate" the economy, on the one hand, and to ameliorate unemployement by "public works," on the other, was the class-conscious response to disaccumulation. In contrast to Kolko, Sklar interprets the new state function as part and parcel of the corporate response to the disaccumulation tendency in general.

Their [the Hoover administration] approach amounted to government-fostered production restriction, secular inflation, and aggressive imperialist expansion, to sustain the flow of profitable investment and capitalist domination of the labor force within the framework of the corporate-industrial system.[6]

Sklar suggests that an adequate capitalist adjustment to the disaccumulation process emerged and developed over the period between the two World Wars. The gradual process of containment of disaccumulation has not been smoothly linear; it is one in which eventually state spending for military production and imperialist expansion, together with increasing production of waste and shoddy goods, needlessly tie capital and labor back into goods production activity.

The formulas for effective state interventionism emerged gradually from the turn of the century through World War II and after. What was needed was a way of using productive capacity without liquidating the exchange-value commodity system of production and distribution. The arms industry serves as a substantial outlet for productive capacity without increasing real income of wage workers at the expense of the property income of the capitalist class. The emergence of disaccumulation leads to the capitalists' reimposition of the accumulation functions within a state-projected framework that decreases the productive capital of society by waste production (e.g., arms). State expenditures involve the realization of surplus value, by tax-enforced purchases from private capital of goods and services that could not otherwise find a market. State expenditures for arms are unproductive for society, but they are essential for the capitalists' realization of surplus value because they absorb labor and provide an outlet for investment that otherwise would be blocked.

But the relation of unproductive state expenditures to the total societal production is the crucial problem. There are two interpretive perspectives—the Keynesian position which sees state intervention as a necessary means for maintaining effective demand and incentive to invest, and the Marxist position which conceives of this intervention as socially contradictory as long as private capital formation is the primary goal. Keynes conceives of production and consumption as societally different problems while Marx tries to relate them. The Marxist position must ultimately claim that increased production of goods for its own sake has societal consequences as a force that blocks disaccumulation and the corresponding development of the production process. The central difference between these two positions pivots on the relationship between the *rationality of state intervention and the reproduction of private accumulation.* The Keynesian position conceives of state intervention as a rational response to growing unemployment and lack of investment possibilities precisely insofar as it restores and reincorporates private accumulation; the Marxist perspective sees state intervention, for just this reason, as a socially irrational means for retarding the disaccumulation process in order to preserve the capitalist social system.

Research confirming the social irrationality of state interventionism is, at present, incomplete.[7] Nonetheless, in the current debates about the social and ecological costs of private economic growth there are numerous studies which document the excessive waste entailed by sustaining "the private enterprize system."[8] Since the empirical evidence for a reformulation of the crisis theory is too diffuse, it is necessary to speculatively construct its rough outlines. The following section should therefore be read as a hypothetical plan that shows how late capitalism has been able to mediate the internal barriers that Marx conceived as contradictory for capitalist development. There is no intent to "deduce" anything from these "laws"—and indeed such a use of Marx's theory would beg the empirical questions that must be studied in order to establish their continued viability. The following extrapolation is used, however, as a speculative reformulation of the crisis theory in its illumination of the emergence and integration of the interventionist state and monopoly capitalism. The variable of the interventionist state is seen, therefore, as the major mediating process that has permitted the ongoing development of American capitalism.

The Structural Crisis of State Monopoly Capitalism (A Speculative Construction)

Marx's model of capitalism postulated competitive conditions and assumed that capitalist development would not totally undermine the law of value. However, monopoly market conditions enable producers to control demand to some extent, too. The discrepancy between monopoly price and value (the labor costs of production) do not permit, then, any general rules, and the original quantitative indicators of the law of value are not therefore operative under monopoly conditions.[9] However, Marx's crisis theory was concerned with the societal processes related to capitalist production and can be used as a guide for the reformulation of the theory under new relations of production. Most importantly, we can hypothesize why capitalist reproduction requires state intervention. But we will try and show that state intervention reflexively promotes centralization of private capital. Hence the structural tendencies that Marx analyzed as the propensity of the rate of profit to fall and the law of increasing economic concentration have become inseparable in the monopoly phase of capitalism. This is because the emergence of a disaccumulation potential necessitated the interpenetration of state and civil society to block its revolutionary social consequences. So, if the "needs" of private capital accumulation, as illuminated by Marx's crisis theory, are hypothetically reconstructed, we can speculate about the structural crisis of late capitalism.

1. The tendency for the rate of profit to fall:

In order to mediate the self-contradictory tendency toward a great mechanization of the goods production sector, at least two conditions must be maintained: first, the constant increase in the productivity of labor and, secondly, the creation of ever greater amounts of surplus value. These goals can be aided by:

    a. State support for education which produces the higher outputs of "educated labor";[10]

    b. State support for research and development which feeds back into capitalist economy in the form of technical innovations which reduce labor *and capital* costs and provide an ever new stream of products.[11]

2. The tendency toward economic concentration:

The market consequences of an economy in which greater economic concentration exists has been the subject for wide inquiry, criticism, and debate.[12] But the social instabilities created by the oligopolistic trend can be partially stabilized by:

    a. Massive state expenditures and planning for the military and aerospace adventures that enable an aggregate demand and investment level to be maintained independent of the flux of market demands on private capital;[13]

    b. As oligopolistic markets do not restructure themselves in the course of periodic economic crises, the massive intervention of the state and the stimulation of a war economy function as a revitalizing force that increases the level of the social productivity of labor;

    c. World-wide surveillance of the "free world" ensures the support of "modernization processes" which permit investment opportunity, new markets, and the internationalization of capital formation processes.

If we reflect on these state functions, however, we begin to recognize that mediation of the structural tendencies analyzed by Marx is not effected cheaply. All of the above state functions entail huge costs which must now be added to the "circulation expenses"[14] of private capital, in that they are the unproductive costs of securing private value production and realization. Insofar as these "circulation costs" are greatly increased, they contradict the societal benefits of a higher productivity of labor.

III: *Toward a Reunification of Critical Theory*

3. The tendency toward increasing misery:

The capacity to mediate this tendency is the improvement of the standard of living in ways which permit the illusion of a trend toward economic equality. Mechanisms that conceal the objective conflict inherent in capitalist development are necessary for the maintenance of social harmony and consumer demand. These goals can be aided by:

a. A labor union movement that exerts a constant demand for higher wages while also functioning as an integrative mechanism for the society by making labor responsive to the needs of capital;[15]

b. Development of a consumerism which sets ever new standards for "the good life" in terms of goods and services—increasingly this "permanent revolution" in commodities and styles requires a massive promotion and advertizing effort;[16]

c. The growth of scientized production processes releases more and more workers from the agricultural and goods production sectors and, despite a growing service sector, the numbers of persons whose income must be maintained by the state has in the last years undergone a rapid expansion. For example, the Brookings Institute Study of the 1972 federal budget shows that incomes maintenance was the most rapidly expanding budget category. In 1960 when the military cost was $80 billion, incomes maintenance was $25 billion; in 1972 incomes maintenance was $85 billion while military remained the same.[17]

Between 1950 and 1960 only one out of every ten new jobs in the U.S. economy was created by private capital.[18] Or as Willard Wirtz reported in the 1964 manpower report, only 5% of the new jobs created between 1957 and 1963 were created by private demand.[19] At the same time, between 1960 and 1970, while the U.S. population increased by 13 percent, the population on welfare increased by 94 percent.[20]

4. The tendency toward increasing severity of crisis:

As the late capitalist accumulation process reaches new levels of productive capacity, while requiring more and more state intervention, the scope of its societal consequences and costs increases. Employment possibilities, allocation of resources for public needs (education, welfare, health, etc.) suffer as a result of the unquestioned primacy of the "free enterprise system." The growing costs of this trend can be mediated by increasing the scope of federal, state, and local government in order to meet both the needs of the government and the needs of the people. But this requires the integration of these economic and ameliorative functions and their "rationalization" by modes of benefit-maximization analysis that becomes more and more necessary for "social planning." New types of fiscal policy therefore permit the state to use the federal budget as a planning mechanism for the balancing of the expenditures that support the economy and those that are for social needs.[21]

Increased state intervention into the economy ($285 billion out of an $860 billion G.N.P. in 1968) to sustain value production results in the ever-growing need for a broader instrumental rationalization of the society guided by the state. Thus, the growth of state intervention is not a neutral system balancing and restructuring.

If we attempt to reconsider the dynamic of late capitalist production, we can begin with the growing divergence between technically necessary, and socially necessary, labor time. This gap is precisely what Sklar is trying to conceptualize with his idea of "disaccumulation" where the potential for reducing labor time and capital input for unit output is becoming more realizable, given the level of development of the means of production. Yet the growth of monopoly markets and state supported "waste production" are so many ways in which the technical composition of capital is inflated (by maintaining more labor inputs than are socially necessary) to maintain a viable value composition of capital. That is, the marginal productivity of capital is ensured by Keynesian pump priming which has, from the Marxist perspective, the socially irrational result of producing unneeded luxury goods that absorb unused capital. In other words, the cost of maintaining monopoly capitalist production in the face of growing disaccumulation requires state enforcement of the primacy of the needs of capital over the social consumption needs (health, housing, urban problems, etc.).[22] To this extent, the Keynesian solution accepts the necessity of blocking the social potentials of disaccumulation in order to retain a capitalist form of economic growth. The crisis of American capitalism is precisely the contradiction between the needs of capitalist profitability and the needs of social consumption.

And yet, ultimately, there is a limit to the scope of state intervention which has been partially conceptualized by James O'Conner's notion of "the fiscal crisis of the state."[23] The fact that the interventionist state is a "poor-house state" provides this limit. It cannot continue to cope with both the needs of the private economy and the needs of the population since its revenues are limited by their source in the tax structure. There is an end to the state's capacity to foot the bills for corporate capitalism—eventually the privileged tax status of the corporate sector must become the source of political conflict. While O'Conner's work is a reapplication of Marx's crisis theory to the conditions of monopoly capitalism, it does not go far enough to show the social contradiction of state interventionist capitalism.

The process of state intervention does not suffer only from lack of resources—it is destructive of resources. The *dynamic* contradiction of late capitalism involves the direct support of waste production thereby retarding the liberating potentials of the disaccumulation process. Rather than seeking new ways of organizing societal production that could meet social needs, the state proceeds on the assumption that stimulating private economic growth is the only way to meet social needs. This assumption is false to the extent to which there is no recognition of the social costs of private capital formation, no assessment of the social waste involved in capitalist state interventionism, and no recognition of the dynamic antagonism of the needs of private capital and the social needs of society. Empirically this dynamic contradiction could be measured in terms of the technically necessary labor time needed for meeting social needs and the artificially extended socially necessary labor time that is now expended to do this. Whereas the competitive phase of capitalist development was revolutionary in its forcing of a correlation between technical and socially necessary labor, state-monopoly capitalism introduces a growing disjuncture between the two. The source of this disjuncture is in what Sklar calls the disaccumulation process, which would, if allowed to develop, undermine the social relations of capital and initiate a new "socialist" relation between production and social needs.

The gap between the technical and socially necessary labor time is structurally related to the emergence of monopoly capitalism where the oligarchic control of markets stops the competitive price mechanism and permits greater concentration and centralization of capital; this retards the accumulation process and promotes a greater pressure toward stagnation than ever before. The capitalist state steps into this context, with its role of the largest consumer of underutilized capital, and supports waste production to such a degree that it produces inflation.[24] A description of the results of monopoly control and state support as the "stagflation" concept of the current state of the American economy indicates the new combination of the classic capitalist tendency toward stagnation and the new state monopoly tendency toward inflation.

The current dilemma of managed capitalism renews, therefore, the relevance of Marx's crisis theory in that the basic problem remains one of appropriating public funds (surplus) to secure private economic growth. American capitalism in the sixties has shown that "built-in stabilizers" produce an inflationary spiral to which the Nixon wage-price freeze was a necessary and escalated response. Yet, numerous apologists for Mr. Nixon's policy admitted that the "new managed capitalism . . . continues to seek inflationary solutions to inflationary problems."[25] Economically, state intervention is now accompanied by inflationary pressures which recurrently result in a liquidity crisis (every year it takes more units of debt to raise the GNP by another dollar). Even if the Nixon wage-price freeze restores enough liquidity, there has been set up a self-contradictory tendency toward a neo-mercantilism that protects American capitalism, no longer able to compete in a "free market." To even hope that the new economic policy will work requires a manipulated revival of patriotism, in which the labor unions have been commanded to play a major role. The costs of maintaining "private enterprise" are now pushed directly onto the consumer and taxpayer.

Therefore, today's capitalism is new only in its unique historical configuration; the basic dynamic that Marx analyzed as deriving from its central contradiction remains the same and reconstitutes the crisis—now on a higher level of development in which the state is a new counteracting and yet reactivating component. Contemporary Marxist analysts who continue to formulate today's objective crisis in political economic terms are merely reapplying Marx's crisis theory to specific historical conditions. In this way, James

O'Conner's identification of the state's fiscal crisis is one way of reformulating the crisis theory. Ernest Mandel, who has made another parallel reformulation of the theory, argues that

The dilemma confronting the state . . . is the choice between crisis and inflation. The former cannot be avoided without intensifying the latter.[26]

Although both of these reformulations stress the political economic indicators to crisis, they also recognize its sociocultural dimensions. The following will attempt to clarify the relationship between these.

The State-Guided Instrumental Rationalization of Society

The growing momentum of human alienation in late capitalism is all the more serious because the source and dynamic of the alienation is not confronted directly. The depth of the crisis of late capitalism may not be recognized by a society that appears to be growing and maintaining an "abundance" for its population. Where the origin and reality of alienation is not recognized, the resultant mode of ideological control of late capitalism constitutes a new type of human domination. While claiming to be the zenith of modern rational society, in reality there is the growth of coercion and various manipulations that derive from an unrecognized and socially unnecessary motive. The crisis of late capitalism is qualitatively deeper insofar as its populations are unaware and uncritical of the forces that further coerce and restrict their life chances.

Contemporary neo-Marxism seems to be gradually converging toward the recognition of a new level and mode of domination. Theorists such as Lukacs, Marcuse, Habermas, Lefebvre, and others, have all emphasized the combination of enforced dependence, cultural manipulation, and growing political powerlessness that comes from the dynamic of late industrial society. These cultural reformulations of the crisis theory have been unable, however, to show the societal dynamic which shapes the objective context of crisis. Many of these theorists have been influenced by Max Weber's more formalistic type of political sociology. While using Weber to broaden their analysis, and despite their immanent critiques of his work, they have not been able to reconnect their cultural criticism to a critique of political economy. Most specifically, they have failed to see the reciprocity of state intervention into the economy on the one hand, and the economic exchange function of the state, on the other.

Today's capitalist state has transformed itself from the ideologically restricted ("free market mechanism") to an expanded penetration of society that permits interest groups of all kinds to represent their "needs" to the "public." This is possible, however, only at the cost of structurally built-in restrictions that narrow the type and nature of needs that can be represented. Where liberal capitalism permitted political representation by constitutionally granting rights to aggregates of *persons*, today's representation is constricted by political institutions that increasingly permit access of needs only in their expression of group interests. (This is what Daniel Bell calls "the growth of group rights" within a "post-industrial society.")[27]

The pluralist model of democracy assumes that all interests have equal access to the government sectors to express their needs. In this model, policies decided ideally follow a pattern of distributive justice in which each interest group is given the measure of justice that it deserves and that is proportional to its size and intensity. In this optimistic vision there is no "ruling class" or repressive political process—only balance of power deliberations in which each interest receives its due.

In opposition to this model, Claus Offe has shown that "consensus formation" begins from a political-economic matrix which delimits or constrains the entire political process of representation.

The pluralistic system of organized interests excludes from the processes concerned with consensus formation all articulations of demands that are general in nature and not associated with any status group; that are incapable of conflict because they have no functional significance for the utilization of capital and labor power; and that represent utopian projections beyond the historically specific system insofar as they do not unconditionally abide by the pragmatic rules of judicious bargaining.[28]

To the extent, then, that the existing process of political consensus formation has internal to it restrictive mechanisms which constrain the types of needs that can be represented and responded to, we must recognize that the *social controls which protect the system priorities are inherent in the political institutions themselves.* The interests of the corporate capitalist sector are not like other interests—their reproduction defines the common system's interest which the political process strives to maintain in a dynamic equilibrium. Consensus formation proceeds, therefore, within a framework that is essentially one of preventive crisis management for corporate capitalism and, to this extent, narrows the nature of political debate to the technical problems of systems maintenance. Consequently, there is a *depoliticizing of politics* which is manifest as:

a national politics which has both parties posturing without joining for debate on issues; manufacturing mass images and construing "democracy" as a plebiscitary decision between sets of administrative appeals. There is no discussion of the dilemmas of the society but rather different packages presented as to how to deliver the services to specific groups.[29]

"Politics" today means the creation of pseudo-issues that can legitimate one administration over its opponent—without involving any of the system's priorities. President Nixon's school busing policy which appeals to the class and race resentments of the population while trying to strengthen his chances for reelection was an example of this. Since there exists evidence that greater spending for black education does not improve it, and that more money goes for busing to maintain segregation than to bring integration seems to be irrelevant to the "political issue."

The very existence of a *political* process is today questionable and it is perhaps more accurately viewed as a planning mechanism for the economy and a service delivery system for the needs of organizable groups. The inflexibility of the federal budget priorities and the limited power that the Congress has over these allocations reveal the regulative nonpolitical character of the American state.[30] Add to this structural inflexibility the further rigidity resulting from decision-making procedures, such as cost-effectiveness or the Planning, Programming, Budgeting System that technically constrain the action of either political party when it comes to power. But perhaps the most serious political distortion is the growth of the nonpublic decision-making procedures of the executive which cannot be checked by the other branches of government. The entire history of the Vietnam war policy, as disclosed by *The Pentagon Papers*, was an example of this, as the authoritarian style of the executive branch, which labeled all persons or groups who questioned the nonpublicness of these decisions as undemocratic, even after repeated instances of deception, is an index of the growing ideological character of American capitalism.

From such tendencies of the American state we must now recognize that the "political" process is a necessary component of late capitalist society. It is equally important as an adjustive and integrative mechanism of the economy (hence, the economy has become politicized) and as a mediation between the needs of the population and the needs of corporate capitalist reproduction (in this sense, the society as a whole has had to adjust to the primacy of economic growth). We have, then, a new social totality which neither meets the analytic separation of the economic and the political (e.g., in Weber), nor corresponds to Marx's crisis theory which conceptualizes capitalism as forcibly separating the factors of value production. The political and the economic have, in a specific way, interpenetrated each other and can no longer be conceptualized as analytically separable. The problem is, now, how to conceptualize the relations and interrelated dynamic of the political and economic processes of late capitalism.

To attempt to express the new configuration in Marx's terms, we could say that the "political" (which is now really a special type of instrumental rationalization) has become both a relation and a factor of production. The capitalist productive process which initially forced a separation of material means and living labor power and resulted in the structural tendencies toward crisis has, during the twentieth century, been reintegrated—not by resolving the capital-labor contradiction, but by generating a self-adjusting state interventionalism whose task is primarily to rationalize the potential conflict between capitalist production and its growing social costs. An acquired system of instrumental rationales has emerged to cope with the conflict between labor and capital.

If the political and economic are inseparably interrelated, the approaches that account for the political process as emergent from the economic must fail in their attempts. We must therefore relinquish analyses that try to define and reconstruct the political in terms of a dominant interest. This is not to say that the current instrumental rationalization has eliminated the structure of capitalist power and privilege or the exploitation and alienation of capitalist accumulation. The point is that the political institutions are institutionalized crisis mediators of economy and society and as such cannot be reduced to the prepolitical economic processes. This argument is made well by Claus Offe:

> If one approaches the empirical power relations obtaining between societal interest groups as an unstable equilibrium kept in balance by the state apparatus, rather than as a prepolitical, natural phenomenon, then the domain of "civil society," with its semblance of autonomy, must be described in terms that bring out its politically mediated nature. In an era of comprehensive state intervention, one can no longer reasonably speak of "spheres free of state interference" that constitute the "material base" of the "political superstructure"; an all-pervasive state regulation of social and economic processes is certainly a better description of today's order. Under these conditions, the official mechanisms sustaining the relationship between the state and society, such as subsidies, co-optation, delegation, licensing, etc., reflect but subtle gradations of political control; as such, they help to maintain the fiction of a clear separation between state and society that has, in fact, become almost irrelevant.[31]

The Marxist economic analysis of "the state," the C. Wright Mills' conception of the "Power Elite," and the numerous variations of conflict and elite analysis are all committed to an approach that attempts to find the basis of power in the socioeconomic distribution of property and influence. From the conflict perspective, the operations of the political institutions can be explained only in terms of their instrumentality to the dominant interests groups. Our new conceptualization would imply, however, that political power cannot be reconstructed in terms of its economic functions; it is a semi-independent sphere to the extent that the political process is now an essential mechanism for maintaining the stability of the social system. But, again, this does not suggest that the political is analytically separable from the economic, or that the domination of capitalism has, in fact, been mediated. It does mean that late capitalism is generating its own contradiction in a new configuration of groups that are increasingly in conflict with the system.

Just as Marx's analysis of early capitalism showed that wage labor and capital were progressively separated by the process of accumulation, so the mediated, yet still objectively contradicted, accumulation process of late capitalism produces aggregates of people whose condition of life can still be conceptualized by the terms "exploitation" and "alienation."[32]

1. State support for high technology industry and services may increase profits but it produces as a by-product a permanent *underclass* that must be maintained by federal, state, and local welfare systems.

2. The growth of the *state* itself has produced a labor sector that now approaches 25 million in all branches of government and associated semipublic industry. These people are making growing wage and welfare demands on the state, whose resources are already overextended.

3. Today's production process, with its expanding need for educated labor, and accelerating status precariousness of the middle classes, generates a *"post-industrial" stratum* of estranged youth, college students, and young workers whose experience of this system leads them to a style of life in which "ripping-off" the system is a central principle. This is the locus of the "new sensibility" that the technocrats are worried about.[33]

4. The *technical intelligentsia* are, of course, produced by a knowledge-dependent society and are expected to accept the priorities of the system. Yet, to the extent to which they are asked to produce waste and planned obsolescence or are constrained in the pursuit and communication of truth by the needs of capital, there is a growing potential for conflict between the scientific intelligentsia and the capitalists. It is a potential which was recognized long ago by Veblen and today seems to be reaching the point of overt conflict.[34]

III: *Toward a Reunification of Critical Theory*

Of course, in traditional terms, all of these groups are part of the "working class" regarding their relation to the means of production. But this criterion is no longer adequate for critical analysis due to the state-monopoly system which has distorted the classic accumulation process. To the relation to production must now be added a sociopolitical criterion of degree of access to the political system which is today an additional element for potential social power.[35] The indices for "class" in state-monopoly capitalism have to be reformulated in line with the fusion and changed relations of the factors and social relations of production. The symmetry of Marx's analysis of the immanent class dynamic of accumulation must now be reconceptualized to account for a new dynamic. The groups listed above are some of the new aggregates produced by the transformed accumulation process. The common source of exploitation and alienation can be clearly reformulated in political economic terms, but their objective power potential is no longer in a one-to-one correspondence to their economic location. Much analysis and political struggle remains to be done before we can link the dialectic of domination to the actual anticipation of enlightenment and emancipation.

Yet consciousness of the intensifying objective contradictions of American capitalism is withheld from these groups by a society that has ended ideology by institutionalizing its repressive power in a "political" process that responds to particularistic needs at the cost of giving up needs that challenge the society's structural configuration. The growing economic exploitation and sociopolitical alienation have been mystified by "the welfare state" system which makes pluralist representation possible at the cost of restricting the scope of needs that could be presented. But even these particularistic needs can be met only partially and in direct correlation with the system's need for the particular group. (For example, the unemployed aerospace scientists and technicians received, by special legislative act, a relief grant that supported them after the federal cut-backs.) However, the very appearance of a political institution that is responsive to particular groups conceals the built-in mechanisms that constrain and block equal political representation. This is the case with the vastly expanded federal, state, and local political system that permits political bargaining about societal conflicts and has stimulated the many minority, regional, occupational, etc., groups to organize themselves in order to assert their special interests; but despite the trend toward more political activity, and conflict between competing interests, the political institution is unable to resolve or meet the needs of these groups. The contradiction inherent in this tendency was discussed in a current editorial in the *Wall Street Journal*:

> What is deeply troubling is that we seem simultaneously to be intensifying conflict and to be weakening our powers of reconciliation. Unless this spiral is broken we risk being torn apart as a nation, with catastrophic consequences for the whole world.[36]

But the dynamic of the society now forces the acceleration of political activity in accordance with the ever-renewed needs of private capital facing stagflation and the growing social dislocations that result from anarchic planning of corporate units. The state must intervene therefore more deeply and more widely and in this way, it is constantly forcing changes in education, welfare, urban problems, and so forth. The interventionist state is the power behind what Jürgen Habermas has called the instrumental rationalization of society; it superimposes more and more technical bureaucratic control over the process of political representation (rendering it a technical ritual that cannot express the primary needs of the society) and constrains everyday life with state-imposed technical rules originating in compromises that are unintelligible to the individual. In this way, both politics and life practice become at the same time more "rationalized" and more irrational from both a societal and a personal standpoint.

Today's technocratic ideology is "beyond ideology," having reduced all utopian components of societal legitimation to the single goal of self-preservation. This technical value is then justified by the various models of "rationality" that now legitimate the management of late capitalism. Hence, legitimation of society is predicated on the promise of survival and mediation of crisis to all those who accept without question the depoliticization of politics and the bureaucratic mystification of the everyday world. Legitimacy is linked to a general technocratic consciousness that sees the social system determined by the immanent logic of scientific and technological progress. From this viewpoint, the logics of technical development are the source of societal constraints and policy decisions, as, for example, in the case of the weapons race which has constantly been perpetuated by a rhetoric which speaks of the technical necessities of our national security system.

Feeding into and reinforcing the growth of this technocratic ideology is the trend toward a policy orientation in the social sciences. The emergence of systems analysis, futurology, the "new political economy," game theory, etc., are all instances of the social scientist's increasing awareness of the technical interest of his field. Another technocratic tendency is the growing demand from the "knowledge industry" and bureaucrats for a system of social accounting. Here, too, the guiding principles are that all "budgets must be balanced, investments must be planned in accordance with profit expectations, and thus human needs are still (conceived as satisfiable only) in relation to effective demand of paying customers."[37] A bill called the Full Opportunity and Social Accounting Act has been introduced in two consecutive sessions of Congress, and the Nixon administration has committed itself to a program of social reports in which the attempt to formulate "national goals" is foremost (July 13, 1969). This continues a tradition which began officially with the 1957 Sputnik-stimulated report, *Goals for Americans*, requested by President Eisenhower.

In a way, the new "rational" ideology is more powerful than that of liberal capitalism since it conceals the practical questions of life and projects no image of the good life. In the so-called value neutrality of the new policy sciences there is assumed a universal value of control of the social system which in practice represses political debate. In a parallel manner the individual's daily life in today's industrial society consists of a series of adjustments to technical imperatives that are presented to him as "natural" conditions of human "survival." Therefore the new ideology and its everyday application results in the repression of communicative possibilities for the individual and the society.

Consequently, there has emerged an entire new field of critical research concerned with the study of "repressive communication." The Frankfurt school's studies of authoritarianism exemplify this new direction for critical inquiry, and systematic exegesis of current research in this area goes beyond our attempt to reestablish the continuity of critical theory.[38]

The Dialectic of Domination and Emancipation

Whereas critical *science* ends with the empirical critique of domination inherent in a specific social context, speculative critique is able to anticipate modes of emancipation. Where the critiques of domination refer to actual inequities, such as alienations and repressions that have been established empirically, the systematic anticipation of emancipation goes beyond this framework and involves a self-positing struggle. There is no "scientific" theory of emancipation in which knowledge of domination can itself supply instrumental means for liberation. This type of linear relationship could result only from an objectivistically based "science," such as "scientific socialism," in which emancipation is defined as the determinate result of objective trends. Such has been the case in the history of socialist class struggle where the end of emancipation—the social ownership of the means of production—is justified by its derivation from the objective necessities of material development. This objectivistic ideal of liberation has resulted in the emergence of state-socialisms that reproduce the domination of capitalist society in another form.

The relation between domination and emancipation is relevant only within a specific context and always involves the mediation of objective institutions by the transformations of the subject. Emancipation therefore implies that self-conscious agents transform themselves in a way that results in the reconstitution of the institutional framework of society—a use of critical theory analogous to that of psychoanalysis. Theory can be used as a general interpretive scheme for the reconstruction of self-development processes that involve domination, but it cannot in itself "force" emancipation. The liberating process requires in addition the elements of propitious circumstances and the patient's own "working-through" of the resymbolized self-experience. If we extend this model to the level of social emancipation we can see how inadequately developed are our conceptions of the necessary conditions for it. This inadequacy is related to the fact that the socialist tradition has usually been accepted as expressing the interest of emancipation in the capitalist epoch. Whereas this tradition did indeed consider social control of production as a universal requisite for the associated goal of man's free development, the dialectic was lost in the actual process of "emancipation." The socialist notion of "class struggle" must now be replaced by a more multi-leveled conception of the struggle against industrial domination.

If we begin from the framework of a unified critical theory, such as the one begun here, we are forced to recognize that the constraints upon optimal development of technological potential are themselves now enveloped in a set of deeper constraints within the character of each individual. The very conception of emancipation requires a new comprehension of the relationship between self-consciousness and social development. Today's job-holder has not only stopped conceiving of himself as part of a social class but he has also accepted the "system" as inherently self-directing. The very idea of regaining control over social institutions and personal development seems abstract. This is the case despite the continued disintegration of bourgeois institutions like the family, schools, and so forth. The creation of adequate conditions for emancipation are tied into a general enlightenment of the population to a much greater degree than radicals usually realize. The struggle against domination begins therefore with the systematic criticism of the basic categories that legitimate industrial domination. In this context the development of a critical scientific community is essential.

But the real process of enlightenment refers to the reinterpretation of their needs by the many people who are currently unable to do so. Thinking about ways in which communicative processes can be stimulated is crucial for the application of theoretical enlightenment to everyday life. Just as corporate state–planning sets up models for the management of resources (including the population), so critical theorists must construct models for the activation of communication about human requirements and the ways in which institutions can be changed to meet them. Black and women's liberation stand here as complex realities that are both exemplary models and constant reminders of the separatist tendency resulting from emancipatory struggles unable to comprehend the possibility of social development. As Alain Touraine has argued, every liberation movement has to resolve the problem of understanding self-identity *and* the dynamic of domination within a resymbolized totality that suggests how self and social development can be actualized together.[39] Failure to comprehend this leads to a separatism that holds to the illusion that emancipation is possible independent of the system. Often this is the end of the liberation process and the beginning of "co-optation."

Although "class consciousness" may be part of this deeper understanding of the common source of domination it can no longer be considered an adequate conceptualization. While location within the economic system remains central to economic and political exploitation and alienation, the social cultural dislocations and reifications form a context in which consciousness is disrupted by more complex relations. Persons who have developed in a society where hierarchical organizations, institutionalized possessive individualism, and technologically altered perceptional experience are part of everyday life are not able to comprehend self and other in terms of class position. Class consciousness is not enough.[40] Finally, emancipated consciousness must achieve the spontaneous reintegration of imagination and perception, and the capacity to relearn and reinterpret within novel situations. It may be that spontaneous reinterpretation of needs and the restoration of social community have always been the authentic revolutionary self-positing of those dominated by a state industrial system. In this case "revolution" is taken to mean the social revolution that transforms social institutions into meaningful patterns of cooperation able to facilitate communicative conditions for man's individuation.

It is necessary to reopen the question left unanswered by the socialist tradition in both theory and practice: What are the processes that can create a social system in which individual and social development can be reconciled without generating a highly centralized and authoritarian system? This question cannot be approached theoretically, but requires a deeper understanding of historical processes. "Working class history" must be broadened to include the entire spectrum of human claims for liberation in the industrial epoch. All attempts to create workers' councils, workers' participation, utopian communities, alternative cultural experiences, and so on, must be reconstructed to understand the story behind contemporary struggles for emancipation. Rather than assume that a concept of emancipation can be derived deductively from theory we must recognize it can be reconstructed only from the experience of the masses who have been trying to liberate themselves from industrial domination for centuries. This story has not been told and socialists do not have the secret in their theory. No self-selected vanguard can express the goals or in any sense "make" the preconditions for revolutionary change by the use of instrumental Marxist-Leninist science. It is important to realize that criticism of domination inherent in state socialism escapes the categories of such a "science" and its claim to be an instrument of emancipation is a basic failure to recognize the dialectic between the critique of domination and the self-positing struggle of emancipation. Theory can become a "material force" only as a part of the communicative process in which the discussions about needs and desires results in a transformed political and everyday practice. But in this sense theorists learn from this communicative process and while they are essential for its symbolic expression they cannot determine its outcome. Hence the ability to hear and to see what is happening in current liberation movements is probably more "radical" than any strategy now conceived. These existing movements are the living laboratory for understanding the possibilities for emancipation. Enlightenment will derive from the comprehension of these movements within a reconstruction of human history. Although the critique of domination can provide the scheme for a general interpretation of the present, creation of the conditions for emancipation goes beyond the reach of this theory and demands a participation in the process of liberation itself. Whereas critical theory can construct models for political struggle, the materials for these models can come only from the actual historical experience of the people who now embody the hope for freedom.

Despite today's mushrooming repression, it is clear to anyone who travels around this country that an American "revolution" (i.e., major structural changes) is the unfinished business of our civilization. Claims for emancipation from unnecessary corporate and state controls are found in every sector and region of the country. While not generally recognizing the common source of their domination and perceiving no general possibilities for a real politics, those calling for reform could be mobilized in many more ways than the traditionalist realizes. Every space, service, or institution that can be enclosed and neutralized from repressive penetration is a new beginning for the creation of values and persons that are not co-optable by the system. The political forms through which major structural changes can be won are not yet clear but the "long march" through the institutions has begun and contradicts the despair of those who long for the "energy" of the 1960s.

The dynamic for this decentralizing communal movement comes from an "overdetermined" set of objective possibilities. First the economic crisis of the state capitalist system enforces an instrumental rationalization process that promotes social-political centralization and a resultant social de-institutionalization; community struggles to reinterpret local needs are made possible by this dynamic.

Given the closure of the political sphere by state-guided instrumental rationalization, the viability of electoral politics as an agency for radical social change is blocked at present. However, in the contradictory social consequences of this new dynamic there is a negative dialectic that shapes an objective possibility for social change. Insofar as the structural tendency of advanced industrial society involves a contradiction that limits its capacity to meet the deepening needs of the population, there is a constant reshaping of the crisis of everyday life. General needs, such as health, education, welfare, environmental conditions—that can only be partially and inequitably met by the state—provide a social space for emancipatory movements.

III: *Toward a Reunification of Critical Theory*

Despite electoral image-making and the sectarian left's incantations to the working class, there are many who have begun to build a new social base for social change.[41] Reacting against hierarchical control and the institutional bad faith of the dominant society, persons in every occupation throughout the United States are creating new, or trying to regain control of existing, social forms to overcome domination. Aware of the inadequacy of bureaucratic structures and services, thousands of people, largely without awareness of their solidarity, are turning to the building of a communitarian movement which is striving to restore control of production and a social community. The free schools, clinics, food co-ops, the urban community control movements, ecology and alternative technology are but a few examples of this movement.

Critical theory begins in this context and is confronted by problems posed by the dialectics of domination and emancipation. In view of the present need of the communal movement for scientific aid, the relevance of a critical university setting cannot be underestimated. Rather than assume that the meaning of "radical education" is to subvert the education process, *there is a need to actualize it by a serious engagement with the self-formation of a critical intelligentsia.*[42] (But the limitations of a liberation movement confined to the context of the university are well known, and all possible bridges between the university and the sociocultural struggles for emancipation should be realized.)

The extension of a genuine liberation movement requires the utilization of many talents, skills, and techniques for labor and capital saving that are now identified with the strategies of corporate capitalism. Unless the people's needs can be responded to by the creation of alternative planning systems and technologies of all kinds it is unlikely that the effort can survive. Therefore, the innovation of ways of relating science and technological systems to the goal of restoring community control of production and social relations is a crucial problem.[43] Until loose federations of communities, collectives, unions, and so forth, learn how to use expertise in finding efficient high technology—low cost techniques for the planning of struggles against local domination—the chance for a genuine movement for social liberation is impeded. Groups such as those in Madison, Cambridge, Berkeley, Santa Barbara, Canyon, etc., that are thinking about how to create local institutions as the base from which a local politics can be generated are the experiments that may show the way. Only a self-conscious experimental praxis can create the models of social development that are capable of reducing control of the dominant system over human life. The timetable for this project cannot and should not be anticipated. The means is the end. The apocalyptic politics and the radical establishment of the 1960s must be overcome in a reordering of emancipatory priorities.

NOTES
AND
INDEX

Notes

Introduction

1. See Jürgen Habermas, Chapters 4–6 in *Toward a Rational Society* (Boston: Beacon Press, 1971). This general perspective is systematically applied by Claus Offe in "Political Authority and Class Structure" in *The International Journal of Sociology*, Spring, 1972.

2. See the discussion of the pathology of the Vietnam war in *Social Policy*, Sept. 1972. For a more generalized analysis of the ideological function of social science see Hans Peter Dreitzel's "Social Science and the Problem of Rationality: Notes on the Sociology of Technocrats" in *Politics and Society*, Winter, 1972.

3. See *The Wall Street Journal*, April 4, 1972, for an assessment of the sources of the American drug problem. It ends with a quixotic plea for a moral reconstruction requiring a religious, charismatic revival. After reflecting on the institutional and structural forces that reproduced the drug problem—privatization of life (i.e., deprivative isolation), growing irrelevance of institutional goals for personal life, etc.—the authors' only recommendation was the abstract anticipation of a moral reconstruction. Social scientists who are unable to confront the structural forces that reproduce conditions leading to "social problems" seem to be part of the problem rather than its solution. This point is made more concretely and provocatively by David Halberstam in *The Best and The Brightest* (New York: Random House, 1972), and Noam Chomsky in *American Power and the New Mandarins* (New York: Pantheon, 1969); both document the incredible "reality gap" between the technical recommendations of scientific estates and the actual events of the 1960s.

4. For example Alvin Gouldner's *The Coming Crisis in Western Sociology* (New York: Basic Books, 1970), or Robin Blackburn's *Ideology in Social Science* (London: Fontana/Collins, 1972).

5. See D. Hymes' (ed.) *Reinventing Anthropology* (New York: Pantheon, 1972)—especially the papers by Hymes and Stanley Diamond—for discussions of the ways in which scientific knowledge is used against peoples. See also Paul Goodman's attempt to communicate this to the National Security Industrial Association in *The New York Review of Books*, 23 Nov. 1967.

6. See Gundar Frank "The Sociology of Development and the Underdevelopment of Sociology," in *Catalyst* #3, Summer 1967, pp. 20–73.

7. This euphoria is expressed poetically by one of Max Weber's most important American followers: "The 20th century Revolution in science and technoculture now moving across the world involves the likelihood of a near total reconstruction of the received sensory, electronic and political environments. . . . In the end, the accelerated advance and universal collectivization, of intelligence, information and insight, upon which all parties to the conflicts are depending—whether they say so, know so, or not—all point to Universal Algebra." Benjamin Nelson, "Scholastic Rationales of Conscience, Early Modern Crises of Credibility and the Scientific Technocultural Revolutions of the 17th and 20th Centuries," in *Journal for the Scientific Study of Religion* VII Fall, pp. 155–177.

8. The present volume attempts to disprove this simplistic attitude by showing that extension of science and technology, as well as the "problems" analyzed by social science, do not proceed from the inherent needs of peoples or institutions but develops in a one-sided partisan manner that reinforces the existing power configurations. Only a critical reexamination of the meaning of "knowledge," "science," "freedom," and "necessity" will restore the societal conditions for the actualization of a social science that can contribute to human enlightenment and emancipation rather than growing disenchantment and domination.

9. See Bertram M. Gross, "Planning in an Age of Social Revolution," in *Annals*, May–June, 1971, p. 260ff.

10. Daniel Bell, "Notes on the Post-Industrial Society: I and II," in *The Public Interest*, Winter and Spring, 1967, # 6 & 7.

11. Kenneth Boulding, *The Meaning of the Twentieth Century* (New York: Harper & Row, 1967).

12. Zbigniew Brzezinski, *Between Two Ages: America in the Technetronic Age* (New York: Viking Press, 1970).

13. Kenneth Galbraith, *The New Industrial Society* (Boston: Houghton Mifflin, 1967).

14. See the October 17, 1969 *Wall Street Journal* editorial article on the "Mindless Market." "Mindless" does not refer to its self-regulating nature as the early Adam Smith implied by his "invisible hand" metaphor, but to the *need for regulation* of the market in order to bring about better response to the "technical imperatives" of our time.

15. William Leiss, "The Consequences of Technological Progress: Critical Comments on Recent Theories," in *Canadian Public Administration*, Sept. 1970, p. 255.

16. This thesis is systematically developed in chapter 7.

17. See J. Habermas, *Knowledge and Human Interest* (Boston: Beacon Press, 1970)—especially the appendix.

18. See Edmond Husserl, *The Crisis of European Sciences and Transcendental Phenomenology* (Evanston: Northwestern University Press, 1970).

19. See Martin Heidegger, *Zeit und Sein* (Niemeyer: 1935); also Werner Marx, *Heidegger and the Tradition* (Evanston: Northwestern University Press, 1971).

20. See J. Habermas, op. cit.

21. H. G. Gadamer, "The Critique of Reason," in *Man and World*, June, 1970.

22. This central thesis is developed in part two.

23. This thesis is developed in chapter 3.

24. The exposition of Hegel's contribution to critical theory is found in Chapters 1 and 3.

25. The development of Marx's reformulation of critical theory is found in Chapters 2 and 5.

26. See the excellent critique of Marx in Albrecht Wellmer's *Critical Theory of Society* (New York: Herder and Herder, 1971).

27. For a criticism of mechanical Marxism see Roger Garaudy, *The Crisis in Communism: The Turning Point in Socialism* (Grove Press, 1970); also Murray Bookchin, *Post-Scarcity Anarchism* (Berkeley: Ramparts Press, 1970).

28. See Chapters 3, 6 and 7.

29. This argument is developed in Chapter 7.

1. Pre-Modern Origins and Hegel's Theory of Cultural Alienation

1. See Arthur Lovejoy, *The Great Chain of Being* (New York: Harper & Row, 1960).

2. This history is treated in *Alienation and the Dialectical Paradigm,* the author's Ph.D. dissertation, Graduate Faculty of the New School for Social Research, 1968. However, the stimulation to pursue the topic derives from conversations with Noel Brann of the University of Maryland. Dr. Brann's as yet unpublished Ph.D. dissertation, *On the Renaissance Passion of Melancholy,* Stanford University, 1965, deals with the topic of Section 4 of this chapter in much greater depth and scholarly detail.

3. The most relevant history of the idea is offered by Nathan Rotenstreich, "On the Ecstatic Sources of the Concept of Alienation," in *The Review of Metaphysics,* vol. 16, 1963, which he expanded in his later *Basic Problems of Marx's Philosophy* (New York: Bobbs-Merrill, 1965).

4. Rotenstreich's essay in *The Review of Metaphysics,* op. cit., pp. 551–552.

5. . . . and at first a shudder runs through him and again the old awe steals over him; then looking upon the face of his beloved as to a god he reverences him, and if he were not afraid of being thought a downright madman, he would sacrifice to his beloved as to the image of a god: then while he gazes on him there is a sort of reaction, and the shudder passes into an unusual heat and perspiration; for as he receives the effluence of beauty through the eyes, the wing moistens and he warms. . . . During this process the whole soul is all in a state of ebullition and effervescence. . . . *The Dialogues of Plato,* translated by Jowett (New York: Random House, 1920), vol. 1, pp. 249–254.

6. This is illustrated by the accounts of Aristodemus and Alcibiades, in the *Symposium,* of Socrates' "trances" which are to be accepted as evidence of his "other-worldliness."

7. Erwin Rohde, *Psyche*, vol. II (New York: Harper and Row, 1966), p. 259.

8. The source of this doctrine is in *Problemata XXX, 1*, which is today questioned as an authentic part of Aristotle's work. (Thus Walter Muri's "Melancholic und Schwarze Galle" in *Museum Helveticum X* 1953 attributes it to Theophrastus.) But until recently scholars thought it was Aristotle's. See Klibansky, Panfsky and Saxl, *Saturn and Melancholy* (London: Thomas Nelson, 1964).

9. This dilemma has become a part of the interpretation of Albrecht Dürer's etching "Melancholia I" which depicts an "ecstatic" who is sitting in what can only be a state of melancholy, surrounded by scientific instruments as well as symbols of "the closed world." See Erwin Panofsky's *Albrecht Dürer* (Oxford: The Clarendon Press, 1948), I, p. 165.

10. See Noel Brann, op. cit.

11. Klibansky, et. al., op. cit., pp. 262–263.

12. Ibid., p. 259.

13. The commentary on the *Ion* is found in the P. O. Kristeller facsimile of the *Theologica platonica* by Marsilio Ficino (Torino, 1962).

14. Quoted in Brann, op. cit.

15. It is important to mention that the word "melancholia" does not appear in Ficino's Commentary on Plato's *Ion*; it appears in the *De vita* where Ficino is again analyzing the poet-priest but this time as a foremost melancholic type. See Klibansky, et. al., op. cit., p. 68ff.

16. Ficino's analysis of Socrates appears in his commentary on the *Phaedrus*. An English translation exists: See Sears Jayne *University of Missouri Studies XIX, 1* (1944).

17. Brann argues that it is not:

Whereas the Platonic *furor divinus* seems to signify a harmonization of the sensual disturbances on the lower level and the agitation of the soul to the higher levels of the spiritual hierarchy, the *furor melancholicus* appears conversely to signify an alienation from the higher levels into the disturbances of the lower sensual levels. Though Ficino effectively fuses these two versions of the spiritual "alienatione" according to the Platonic scheme of "amor copia" and "amor inopia," he does not effectively identify them. . . . It should be noted that the *furor amatorius* comprises the nadir. Nor does the embodiment of both these states at once in Socrates resolve the dilemma. On the contrary it seems to present a new one. If Socrates is "ne commotus quidem animo," according to the tranquil ideal of "amor copia," a logical difficulty presents itself in which a melancholy Socrates by virtue of his corporal existence is at the same time a prime example of "Stoic" tranquility by virtue of his spiritual existence.

18. The account of this history is made effectively by Klibansky, et. al., op. cit.

19. Another illustration of this distinction is St. Teresa of Avila (1515–1582) who distinguishes between "a rapture which is called ecstacy" and a "false rapture" which deluded her nuns (at the convent of St. Joseph) when

they allowed themselves to be carried away by "impetuous longings after our Lord, which they were not able to control." *The Foundations,* translated by David Lewis (London, 1913), p. 51ff.

20. Wm. James, *Varieties of Religious Experience* (New York: Modern Library, 1958), pp. 128–29, 136–37.

21. Giordano Bruno, *The Heroic Frenzies,* translated by Paul Eugene Memmo, Jr. (Chapel Hill: The University of North Carolina Press, 1966), p. 135.

22. This is from Hegel's first published writing in 1801. Quoted in Walter Kaufmann's *Hegel: A Reinterpretation* (Garden City: Anchor, 1966), pp. 49–50.

23. Quoted in Kaufmann, ibid.

24. Hegel, *The Philosophy of Right,* translated by Tom Knox (Oxford: Clarendon Press, 1952), p. 11.

25. Hegel, *Phenomenology* (New York: MacMillan, 1961), p. 289.

26. Ibid., p. 10.

27. Hegel, *Philosophy of Right,* op. cit., p. 12.

28. W. Kaufmann, *Commentary on Hegel* (Garden City: Doubleday, 1965), pp. 116–17.

29. Ibid., pp. 40–50.

30. Hegel, *The Philosophy of Right,* op. cit., p. 226.

31. Ibid., p. 26.

32. Ibid., p. 26.

33. Hegel, *Phenomenology,* op. cit., p. 514.

34. Hegel, *On Christianity* (New York: Harper and Row, 1961).

35. Ibid., pp. 140–41.

36. Ibid., p. 294.

37. Ibid., p. 301.

38. Ibid., p. 251.

39. Ibid., p. 261.

40. Ibid., p. 312.

41. Ibid., p. 296. The notion of "spiritual causality" is the unique causality referred to above as the "causality of fate."

42. See Max Scheler, *Man's Place in Nature* (New York: Noonday Press, 1962), but most specifically Ernst Cassirer's essay, "Spirit and Life," appended to *The Philosophy of Ernst Cassierer,* P. A. Schilpp, ed. (Evanston: Library of Living Philosophy, 1949).

43. See footnote #25, Chapter 3 for a discussion of Dilthey.

44. See Kaufmann, *Commentary,* op. cit., p. 44.

45. Hegel, *The Phenomenology of Spirit* (1807) (New York: MacMillan, 1961).

46. Ibid., 135.

47. Ibid., p. 252.

48. For example, in *The Divided Self* (New York: Pantheon, 1969), R. D. Laing develops some of the implications of Hegel's analysis. Also, Helm Stierlin's "The Dialectic of Related Loneliness" in *Psychoanalysis and the Psychoanalytic Review,* Winter, 1965, picks up Hegel's analysis and uses it for an inquiry into the structure of human experience.

49. See Hannah Arendt, *Between Past and Present* (New York: Meridian, 1961), pp. 143–171.

50. See M. B. Foster, *The Political Philosophies of Plato and Hegel* (Oxford: At the Clarendon Press, 1935), for a critical comparison of the relationship of Hegel and Plato.

51. See Hans Jonas, *The Phenomenon of Life* (New York: Harper and Row, 1966), pp. 211–234 for a treatment of the topic of "cosmos" and its importance in Western thought.

52. Hegel's use of the term "leap" in the preface of the *Phenomenology* is a crucial parallel to Marx's "leap into freedom."

53. Hegel, *History of Philosophy*, op. cit., vol. I, pp. 150–152.

54. Ibid., p. 153.

55. Quoted in Marcuse's *Reason and Revolution* (Boston: Beacon Press, 1964).

56. Hegel's *Phenomenology*, op. cit., p. 73.

57. Ibid.

2. Marx's Critique of the Alienation of Work

1. Schlomo Avineri, *The Social and Political Thought of Karl Marx* (New York: Cambridge University Press, 1968).

2. C. D. Easton and K. H. Guddat (eds.), *Writings of the Young Marx on Philosophy and Society* (New York: Doubleday, 1967), pp. 400–401.

3. In this chapter I am stressing the more dialectical formulations of Marx, not attempting to reconcile them with the more mechanical aspects.

4. See Georg Simmel, *Die Philosophie des Geldes*, 2nd ed. (Berlin: Duncker & Humblot, 1907).

5. See George Lukacs, "Reification and the Consciousness of the Proletariat," *History and Class Consciousness* (Cambridge, Mass.: M.I.T. Press, 1968), who rediscovered it.

6. Marx, *Capital*, Vol. I, Chapter 7, p. 178.

7. Ibid., p. 178.

8. See Easton and Guddat, op. cit., p. 143ff.

9. See David McLellan, *Marx Before Marxism* (New York: Harper & Row, 1970), p. 95.

10. Ibid., p. 103ff.

11. See Avineri, op. cit., p. 25.

12. This theme was developed by Jürgen Habermas in his *Strukturwandel der Offentlichkeit* (Nenwied: Luchterhand, 1968).

13. These formulations of the purpose of critique, as against criticism, abound in the writing and letters of the 1843–1848 period. (See Easton & Guddat, op. cit., pp. 211–15, 249–264, etc.)

14. These presuppositions revealed by Marx's reflections have been given a systematic exposition in C. P. McPherson's *The Theory of Possessive Individualism* (New York: Oxford University Press, 1964).

15. Thus, the interesting critique of Marx's theory of labor, as developed by Hannah Arendt in *The Human Condition* (Garden City: Doubleday,

1959), Chapter 5, was anticipated by Marx himself in these early manuscripts. Arendt is misled by the organic metaphors when she argues that Marx reduces work to the natural processes of labor. But as the last section of her chapter shows, she is in part right in her assertion that action is reduced to an analogue of work.

16. The source of these reflections is again the work of the 1843–48 period.

17. While he began this analysis in the early manuscripts, Marx completed these investigations only toward the end of the ten-year interval between 1848–1857 in a series of essays and monographs called the *Grundrisse der Kritik der politischen Ökonomie.*

18. These transcendentally-formulated conceptions of communism and free human production are found in the early manuscripts. See Easton and Guddat, op. cit., p. 264ff.

19. Marx, *Capital,* I. p. 80.

20. Marian Bowley, "Some 17th Century Contributions to the Theory of Value," *Economica,* May 1963.

21. Marx, *Capital,* Vol. I, p. 41. See also letter to Engels, August 24, 1867, where he claims the best in *Capital* to be the distinction between the two-fold character of labor and the treatment of surplus value.

22. For the development of this structural argument, see Chapter 7 below.

23. *Capital,* op. cit., p. 47.

24. Karl Marx, *Text zu Methode und Praxis, III: Der Mensch in Arbeit und Kooperation,* (Aus den *Grundrisse*) (Hamburg: Rowohlt, 1967), pp. 88–89.

25. See Raya Dunayevskaya, *Marxism and Freedom* (New York: Twayne, 1958).

26. An excellent analysis of the inner ambiguity of Marx on this question appears in Albrecht Wellmer's *The Critical Theory of Society,* op. cit.

27. Stanley Moore, *Three Tactics: The Background in Marx* (New York: Monthly Review Press, 1963).

28. For example see Friedrich Engels, "Critique of a Draft for the Erfurt Program."

29. Karl Marx's letter to Domela-Niewenhuis, February 22, 1881, in Hal Draper (ed.) Karl Marx and Friedrich Engels, *Writings on the Paris Commune* (New York: Monthly Review Press, 1972).

30. Hal Draper (ed.) ibid., p. 76.

31. See Martin Buber's analysis in *Paths in Utopia* (Boston: Beacon Press, 1958); Murray Bookchin's critique of Marxist centralism in *Post Scarcity Anarchism* (Berkeley: Ramparts Press, 1971); Hannah Arendt's *On Revolution* (New York: Viking, 1962), especially Chapter 6.

32. See Bookchin, op. cit., pp. 149–220.

33. Hegel, *Lectures on the History of Philosophy* (London: Kegan Paul, Vol. I 1892–5) p. 150.

34. Hegel, *The Philosophy of Right,* op. cit., p. 53.

35. See Henri Lefebvre, *The Sociology of Marx* (New York: Pantheon, 1968), p. 45.

36. Quoted in Kaufmann, *Hegel: A Reinterpretation* (New York: Anchor Books, 1966), pp. 49–50.

3. *Transcendental Reflection and Positivism*

1. H. Marcuse, *Reason and Revolution* (Boston: Beacon Press, 1960), p. 16.
2. J. Habermas, *Knowledge and Human Interest*, op. cit., p. 68.
3. Immanuel Kant, *The Critique of Pure Reason*, trans. Norman Kemp Smith (New York: St. Martin's Press, 1961), pp. 152–54.
4. F. Hegel, *The Phenomenology of Mind*, op. cit.
5. Klaus Hartmann, "Taking the Transcendental Turn," *Review of Metaphysics*, December 1965.
6. These arguments are reconstructed in a precise manner in Jürgen Habermas, op. cit.; also see Josef Maier, *On Hegel's Critique of Kant* (New York: AMS Press, 1966).
7. Habermas, op. cit.
8. See Chapter 1 for development of Hegel's method of cultural critique.
9. Contemporary positivists have begun to see that Kant's problematic is central to the subject they are analyzing. See P. F. Strawson, *Individuals. An Essay in Descriptive Metaphysics*, (London: Methuen and Co. 1959).
10. See Leszek Kolakowski, *The Alienation of Reason: A History of Positivist Thought* (New York: Doubleday, 1968).
11. See Alvin Gouldner, *The Coming Crisis in Western Sociology*, op. cit.
12. M. Mandelbaum, *History, Man and Reason* (Baltimore: The Johns Hopkins Press, 1971), p. 11.
13. Mandelbaum, ibid., p. 12.
14. See Georg Henrik von Wright, *Explanation and Understanding* (Ithica: Cornell University Press, 1971), pp. 8–11; and Albrecht Wellmer's *Critical Theory of Society* (New York: Herder & Herder, 1971), pp. 13–16ff.
15. See Wellmer, ibid.
16. Hemple, "Problems and Changes in the Empiricist Criterion of Meaning," in *Aspects of Scientific Explanation* . . . (New York: Free Press, 1965).
17. Wellmer, op. cit.; Habermas, op. cit.
18. See Ernst Cassirer, *The Problem of Knowledge* (New Haven: Yale University Press, 1950), pp. 41–42, 85–87.
19. Jürgen Habermas, op. cit., pp. 67–90.
20. Ibid., pp. 87, 330.
21. A. Cicourel, *Method and Measurement in Sociology* (New York Free Press, 1964), especially Chapter 1.
22. For example Martindale's statement, "It is unfortunate that Weber never developed his methodology apart from the theoretical and philosophical issues . . . ," is a typical American attitude; see *The Nature and Types of Sociological Theory* (Boston: Houghton Mifflin, 1960), p. 380.

23. Heinrich Rickert, *Kulturwissenschaft und Naturwissenschaft* (Leipzig: Mohr, 1899).

24. The distinction between act-meaning and action-meaning made by Abraham Kaplan in *The Conduct of Social Inquiry* (Chicago: Chandler Press, 1964), is a useful interpretation of Weber's distinction between value and motivational interpretations.

25. For Dilthey the movement of interpretation is circular: in going from "outer" to "inner" we presuppose some common whole (e.g., language, knowledge of societal norms, etc.), which makes it possible for us to grasp the relations of the symbolic representation. Some whole must precede the part but an understanding of part immediately has implications for our grasp of the whole. This rather trite-sounding concept, which Dilthey calls the "circle of interpretation," and later writers call the "hermeneutic circle," is actually a transcendental reflection upon the subjective conditions which made interpretive understanding possible. Dilthey's application of it is best illustrated by his discussion of the problems of writing an autobiography. Here the "object" studied and the interpreter are one and the same and thus there is a maximum access to the "data." For Dilthey autobiography is a model for all human sciences. This interpretation of Dilthey is based on his last essays (edited by B. Groethuyen in 1926 as Vol. VII of Dilthey's *Gesammalte Schriften*). Their linkage to Hegel was pointed out by Albert Salomon in his course on Wilhelm Dilthey (Spring semester, 1964) at the Graduate Faculty of the New School. A selected English translation of parts of these essays is to be found in H. P. Rickman's *Wilhelm Dilthey: Pattern and Meaning in History* (New York: Harper & Row, 1961). The essay which is most important for the development here is "The Construction of the Historical World in Human Sciences."

26. See Habermas, op. cit., Chapters 7 and 8. Habermas is concerned primarily with the relations of hermeneutic logic to the logic of induction in the natural science, on the one hand, and to the development of one-sided hermeneutic logic in phenomenology and analytic philosophy on the other. The same concern is shared by Karl-Otto Apel, whose recently translated *Analytic Philosophy of Language and the Geisteswissenschaften* (New York: The Humanities Press, 1967), documents the convergence of these traditions.

27. The concept of "cognitive interest" derives from Kant. See Habermas, op. cit., chapter 9.

28. See T. Parsons, *The Structure of Social Action* (New York: Free Press, 1949), chapter 16.

29. Max Weber, *Aüfsatze zur Wissenschaftslehre* (Tubingen, 1922), pp. 189, 193, 214.

30. Parsons, op. cit.

31. See Jürgen Habermas's "Zur logik der Sozialwissenschaft," in *Philosophische Rundschau*, February 1967.

32. The elements of a systematic critique of Weber had already been expressed by Adorno in his 1947 statement entitled "Soziologie und Empirische Forschung," and in Jürgen Habermas's 1963 essay, "Analytische Wissenschaftstheorie und Dialektik." These and later responses by Karl Popper, Hans Albert, Ralf Dahrendorf, et al., were collected and published in

1969 by Luchterhand under the title *Der Positivismusstreit in der Deutschen Soziologie*; an English translation of this volume has been under way for some time. Perhaps the most informed discussion of this debate is George Lichtheim's essay, "Marx or Weber: Dialectical Methodology," which now appears in his new collection, *From Marx to Hegel*, (New York: Herder and Herder, 1971), pp. 200–219.

33. The Lowith and Mommsen critiques of Weber appear in Dennis Wrong (ed.), *Max Weber* (Englewood Cliffs: Prentice-Hall, 1970); the Marcuse and Habermas critique appear in Otto Stammer, *Max Weber and Sociology Today* (New York: Oxford University Press, 1971).

34. See George Lukacs, *History and Class Consciousness*, op. cit.

35. Whereas a critique of Marcuse is found in chapter 6, the most interesting critique of Sartre is in Jürgen Habermas, *Theorie und Praxis* (Frankfurt: Suhrkamp, 1971), which will be published in translation by Beacon Press.

36. See L. Althusser, *For Marx* (New York: Pantheon, 1969), or *Reading Capital* (with Etienne Balibar) (New York: New Left Books, 1970). For a penetrating critique of Althusser see John Gerassi, "Reading Althusser," in *The New Left Review*, #65.

37. Discussion of this complex logical issue is developed in Gotthard Gunther, *Idee und Grundrisse einer nicht-Aristotelischen Logik*, Verlag von Felix Meiner, 1959.

4. *The Dialectical Foundations of Critical Theory: Jürgen Habermas's Metatheoretical Investigations*

1. For example, the critical articles of Goran Therborn in the *New Left Review*, #63 and #67.

2. Max Horkheimer, "Traditional and Critical Theory," in *Critical Theory*, 2 vols. (New York: Herder and Herder, 1973).

3. Albert Wellmer, *The Critical Theory of Society* (New York: Herder and Herder, 1970), p. 14.

4. See Martin Jay's forthcoming book on *The Dialectical Imagination*, (New York: Littlejohn & Co., 1972), which was initially a Harvard Ph.D. dissertation in history presented in 1971. One of the many excellent aspects of this study is Jay's constant documentation of the changing political consciousness of the Frankfurt School members.

5. Wellmer's book, op. cit., develops this critique of Marx's secret positivism in a brilliant fashion.

6. See George Lichtheim, *From Marx to Hegel* (New York: Herder and Herder, 1971), p. 174ff.

7. The main theoretical works in Habermas's developing corpus are *Theorie und Praxis: Sozialphilosophische Studien* (Neuwied: Luchterhand, 2nd ed. 1967); *Erkenntniss und Interesse* (Frankfurt: Suhrkamp, 1968), and the yet unpublished *Towards a Communication Theory of Society*, presented at the Christian Gauss Lectures at Princeton University in the Spring of 1971. See Jürgen Habermas, "Zur Logik der Sozialwissenschaft," *Philo-*

sphische Rundschau, February, 1967, for a critique of hermeneutics and linguistics. For the critique of systems theory which is currently creating a sensation in Germany, see J. Habermas and N. Luckmann's *Theorie der Gesellschaft oder Sozialtechnologie—was leistet die Systemforschung?* (Frankfurt: Suhrkamp, 1971).

8. See T. Adorno's *Zür Metakritik der Erkenntnisstheorie*, or Jürgen Habermas's essay, "Knowledge and Human Interests," which appears as an appendix to *Knowledge and Human Interests*. But, most importantly, Habermas's forthcoming *Toward a Communication Theory of Society* (Boston: Beacon Press) develops a penetrating critique of Husserlian phenomenology as unable to ground its theory intersubjectively.

9. Marx, "Critique of the Hegelian Dialectic and Philosophy in General," in *The Writings of the Young Marx on Philosophy and Society*, L. Easton & K. H. Guddat (eds.), (Garden City: Doubleday, Anchor, 1967), p. 321.

10. Albrecht Wellmer, op. cit., pp. 83–84.

11. The concept of instrumental rationalization has been defined on p. 265ff.

12. Habermas, *Knowledge and Human Interests,* op. cit., p. 196.

13. Ibid.

14. Ibid., p. 245.

15. Ibid., pp. 242, 258.

16. Ibid., pp. 262–273

17. Ibid., p. 284.

18. Ibid., p. 168.

19. Ibid., p. 191ff.

20. Ibid., p. 258.

21. The elements of Habermas's theory were developed in a series of articles: "Toward a Theory of Communicative Competence," in P. Dreitzel (ed.), *Recent Sociology* #2; "On Systemically Distorted Communication," In *Inquiry*, Vol. 13 (1970), #4, pp. 205–218; "Summation and Response," in *Continuum*, Spring–Summer, 1970; and finally, in the forthcoming *Toward a Communication Theory of Society* (Boston: Beacon Press). However, parts of this section are reconstructed on the basis of the Christian Gauss lectures at Princeton in the Spring of 1971 and are therefore an inadequate statement of Habermas's position on this issue.

22. It is this inherently contemplative mode of phenomenological theorizing which permits the unquestioned naive realism of everyday life. In *The Social Construction of Reality* (Garden City: Doubleday, 1966), Berger and Luckmann's conception of the necessity for the stabilization of the everyday world (objectivistically rooted in the biosocial needs of man) can now be seen as a noncritical justification of "necessary" false consciousness. To claim that reification is a social necessity is ultimately self-contradictory. That is, the built-in claim to validity of all constitutive acts, on the one hand, and the obvious false consciousnesss of the natural attitude, on the other, is not questioned in Berger and Luckmann's dialectical theory. This is because of the objectivistic moment of objectivication which permits false consciousness to be legitimate due to its bio-socially rooted function.

This justification of the legitimacy of false consciousness identifies the social construction of reality as a deeply conservative and potentially ideological social theory in which the terms "alienation" and "reification" have lost their critical meaning.

23. Habermas, "Summation and Response," in *Continuum*, op. cit., p. 131.

24. Habermas's critique of it appears in *Theorie und Praxis*, op. cit., pp. 188–200, where he summarizes the economic critique of the "law."

25. See pp. 182–183.

26. Of course it is originally suggested by Hegel's notion of the "causality of fate."

27. See Gar Alperovitz's "Notes Toward a Pluralist Commonwealth," in *The Review of Radical Political Economics*, Vol. 4 #2 Summer 1972. This article is excerpted from his forthcoming book, *A Long Revolution*, which promises to be an important analysis of alternative programs for socioeconomic development.

5. Marx's Crisis Theory: The Contradictions of Capital Accumulation

1. Marx, *Theories of Surplus Value*, Part II (Vol. IV of *Capital*) (Moscow: Progress Publishers, 1968), pp. 509, 513.

2. Marx, *The Grundrisse*, D. McLellan trans. (New York: Harper & Row, 1971), pp. 20ff, 41, 151.

3. For example, Talcott Parsons who, in the introduction to *Structures of Social Action*, op. cit., claims that Marx's work doesn't fall within the scope of sociology. But Parsons also isolates analytically and/or excludes social organization from the economic. See T. Parsons and N. J. Smelser, *Economy and Society* (New York: Free Press, 1956), p. 21. Marx's analysis, on the other hand, proceeds by showing how the economic development establishes restrictive conditions upon the political and social. This type of sophistication is only now being recognized by the critics of "pluralist" analysis.

4. The most obvious reason for Chapter 10 of *Capital I*, in which Marx shows that the struggle for a shorter working day has been aided by changes within the productive process itself, is that he was impressed by the events of the late 1850s and 1860s: the American "holy war of labor," the civil war, together with strikes throughout Europe, convinced Marx that the revolutionary struggle was aided directly by the developing conditions of production. At this point, he added Chapter 10 on the working day. See Raya Dunayevskaya, *Marxism and Freedom* (New York: Twayne 1964), p. 88ff. The relationship of a theory of revolution and the critique of political economy remained unclear in Marx. See S. Moore, *Three Tactics* (New York: Monthly Review Press, 1963). But most notably, see the highly suggestive unfinished argument of Martin Nicolaus, "The Crisis of Late Capitalism," in *The Revival of American Socialism* George Fischer, et. al., (eds.) (New York: Oxford University Press, 1971). It is important to add

that Nicolaus rejects his own argument on the basis of the May 1968 events in Paris, but the repudiation is not as clear as the initial argument which shows how the crisis theory and the revolutionary theory never came together in Marx's work.

5. See Marx, *The German Ideology*, (New York: International Publishers, 1948), pp. 56ff.

6. For a vivid description of the dislocating consequences of the bourgeois revolution, see Karl Polanyi, *The Great Transformation* (Boston: Beacon Press, 1944).

7. The "uniqueness" of American capitalism is outlined nicely by A. Schonfeld in his comparative economic analysis in *Modern Capitalism* (New York: Oxford University Press, 1966).

8. For example, see K. W. Kapp, *The Social Costs of Private Economy* (New York: Schocken, 1970), and Ralph Nader's recent research into the wastefulness of private corporate power. Perhaps more interesting are the highly hopeful speculations at the 1971 futurology conference where several speakers questioned the rationality of the profit motive!

9. See Sweezy, *The Theory of Capitalist Development* (New York: Monthly Review Press, 1968), Part 3, for a general discussion of the crisis theory.

10. See Assar Linbeck, (foreword by Paul A. Samuelson), *The Political Economy of the New Left* (New York: Harper & Row, 1971).

11. For an intelligent and penetrating discussion of the methodological status of Marx's "laws," see Ronald L. Meek, *Economics and Ideology* (London: Chapman & Hall, 1967). The following is indebted to Meek's analysis in numerous ways.

12. In this stress of the difference between the material and value production processes, I am following the emphasis of Paul Mattick in *Marx and Keynes: The Limits of the Mixed Economy* (Boston: Porter Sargent, 1969), and Ernest Mandel, *The Formation of the Economic Thought of Karl Marx* (New York: Monthly Review Press, 1971), p. 83ff.

13. Rudi Schmiede and David Jaffe's "State Expenditure and the Marxian Theory of Crisis" (unpublished).

14. This misconception is rather common. One interesting occurrence of it is in Jürgen Habermas, *Theorie und Praxis*, pp. 188–200.

15. Marx, *Capital I*, Chapter 25.

16. For an interesting comparison of Marx and Weber, see Anthony Giddens, *Capitalism and Modern Social Theory* (New York: Cambridge University Press, 1971). However, Giddens fails to recognize that critique of Weber's concept of rationalization in Marx's own work.

17. For example, see the recent study of the American automobile industry and the societal costs that its critical expansion entails, *The Road and the Car in American Life*, by John B. Rae (Cambridge, Mass.: M.I.T. Press, 1972) and *The Automobile Industry Since 1945*, by Lawrence J. White (Cambridge, Mass.: Harvard University Press, 1972).

18. This interpretation of the law is utilized in Habermas's summary of the critique of the law dealing with the tendency of the rate of profit to decline. Op. cit., #14.

19. See Marx, *Capital*, Vol. III, pp. 211–32.

20. Baran & Sweezy, *Monopoly Capital* (New York: Monthly Review Press, 1966), p. 72.

21. See Joseph Gillman's, *The Falling Rate of Profit* (London: Dobson, 1957), to defend the law's viability. Otherwise, one of the most interesting criticisms of the law is in M. Blaug's essay in *Marx and Modern Economics*, D. Horowitz, (ed.) (New York: Monthly Review Press, 1968).

22. Ronald Meek, op. cit., p. 136. Meek is working out here the implications of Roman Rosdolsky's "Zur neuren kritik des Marxschen Gesetzes der fallenden Profitrate," in *Kyklos*, Vol. 9, #2, 1956.

23. Meek, ibid., p. 142.

24. The literature on this point seems universally to recognize that Marx's formulation was often very open-ended and did not stress absolute impoverishment as much as it seems, given some passages of the text. For example, see R. L. Meek, *Economics and Ideology* (London: Chapman & Hall, 1967), pp. 112ff; Ernest Mandel, *The Formation of the Economic Thought of Karl Marx* (New York: Monthly Review Press, 1971), p. 147ff. Mandel's analysis summarizes nicely most of the contemporary work on this issue.

25. Quoted in Mandel, ibid., p. 147.

26. See Marx, *Capital*, Vol. I, p. 644.

27. See Isaac Balbus, "The Concept of Interest in Pluralist and Marxian Analysis," in *Politics and Society*, Vol. 1, #2, February 1971.

28. R. Dahrendorf, *Class and Class Conflict in Industrial Society* (Stanford: Stanford University Press, 1959).

29. C. Wright Mills, *The Power Elite* (New York: Oxford University Press, 1956).

30. The most penetrating analysis of the limitations of contemporary class analysis appears in Claus Offe's "Political Authority and Class Structures—An Analysis of Late Capitalist Societies," in *The International Journal Sociology*, Spring, 1972.

31. See Gabriel Kolko, *Wealth and Power in America* (New York: Praeger, 1962).

32. The so-called "crisis of federalism" is the result of a profit hierarchy within the capitalist class which polarizes the corporate elite and the local propertied capitalist class. For a theoretical discussion of the economic consequences of intra-capitalist conflict, see Paolo Leon, *Structural Change and Growth in Capitalism* (Baltimore: The Johns Hopkins Press, 1967), especially Chapter 3.

33. *Wall Street Journal*, March 13, 1968, p. 1.

34. Senate Subcommittee on Antitrust and Monopoly, Hearings on *Economic Concentration*, 1964–65, pp. 114–115.

35. A significant current study of economic concentration is Ralph Nelson's *Merger Movements in American Industry, 1895–1956*, National Bureau of Economic Research, (Princeton: Princeton University Press, 1959).

36. Examples of suppression and concealment of emergent technological capacities by huge economic power centers are the extension and control of scientific research through patent laws, contracts binding discoveries as cor-

poration "property," the classification of information by governments, and, finally, the industrial espionage which effectively restores an illegal form of communication in order to overcome the blocking of scientific communication.

37.   Suppression of the developments of science by private economic power is a taken-for-granted reality of the scientific community, despite the fact that this contradicts the idealization inherent in the ideal of scientific inquiry itself.

38.   Marx, *Capital*, Vol. III, p. 264.

39.   See Wellmer, op. cit., especially Chapter 2.

40.   J. A. Schumpeter, *History of Economic Analysis*, (New York: Oxford University Press, 1954), p. 1131ff.

41.   See Roman Rosdolsky, "Das Kapital in Allgemeinen und 'die vielen kapitalien,'" in *Kyklos* #2, 1953, also Ernest Mandel, *The Economic Foundations of Marx* (New York: Monthly Review Press, 1971). Chapter 7.

42.   Ibid.

43.   Adolf Lowe has beautifully expressed these unique components in his *On Economic Knowledge* (New York: Harper & Row, 1965), p. 180ff.

44.   Ibid., p. 187.

45.   Marx, *Capital*, Vol. III, p. 250.

46.   See Paul M. Sweezy, *The Theory of Capitalist Development* (New York: Monthly Review Press, 1942), p. 156ff.

47.   R. Schmeide and D. Jaffe, op. cit.

48.   This passage is translated in Martin Nicolaus's "The Unknown Marx," *New Left Review* #48, pp. 56–57. The extended passages from which it is taken are found in the *Grundisse der Kritik der politischen Okonomie* (Berlin: Dietz Verlag, 1953), pp. 318–19, 336–47.

49.   Perhaps the most significant appearance of these logical schema is in the very earliest part of the *Grundrisse* (August 1857) in which Marx analyzes "The General Relation of Production to Distribution, Exchange and Consumption." This point is translated by David McLellan in *The Grundrisse*, (New York: Harper & Row, 1971), p. 1ff.

50.   Marx, *Capital*, Vol. III, p. 244.

6. Cultural-Marxism: The Contradictions of Industrial "Rationality"

1.   See Martin Jay, *The Dialectical Imagination* (Little Brown, 1973), for an excellent intellectual history of this school. Also see D. Howard & K. Klare (eds.), *The Hidden Dimension* (New York: Basic Books, 1972), for studies of European Marxism after Lenin.

2.   This reconstruction of Lukacs's Theory of Reification is based on his *History and Class Consciousness* (Cambridge, Mass.: M.I.T. Press, 1971). For a more adequate treatment of Lukacs' Theory of Reification, see the essay of the same title in Telos #11, Spring 172.

3.   See Adorno & Horkheimer, *Dialektik der Aufklärung* (Amsterdam:

Querido, 1947), p. 305 (now translated as *Dialectic of Enlightenment* (New York: Herder and Herder, 1972).

4.   For a sympathetic interpretation of the Frankfurt School's conception of praxis, see Paul Breines (ed.), *Critical Interruptions* (New York: Herder & Herder, 1970), especially the essays by Breines, Weber, and Shapiro. For a critique from a Leninist position, see Goran Theborn's article in *New Left Review* #63. For a defense of the School, see my discussion in *Telos* #7, Spring, 1971.

5.   For the critics of Marcuse that I consider constructive and in line with the intent of his work, see the analysis of Claus Offe, Bergman, et. al., in J. Habermas (ed.) *Antworten auf Herbert Marcuse* (Frankfurt: Suhrkamp, 1968); also see William Leiss, *The Domination of Nature*, (New York: George Braziller, 1972); J. Shapiro, "From Marcuse to Habermas," *Continuum*, Spring–Summer, 1970, and J. Habermas, "Science and Technology as Ideology," *Toward a Rational Society* (Boston: Beacon Press, 1971).

6.   The critique of Marcuse which departs from this viewpoint is found in: P. Piccone and A. Delfini, "Marcuse's Heideggerian Marxism," *Telos* #6, Fall 1970; and R. Ahlers, "Is Technology Instrinsically Repressive?" *Continuum*, Spring–Summer 1970.

7.   This argument is developed in "The Concept of Essence," in *Negations* (Boston: Beacon Press, 1968).

8.   This point has been made by Jeremy Shapiro's critique of Marcuse in *Continuum*, Spring–Summer, 1970, p. 67.

9.   See Hegel, Preface to *The Phenomenology of Mind*, op. cit.

10.   Marcuse, *Five Lectures* (Boston: Beacon Press, 1970), p.46.

11.   Marcuse, *Eros and Civilization* (Boston: Beacon Press, 1955), p. 52.

12.   Ibid., p. 32.

13.   Ibid., pp. 96–97.

14.   Marx, *Grundrisse*, David McLellan (ed. transl.) (New York: Harper and Row, 1971), p. 23ff.

15.   Marcuse, *One Dimensional Man* (Boston: Beacon Press, 1964), p. 15.

16.   Ibid., p. 29.

17.   Ibid., p. 34.

18.   Ibid., p. 35.

19.   Ibid., pp. 168–69.

20.   Ibid., p. 10.

21.   Marcuse, *Five Lectures*, op. cit., pp. 47, 51. Marcuse thus imputes uniformity to all socialization processes. A more sophisticated approach would recognize the possibility of class socialization processes.

22.   The notion of "mimesis" appears throughout Marcuse's work as it does in the entire writing of the Frankfurt School. It usually implies the type of adaptive behavior which is typical of one-dimensional culture and represents an index to the loss of critical reason.

23.   Marcuse, *One Dimensional Man*, op. cit., p. 56.

24.   Ibid., p. 11.

25. C. Wright Mills, *Power, Politics and People* (New York: Oxford University Press, 1963), pp. 405ff.

26. Marcuse, *One Dimensional Man*, op. cit., p. 74.

27. This section is based on an interpretation of Habermas's *Toward a Rational Society*, op. cit. But it also presupposes the categorical analysis of Chapter 4 above.

28. The term "dedifferentiation" is used by J. P. Nettl and R. Roland Robertson in *International Systems and the Modernization of Societies* (London: Faber and Faber, 1968), p. 46ff. The term refers to "a structural homogenization which involves a fusion of collectivities and roles previously separated on a specialized basis." The intent is to generate a Marxist critique of Parson's structural functionalism. This analysis expresses Habermas's thesis, although Habermas himself does not use the term.

29. For I.B.M. advocacy of national planning, see *I.F. Stone's Weekly*, January 26, 1970. For Litton Industries management service, see *The Wall Street Journal*, Feb. 20, 1968 (planning of Greece's economic development) and November 9, 1967 (planning of Army data processing setup).

30. Habermas, *Toward a Rational Society*, op. cit., p. 107.

31. J. Shapiro, "One-Dimensionality: The Universal Semiotic of Technological Experience," Paul Breines (ed.), *Critical Interruptions*, op. cit., pp. 137–138.

32. H. Lefebvre's critique of "The *Quotidian*," in modern life has pioneered this new focus for critical theory. See his *Everyday Life in the Modern World* (London: Allen Lane, The Penguin Press, 1971). Also see Bruce Brown, "The Critique of Everyday Life," in *Liberation*, April, 1972, and Agnes Heller, "The Marxist Theory of Revolution and the Revolution of Everyday Life," in *Telos* #6, Fall, 1970.

33. These investigations go beyond the scope of the current book which is mainly concerned with a reconstruction of the theoretical traditions of critical theory. While Chapter 7 begins to apply the theory to the macrodynamic of American capitalism, the analysis of the change in cultural processes will require, first, a more careful macroanalysis and, secondly, a more detailed analysis of sociocultural processes.

7. *The Crisis of American Capitalism: A Preliminary Conceptualization*

1. See Alain Touraine's analysis of the new forms of social domination that result from a higher level of the accumulation of capital in *The Post-Industrial Society* (New York: Random House, 1971).

2. Oskar Lange and Fred M. Taylor, *On The Economic Theory of Socialism* (New York: McGraw-Hill, 1964), pp. 99–100. See also Frank Roosevelt, "Market Socialism: A Humane Economy?" in *Journal of Economic Issues*, April 1971.

3. K. William Kapp, *The Social Costs of Private Enterprise* (New York: Schocken, 1971), p. xiii ff. See also Michael Tanser, *The Sick Society* (New York: Holt, Rhinehart and Winston, 1971).

4. Gabriel Kolko, *The Triumph of Conservatism* (New York: Quadrangle, 1963), p. 3.

5. Martin Sklar, "On the Proletarian Revolution and the End of Political-Economic Society," in *Radical America*, May–June 1969. I am also indebted to numerous reformulations suggested by Sklar for this section.

6. Sklar, ibid., p. 12; also see W. A. Williams, *The Contours of American History* (New York: Quadrangle, 1961).

7. Such confirmations from a Marxist perspective have been attempted by Kidron and Baran and Sweezy. However, Kidron's (latent) Keynesianism is revealed by Rudi Schmeide and David Yaffe's "State Expenditure and the Marxian Theory of Crisis," (unpublished manuscript) who also puts Sweezy into this category. The same point is maintained in the R. Lubitz's generally hostile review of Baran & Sweezy's "Monopoly Capital" in *The Public Interest* #21 Fall, 1970.

8. Studies of social waste are K. W. Kapp, op. cit., *The Closed Enterprise System* (New York: Bantam Books, 1972); Ralph Nader's *Study Group Report on Anti-Trust Enforcement*, by M. J. Green with Beverly C. Moore and Bruce Wasserstein (New York: Grossmann, 1972); R. L. Heilbroner et. al. *In the Name of Profit* (New York: Doubleday 1972).

9. See P. Sweezy, *The Theory of Capitalist Development* (New York: Monthly Review Press, 1942), p. 55.

10. Edward Denison, *The Sources of Economic Growth* (New York, 1962) who shows that the contribution of educated labor to economic growth in the 1929–1957 period is 5 to 8 times that of the importance of physical capital.

11. State support for research and development is directly linked to United States "superiority." Gilbert Burch, "Famine Years for the Arms Makers," *Fortune*, May 1971.

12. Critiques of the irrationality of monopoly markets could begin with Baran and Sweezy's *Monopoly Capital*, op. cit., but Nader's analysis (see note 8 above) is also useful. See also P. M. Sweezy's "On the Theory of Monopoly Capitalism," in *Monthly Review*, April 1972, for a summary of the elements for a theory of monopoly capitalism.

13. I realize that my argument assumes that the U.S. economy cannot be turned around from its commitment to the highly wasteful military oriented economy. This is a crucial and speculative assumption. Although some types of peace-time transitions may be possible, such as support for mass transit, one constraint that will, I believe, block a wholesale transition is the extremely high technology level of the semi-public corporate sector which cannot be converted into production for social needs. A second constraint is the basic contradiction of capitalist economic growth which is societally forced into meeting social needs only by creating the capacity to increase markets. In this situation, the Achilles' heel of capitalism is precisely that it is not primarily organized for the material production of use-values to meet social needs, but is constrained in meeting these needs only insofar as they can be turned into markets.

14. See P. M. Sweezy, ibid., p. 22.

15. See Stanley Aronowitz's critique of the labor movement, in "Which Side Are You On?" in *Liberation*, December 1971.

16. Again the last chapters of Baran and Sweezy's *Monopoly Capital*, op. cit., are important on these questions.

17. See The National Urban Coalition study of the 1972 federal budget: *Counter Budget* (New York: Praeger, 1971); see also the editorial article on The Brookings Institute analysis in *The Wall Street Journal*, May 14, 1971.

18. See Robert L. Heilbroner, *The Limits of American Capitalism* (New York: Harper and Row, 1966), p. 52.

19. See B. Seligman, "Automation and the Union," in *The Radical Papers*, I. Howe (ed.) (New York: Anchor, 1966), pp. 210–211.

20. Cited in Baran and Sweezy, *Monopoly Capital*, op. cit., p. 3.

21. See the very important analysis in Herbert Stein's, *The Fiscal Revolution in America*, (Chicago University Press, 1969).

22. See Baran & Sweezy, *Monopoly Capital*, op. cit., and Michael Harrington's *Socialism* (New York: Saturday Review Press, 1970), especially Chapter 12. See also P. Mattick, *Marx and Keynes* (Boston: Porter Sargent, 1969).

23. O'Conner, "The Fiscal Crisis of the State," in *Socialist Revolution* #1, Feb., 1970 and 2, April, 1970.

24. Ernest Mandel, *Marxian Economic Theory*, Vols. I & II (New York: Monthly Review Press, 1968).

25. David Deitch, "The Watershed of the American Economy," *The Nation*, September 13, 1971.

26. Mandel, op. cit.

27. See Daniel Bell, "Unstable America," in *Encounter*, June 1970.

28. Claus Offe, "Political Authority and Class Structure," *The International Journal of Sociology*, Spring 1972.

29. C. Offe, ibid.

30. See J. O'Conner, "The Fiscal Crisis of the State," op. cit.

31. Offe, op. cit.

32. See also M. Green, J. M. Fallows, and David R. Zwich, *Who Runs Congress?* (New York: Bantam Books, 1972). I am here following the guidelines of James O'Conner's excellent "Some Contradictions of Advanced U.S. Capitalism," in *Social Theory and Practice*, Spring 1970.

33. See Daniel Bell article, "Unstable America," in *Encounter*, June, 1970, and "The Cultural Contradictions of Capitalism," in *The Public Interest*, Fall, 1970.

34. See T. Veblen's *The Engineers and the Price System* (New York: B. W. Huebsch, 1921); also see H. Gintis, "The New Working Class and Revolutionary Youth," in *Continuum*, Spring–Summer, 1970. See also, H. L. Nieburg, *In The Name of Science* (New York: Quadrangle, 1970).

35. This formulation follows the ground breaking work of Claus Offe, *Political Authority and Class Structure*, op. cit.

36. Samuel Lubell's editorial article, "The Hidden Crisis in American Politics," in *The Wall Street Journal*, September 1, 1970. This article is an

excerpt from a book of the same title to be published by W. W. Norton and Co.

37. Peter Dreitzel in the introduction to *Recent Sociology #2*, (New York: Macmillan 1971).

38. See Martin Jay, *The Dialectical Imagination*, op. cit.; Bruce Brown, *Marx, Freud and the Critique of Everyday Life: Toward a Permanent Cultural Revolution*, to be published by Monthly Review Press. Also see Peter Dreitzel, *Recent Sociology #2*, op. cit.

39. Alain Touraine, "Crisis and Conflict," in *International Journal of Sociology*, Fall 1971.

40. See Murray Bookchin, *Post-Scarcity Anarchism*, op. cit.

41. The vast size of this movement is generally unrecognized. The current efforts are very different from the new left of the sixties and is consciously opposed to either political attempts to gain "power" (as a first priority) or wide publicity in the media "spectacle." Thus outside of a few "professional new leftists," who now constitute a sort of "radical establishment," most of the imagination of the American "left" is, I believe, involved in the building of alternative institutions and a culture for liberated communalism. Some of the most interesting statements about this movement are found in Murray Bookchin's *Post-Scarcity Anarchism*, op. cit., and Daniel Foss' *Freak Culture* (New York: Dutton, 1972). For a descriptive account of the origins of this movement see Robert Houriet, *Getting Back Together* (New York: Avon, 1972).

42. Cf. Herbert Gintis, "The New Working Class and Revolutionary Youth," in *Socialist Revolution*, May, 1970.

43. Critical research projects are now being carried out in some of the left "think tanks" such as the Cambridge Institute; The Critical Studies Institute (Santa Barbara); The Synergy Institute (Stanford); The Anarchos Collective (N.Y.C.); The Ecos Project (San Francisco); The New Alchemists (Woods Hole, Mass.); The Institute for Policy Studies (Washington, D.C.) etc. But this need is also recognized and met in the following publications: *The Mother Earth News; Synergism; The Whole Earth Catalog; Communitas; Black Bart Brigade; Clear Creek; Anarchos; Liberation; Ramparts; The New Alchemists; Alternative Life Styles*, etc.

INDEX